Dilemmas of Leadership

'The most important leader you study in this book is . . . yourself.' With these words, the authors indicate the emphasis on personal development in *Dilemmas of Leadership*. This textbook provides a reflective leadership development course for would-be leaders, through which readers explore and refine their understanding of leadership, and their own leadership goals and objectives.

Acting as guides, the authors examine skills which enable effective 'map-reading, map-testing and map-making' to support the journey of exploration that the book provokes. Covering areas such as the metaphoric territories of transformational leadership, team leadership, strategy formation and implementation, symbolism, diversity, ethics and the leaders of the future, the authors emphasise a critical approach which seeks out and addresses important and hard-to-resolve dilemmas, with which all leaders have to grapple. These include:

- dilemmas of trust and control
- the economic consequences of principled actions
- dependency patterns induced through 'strong' leadership
- the dilemma of self-destructive leadership.

With the use of case examples and test-yourself vignettes designed for use within leadership courses, and with a structured, insightful writing style, this text is essential reading for all those with an interest in leadership.

Tudor Rickards heads the Organisation Studies group at Manchester Business School where he holds the position of Professor of Creativity and Organisational Change. He has published extensively in these areas, and has held visiting positions in Kiel, New York, Athens and Canterbury, New Zealand.

Murray Clark is a principal lecturer and programme leader for the DBA at Sheffield Hallam University. His research interests in leadership and the development of trust in work relationships originated from his prior experience as a colliery manager. He is a visiting fellow at Manchester Business School.

Dilemmas of Leadership

Tudor Rickards and
Murray Clark

Routledge
Taylor & Francis Group

LONDON AND NEW YORK

First published 2006
by Routledge
2 Park Square, Milton Park, Abingdon, Oxon OX14 4RN

Simultaneously published in the USA and Canada
by Routledge
270 Madison Ave, New York, NY 10016

Routledge is an imprint of the Taylor & Francis Group

© 2006 Tudor Rickards and Murray Clark

Typeset in Times New Roman and Franklin Gothic by
Florence Production Ltd, Stoodleigh, Devon

Printed in the United Kingdom by
The Alden Group, Oxford

British Library Cataloguing in Publication Data
A catalogue record for this book is available from the British Library

Library of Congress Cataloging in Publication Data
A catalog record for this book has been requested

ISBN 0–415–35584–2 (hbk)
ISBN 0–415–35585–0 (pbk)

Contents

Acknowledgements

We gratefully acknowledge the encouragement and support from many individuals and their organisations. Among those we would particularly like to acknowledge: John and Sylvia Arnold, Paul Bamford, Margaret Cannon, Laszlo Czaban, Paul Evans, Simon French, Dawn Gibbins, Andy Gill, Francesca Heslop, Phil Johnson, Ian Lawson, Leadership electives (especially MBA cohorts of 2004–6 at Manchester Business School, business courses at Sheffield Hallam University, including its Irish cohorts, and at Christchurch, Canterbury), Mark Lewis, Stephen McKeown, Kelly Marks, Susan Moger, Luiz Monthaniero, Tom Mullarkey, Richard Phillips, Margaret Quinn, Monty Roberts, Sara Ruks, Leigh Wharton and Richard Whitley.

Introduction

A search for a leadership text

In our work on business leadership with international MBA and executive classes, we teach from and recommend many excellent textbooks. Yet we were never able to find a text from which we could work exclusively. This was the motivating impulse that resulted in *Dilemmas of Leadership*.

We knew and admired a range of texts that presented contemporary ideas on leadership in a clear and authoritative manner. Yet individually, each text lacked at least one of two fundamental features. First, we wanted a text that acknowledged differences across cultures (North American, Latin American, European and Asian cultures figure prominently among our students). Our students had worked as or were seeking employment as leaders in public and private organisations, sometimes with very large and sometimes with very small firms (perhaps as founder/owners of start-ups). Second, and at least as importantly, was the manner in which knowledge was presented. We did not want our readers to be passive recipients of textbook knowledge, however authoritative its originators might be. We were aware that those texts we most respected also tended to set up a dependency relationship. The authors wrote from a position of influence, or thought leaders if you like, and the readers consequently found themselves in the positions of followers. We had run up against a dilemma, and as we will also show, dealing with dilemmas is a very powerful means of supporting leadership development.

Dealing with the dependency dilemma

The more authority we brought to our subject, the more we saw the dangers of reinforcing the dependency dilemma. This is a familiar challenge facing educators, whether they are located in primary schools or in the greatest research universities of the world. The resolution of the dilemma is through the encouragement of what is variously described as *self-directed learning* or *active learning*. In our context, we saw the challenge as providing the means through which we could offer a leader (or would-be leader) an encounter with their own wished-for leadership future. In a tongue-twisting way, we told ourselves that we wanted each reader to become a better leader. The dilemma might be reformulated as the question 'Who owns the learning?'

From reader to rider

In one of his poems, W. H. Auden weaves a story of a reader confronting a rider undertaking a mysterious journey. The reader is passive and not inclined to take the risks of the rider. Do you suppose, the reader asks the rider, that 'diligent looking' will 'discover the lacking'? In other words, why become so involved, when you can never be sure that searching will help you discover what you are looking for? Auden is comparing the passive kind of knowledge of the reader, with the inevitably risky knowledge of the rider, or the person who becomes involved in a personal search.

We want our readers to become riders, who set off on their own journeys of exploration, engaging in 'diligent looking', even though the looking may not completely 'discover the lacking'. We welcome readers who start by asking what are the contemporary ideas about leadership, and who continue by relating the information to their own leadership experiences and aspirations. The personal search is how the reader becomes both a rider and a leader. Borrowing a style influenced by Auden's poem, we offer the following lines to capture our 'take' on the dilemma.

'O where are you going?' says reader to leader
'And who is in charge of the compass and maps?'
'The charts are unfinished' said leader to reader,
'You must journey alone to fill in the gaps.'

In *Dilemmas of Leadership,* we have provided the unfinished maps of leadership, and have offered a few tips on map-reading. Our invitation to each reader/leader is to go on, to search for what is lacking. Our design is intended to be as powerful a support for the process of personal search as we have been able to achieve.

More about dilemmas

It is one thing to talk about a dilemma, and another to elevate dilemmas to pole position in a book title. The decision is even more apparently paradoxical, if the book is about leadership. Aren't leaders supposed to be typified by decisiveness in action? What sort of leader is it who struggles with conceptual issues such as dilemmas? Some readers may already be impatient for us to get on with the important stuff about leadership, and leave behind what sounds far too abstract and conceptual to be of much practical value. There may even be other readers who have developed the habit of skipping what appears to be abstract and therefore impractical, and who have jumped ahead to Chapter 1. That's another style of learning, and they too will get to understand a lot more about dilemmas, and why they are important for leaders. This introduction is for the reader who likes some orientation before setting out on a journey, and probably prefers to see a film from the very beginning, rather than arriving in time for the first action scenes.

Still with us? Good. In the book we define dilemmas as *hard-to-resolve but important issues*. Every leader faces dilemmas, because leadership involves tough decisions, for which there are no obvious answers. We argue that anyone can prepare for tough decisions, in ways which make for better informed decisions. This is the basis for personal leadership development. The preparation is a form of *mental rehearsal or visualisation*. The approach is based on developing an awareness of your own motivations and values against which you would evaluate those actions. It is a version of the mental rehearsal practised by skilled advocates, negotiators and military leaders (who, like business leaders, have to think and act decisively as part of their work). In summary, we offer a series of exercises which develop your skills at mental rehearsal. The approach is based on dealing in rehearsal with the thought challenges as dilemmas, on the grounds that when you really need to act decisively, you will be well prepared. Rehearsal and practice will support decisiveness when needed.

Note that dilemmas may be regarded as a special sort of problem. Unlike most problems, however, they do not permit a process of 'solution finding'. The outcome of studying a dilemma is deeper understanding of why a leadership decision under such circumstances is not so much a solution as a commitment to act, regardless of the consequences. Some of the dilemmas have been addressed in other texts; others have been (as far as we can establish) ignored. Examples of the better known dilemmas examined in the book are the consequences of charismatic influence and of fairness versus effectiveness under conditions of workplace diversity. Examples of less obvious dilemmas would be those involving trust and delegation.

Maps, myths and mandrills

Map-reading, map-testing and map-making

Our approach in the book has been described as a mental rehearsal. To make the rehearsal more vivid we also describe the process as going on a mental excursion or safari with help and support from experienced guides who will also be supplying some maps for the journey. But the process of personal development is not well served by telling you what to do. Instead, we suggest that your journey involves studying the maps (selected information about a journey) only as a first stage. You will then be invited to test the maps for their relevance and accuracy. That is a metaphoric way of helping you develop your skills to be informed or capable of critical evaluation of all sorts of leadership information. Finally, for each journey, you will be able to construct your own maps, which put you more in charge of future journeys. These will be the real leadership challenges, calling for the benefits of prior mental rehearsal. The approaches will benefit from skills at recognising and dealing with dilemmas.

The myths of leadership

A myth is a story which persists over time, and plays a part in the way social groups make sense of their identities and practices. Leadership stories have played such a role for centuries in societies. To understand the maps of leadership we have to engage in map-reading, which takes into account the myths of leadership. This approach helps us evaluate the beliefs surrounding leadership. One important example which has renewed attention in leadership studies in the past few decades is the myth of the so-called heroic leader.

A related issue is that of the leader who sets out to create a story or myth. The story may be centred on the leader's powers (the prophet, great guide, corporate rescuer and so on). Or the story may be one which (in a much used term) creates a vision for the organisation. The processes have become known as ways in which a leader creates sense or meaning for the group. We show how such understanding helps leaders in their map-making activities.

Mandrills and leadership

The mandrill is a type of baboon. It serves as an excellent example of a story which helps us make sense of human leadership styles. There are important reasons why we have to be careful when we make connections between humans and other species. However, these concerns can be addressed if we follow the principles of intelligent map-reading and map-testing, before making too quick a move to personal map-making. The mandrill story seemed to us to acquire myth-like status as we took our leadership course members to visit a local zoo. Time and again, the students and executives returned to the mandrill story, as they reflected on the experience.

The mandrill story is given in more detail in Chapter 5. The interpretation of mandrill 'leadership' made by the onlookers was as a dilemma. The leadership style was seen as one which required so much energy by the leader preserving its position that it was ultimately self-defeating. The power of the story or myth is strengthened because of the sense made by the observers of their own leadership experiences. They felt they recognised afresh well-known patterns of human behaviour they had previously witnessed.

A statement of aims

Our main aim has been to provide a management text and supporting materials for readers to use in order to develop a more informed and critical understanding of leadership, in the service of their own future leadership careers.

Another important aim is to show that such a treatment rescues leadership from the twin dangers of poorly connected theoretical models and practical observations and experiences (this is yet another dilemma of leadership).

We also wish to offer teachers of leadership a means of delivering such ideas either as a stand-alone course, or incorporated into their own materials for existing courses.

Boxes

Additional material is provided in the boxes to be found in each chapter. Tinted boxes contain summary information on a specific aspect of the main text and the non-tinted boxes provide *exercises* to reinforce *issues* discussed in the chapters.

References

A selection of key references is provided. Our notes for each chapter generally drew on about a hundred references which we were able to reduce to the ones we felt were most central (including the criterion of accessibility to readers under current information-collecting conditions). (The complete set of references is available as a supplementary resource for researchers and trainers on the companion website described below.)

Support systems for the reader

Despite our insistence that primary responsibility for the learning rests with the reader/leader, we are also aware of the benefits of learning within a community of practice. Some readers will themselves be educators, with a primary concern of facilitating the journeys of their own business students. The book permits use as a text for business courses at graduate and undergraduate level, and has an international emphasis that appeals to participants on multicultural courses.

Companion website

The companion website for the book has been designed for teachers and students. The site can be visited at http://www.routledge.com/textbooks/0415355850. The site provides a lecturer resources section, with downloadable materials including course outline, lecture plan and Microsoft Powerpoint slides. These have been designed for use as stand-alone lecturer slides, which are easily modified for lecturers who wish to customise the materials (i.e. 'build their own maps for their leadership expeditions'). The site also contains the more comprehensive list of leadership materials used in preparation for this book, and suggestions for 'going more deeply' into the leadership challenges posed in each chapter.

1 Leadership journeys, stories and maps

Orientation

Your new and future leadership maps

Throughout this book you will be finding ways of rethinking your leadership future. It is a good idea for you to set up a benchmark at the very start which you can refer back to after you have worked your way through the book. We encourage you to spend some time drawing up a personal statement on your views about leadership. The only person who will be examining it will be yourself, which makes it more enjoyable. As you write you may even find the 'conversation with yourself' producing a few surprising ideas (Box 1.1).

Box 1.1 Your new and future leadership maps

Use your own preferred approach to produce a reference document for yourself, outlining your ideas and beliefs about leadership at present. The main purpose is to provide a benchmark to refer back to after you have worked your way through the book. The following questions are suggestions to help you produce ideas. Do not restrict yourself to these questions. Feel free to note that you don't know but would like to find out something! You may find it convenient to clip the notes you make to this page for future reference.

- We assume leadership is important to you personally. Why?
- What questions about leadership would you hope to find answers for in this book?
- Are there theories about leadership that have influenced your thinking and/or actions? (Note the main ones.)
- What do you think are your personal leadership strengths and weaknesses at present?
- Which are the leaders you most admire? Why?
- What sort of leadership future would you wish for yourself?

Starting the leadership journey: two leadership challenges

Our intention in setting you the benchmark exercise is to provide you with a chance to think about leadership without any initial interference from us. We want to repeat this process for two more challenges. The first is a way of demonstrating the possible benefits of having an approach to leadership dilemmas when confronted by an unexpected challenge. The second challenge is a simpler one and helps check that our expectations as your guides on this leadership journey are aligned with your own expectations.

The Departure Lounge Dilemma

The Departure Lounge Dilemma serves as an example of a dilemma which could be poorly handled by many inexperienced leaders. There are various approaches for dealing with the dilemma which you will have more information about by the end of the chapter.

The challenge requires you to imagine yourself as a recent graduate in business studies. You have recently started work as a personal aide to the leader of an international organisation. The opportunity for progressing is obvious, and you are keen to demonstrate your worth to the company. You were hired after various psychometric tests and interviews. Your employers were looking for someone with broad knowledge of international business and change programmes. An ability to analyse complex situations was also considered important.

Our story begins as you are waiting for a plane in the international departure lounge. A few minutes ago you were handed a copy of a new best-seller, *Leadership is for Winners not Whingers*. It shows how great leaders are great motivators, like great sports coaches. The book was warmly recommended by the head of another international organisation. At the meeting you are travelling to, your new boss is planning to obtain copies of the book for her executives. She will then announce her intentions of using its approach as a cornerstone for future strategy. You are to draft this part of her speech, and you have the length of the eight-hour flight to decide what she will say. There is no one else you can turn to for help.

You are experienced in taking in information rapidly, and can easily say what the book is all about. That is indicated by the potted summary on the back cover of the book. You are used to writing essays summarising business books. This is an example of a realistic leadership dilemma. As a potential leader you should show your special skills. Perhaps these would allow you to evaluate the book and help your company discover a better way forward, either through rejecting it, or understanding how to use it.

How would you go about examining the book, with that intended goal? If your mind has gone blank momentarily, you may be like the young aide in our story, who may feel that his or her leadership prospects have been suddenly downgraded. This chapter outlines the approach of map-reading and map-testing that we will be following in subsequent chapters. When you have read the chapter you will understand the approach *in principle*. This will enable you to understand the recommended way for dealing with dilemmas such as the one described in the departure lounge (Box 1.2). Subsequent chapters give you plenty of practice in tackling leadership dilemmas. By the time you have read the book you will have become experienced and skilled in real-life leadership challenges.

Box 1.2 The Departure Lounge Dilemma

You have to evaluate a business book quickly. The book (*Leadership is for Winners not Whingers*) argues that business leadership is the same as any other form of leadership. The business leader can produce winners using the same methods as those used by sports coaches. The leader places winning above everything else. This simplifies the goals of the organisation. The approach is a strong motivation to followers. It enables them to understand what is needed, and why. Such focus also identifies losers such as anyone disagreeing with the winning formula. Losers may be given a chance to change their ways and become winners. If that does not happen quickly enough then losers have to be moved so as not to weaken the winning process.

Spend a few minutes thinking how you would evaluate *Leadership is for Winners not Whingers*. Your notes will help you benchmark any change in approach as you study *Dilemmas of Leadership*.

Overview

Map-reading, map-testing and map-making

The rest of this chapter outlines the basic approach for dealing with leadership dilemmas to be found in subsequent chapters throughout the book. It suggests how each reader may see the process as preparing for a personal leadership journey. The process is described through the metaphors of map-reading, map-testing and map-making. The maps refer to the core ideas to be found through studying the work of leaders and leadership researchers.

Another orientation challenge

A second orientation challenge is provided in the form of a brief thought-experiment. We have included it as a way of introducing the principles of conceptual map-making before we provide detailed maps of leadership and its dilemmas. The challenge invites you to consider your expectations prior to reading this book of what you will take from it.

The platform of understanding

This section in the chapter deals with the 'how and why' of map-making. It introduces the concept of a *platform of understanding* without which maps would be useless.

More about map-testing and map-making

The following sections supply suggestions for improved map-testing and map-making. Map-testing draws on the basic principles of research investigation and includes checks for accuracy and validity of claims being made. The third set of skills involve a personalisation of the map. That is to say, the map-reader becomes map-maker. The emphasis shifts from the study of someone else's map to constructing a personal one. The personal map will draw on the elements of the map or maps you have studied and evaluated.

Finding and dealing with dilemmas

The leadership journey is made easier if you develop your map-reading and map-testing skills. However, the journey is always going to pose tough challenges. In this section we go into more detail into the nature of leadership as dealing with hard-to-resolve issues or dilemmas. Dealing with dilemmas is a version of map-reading, -testing and -making, when the territory is tougher and poorly charted.

Introducing an overview map of leadership

Towards the end of the chapter you will find an overview map of leadership. We use it to take a high-level view of other maps. This enables us to explore how such maps may be constructed. It offers a *platform of understanding* for the rest of the book. In addition, it provides enough introductory materials for you to return to the Departure Lounge Dilemma and apply a few skills of map-testing in dealing with it. You will become more practised in such skills as you work though the remaining chapters of the book.

This section offers you a thought experiment. We take you on an imagined journey to a zoo, and then back to reflect on your personal expectations for other journeys to be taken as you read the rest of the book.

Dangerous and important creatures

There is a little joke that curators play on visitors to various zoos around the world. With some adjustment, the joke fits nicely into our book on the dilemmas of leadership. The joke goes something like this. You are walking through the zoo, enjoying the feelings triggered by the sights, sounds and smells. You come across a path leading to an enclosure, and a sign saying 'come in to see the most dangerous animal in the world'. If you are puzzled, you will certainly be tempted by the invitation. When you arrive in the enclosure, you are confronted with a mirror in which you see your own reflection. That is the joke. To help those visitors who do not see the joke immediately, a caption by the mirror reads: 'The most dangerous animal in the world, *homo sapiens*, which has destroyed many other species, and is endangering many others, including its own.'

The joke works because it produces a creative jolt to the visitors. When visitors arrive at a zoo their focus is on the interesting and unusual creatures in their cages. As spectators they watch comfortably from the outside of the experience. It is a position from which a certain kind of learning is possible. The joke jolts the visitor back to another kind of reality, and another kind of learning in which we put ourselves temporarily as the focus of attention. We face the important and challenging implications of our own responsibilities and actions as human beings, and arguably as custodians of the future of the planet.

As authors, we were conscious of the parallels in our role with that of zoo curators. Books on leadership offer experiences to readers, like visits to zoos. We were aware that there were plenty of leadership zoos (books), seeking to inform and educate visitors (readers) through their carefully structured exhibits. As in real-life zoos, there is a remarkable appetite for new experiences, and there is a ready audience attracted to new zoos, displaying the leadership exhibits each with particular emphasis. We happen to be among those who continue to be attracted to new leadership zoos (books). However, we were all too aware of the difficulties of offering a new experience that was a significant departure from many other earlier zoos (books).

A first challenge for your own leadership journey

The joke helps introduce another challenge we offer you on your own leadership journey. The challenge involves two questions about your leadership journeys, and how the book may help you as you engage in them.

The first question is 'Whom do you consider to be the most important leader you will learn about in this book?'

The second is 'What or whom do you consider likely to be the most important guides for your leadership journeys?'

Our suggestion is that you spend a few minutes thinking about the challenge to orient you for the journeys you will experience in subsequent chapters (Box 1.3).

Box 1.3 Find the leader challenge

You often learn more if you are well prepared. This challenge invites you to prepare for your 'journey'. The exercise is one in which you think about your 'map' (the book). We have expressed the challenge so as to suggest there is no right answer.

- *Question 1:* Whom do you consider to be the most important leader you will learn about in this book?
- *Question 2:* What or whom do you consider likely to be the most important guides for your leadership journeys?

As you think about the questions of any challenge (such as the most recent find the leader one) you are influenced by your existing beliefs (or maps) of the subject being thought about. The process of inquiry also prepares you for map-reading, map-testing and map-making.

Question 1 readies you for studying a new map, and encourages you to test its ideas against your expectations (map-reading and map-testing). Question 2 begins the preparation for your own leadership journey (map-making).

When you considered who would be the most important leader you will study, you may have wondered whether the book will offer something very important from accounts of famous and successful business leaders.

That is a reasonable idea, particularly in light of the contents of many books on leadership. We would like to think that our zoo story hinted at another answer. It suggested that maybe the most important leader you will be studying is yourself. If you reached that conclusion you may have thought even more deeply to consider whether you should be more concerned with the leader you are now, the leader you believe you will become, or the leader you would like to become.

The second question also suggests several possibilities. We could understand the reasoning if you had decided that we, as authors, were setting out our roles as your guides.

However, there are again other possibilities. The contents of the book include a compendium of maps and tips for map-making. The book itself could be seen as the *Rough Guide* or *Baedeker* is to the traveller in unfamiliar regions. The book itself is, according to this view, an important guide.

However important these influences are, there is at least one other important possibility that we hope you considered. The theme of the most important leader returns. Did you think about yourself as the ultimate guide to your own leadership journey? We hope so, for that has been something that has guided our thinking.

The maps we provide are those from people we consider thought leaders – influential experts on the territories they have mapped. As authors we have more often assumed the role of guides than of experts on leadership theory or practice. As a reader, you have the choice to take over some of the duties as a self-guide as you set out on your own journeys of leadership development.

The rest of the chapter continues the orientation process, preparing you for the more specific leadership journeys you will encounter, supported by the maps in the subsequent chapters of the book.

A first lesson in map-reading: the platform of understanding

To read maps expertly, it is worth knowing how maps are constructed. We are mainly interested in the 'maps' of leadership, although the processes have similarities to the actual processes of cartography.

Throughout the book the reader will find leadership stories, and opportunities to relate them to personal experiences, beliefs and goals. In general terms, this is the well-known educational method of self-directed learning.[1] Our specific treatment may be thought of as detailing a process within which you take the most trusted general maps available, and construct from them personal maps for personal leadership journeys. The general map is that of received wisdom of a specific topic. Construction of the new maps calls for skills in map-reading (which we provide) and of interpretation. The map-making process also involves skills in reaching conclusions about weaknesses and gaps in the maps.

Platforms of understanding

If you discover an interesting article about leadership, you are looking at a map that might be of value to you. But how to make sense of it? For that, it helps to understand how maps are constructed and authenticated.

The received wisdom on which a general map is based is described as a *platform of understanding* (sometimes abbreviated to POU). A POU is essentially a social construction, whose limits are set by experts and other gatekeepers ('knowledge guardians' or 'intellectual bodyguards') within a defined social group. High-level platforms of understanding are what have sometimes been described as sociological paradigms or world-views. We will be most concerned with leadership platforms of understanding, accepted by the community of leadership gatekeepers who have subjected the POUs to rigorous study (map-testing).

Although the context of establishing a platform of understanding changes from study to study, and over time, a general principle behind the searches remains: *a process of consensus-forming occurs around any conceptual theme of interest to a group of practitioners or researchers.* This process is shaped by various influence leaders, including editors, reviewers of technical articles, sponsors of research and journalistic popularisers of earlier work. The complex cluster of knowledge brokers and their shared ideas has become known as a *paradigm*, a term popularised in Thomas Kuhn's important work on scientific paradigms and scientific revolutions.[2] The convergence process gives coherence to a paradigm. Where competing views fail to converge, the paradigm disrupts, and one or maybe more than one new paradigmatic clusters begin to form. There is scholarly debate about the nature and functioning of social systems, and the credibility of paradigmatic analyses. For our purposes, however, the notion of a *platform of understanding* serves as a metaphor for a widely accepted starting point for examining a field of knowledge. Readers unfamiliar with the concepts of sociological paradigms will be close enough in their interpretation to treat them as rather special and well-documented maps.

A platform of understanding should be treated as a valuable starting point for understanding *currently accepted views* on a subject. Students are examined for evidence of their platform of understanding on the topics indicated in the examination questions. The process is not unlike showing that you have remembered a map you have been taught. However, the student who engages in *exploring the assumptions* of the POU receives extra credit. In practical and professional fields, examiners often ask for integration of theory with personal experiences.

How testing a POU can reveal important dilemmas

Many platforms of understanding present the field as a map without any hidden conceptual dangers to the traveller. The most respected POUs, however, indicate those dangers, perhaps as unresolved issues or paradoxes. In Chapter 2, we have an excellent example of how this happens. The reviewer (and map-maker) Alan Bryman shows how a definition of leadership was repeatedly cited and accepted for three decades, after its appearance in a particularly important reference source. The maps all defined leadership as *a process which influenced a group in attempts at setting and achieving its goals*.[3]

Bryman showed that such maps of leadership were based on a definition that was not adequate for distinguishing leadership from management. This produced a role-differentiation dilemma which was to attract a lot of scholarly attention. (We will later show how such a dilemma can be approached, through further efforts at map-reading, -testing and -making.) Bryman suggested that new definitions of leadership were putting more emphasis on the management of meaning and the active promotion of shared values. In our terms, he helped establish a new map of leadership (which became known as the theory of new leadership, covered in later chapters).

Learning about map-testing

Each chapter (after this one) deals with an important leadership issue, with its associated dilemmas. We approach the issue through summarising the platforms of understanding that we consider to have the most credibility. Before testing them, we also selected a rather wider sample of more contextual materials. These were more specific in scope, perhaps illustrating an aspect of leadership without the deeper and shared knowledge structure of the POUs. If we remind you of the very first orienting challenge, the book *Leadership is for Winners not Whingers* seems likely to have been considered as contextual material. Our testing procedure can be found under the general section of integration in each chapter. There, we work with the platforms of understanding and contextual materials, searching for deeper understanding. The combination generally offers up dilemmas and other ways of challenging surface assumptions and beliefs.

This approach is one with which research investigators are familiar. Like other forms of skill, the more you practise applying sound principles, the more you acquire good habits of analysis that will help as you encounter dilemmas of leadership (if you find this concept relatively distant from your normal approach, you should be able to demonstrate its value by the end of the book). We have chosen to perform much of the testing and integrating of materials, offering you as reader opportunities from time to time to tackle some specific challenge.

One map or more?

For practical travel purposes, you may be perfectly satisfied with one map for your journeying needs. However, to test conceptual maps for their credibility, it often pays to compare maps, one with another. Then, previously hidden aspects may be discovered. This is the rationale for our selecting and testing *two* platforms of understanding wherever possible in this book, each dealing with rather similar territory. The process is a familiar one to researchers in the social sciences, under the formidable name of triangulation.

Triangulation is an element within the process of critique (a formal name for the map-testing process). Working with even more than two maps permits more possibilities for map-testing but with diminishing conceptual gains, and many more practical difficulties. As it happens, in our search for convincing platforms of understanding, we rarely had the luxury of finding more than two from a larger number of candidate maps.

Integration

Let us recall the purposes of assembling platforms of understanding and contextual materials, and studying them. They are providing us with rich sources of ideas about leadership, selected in each chapter around a particular 'territory' often indicating important leadership dilemmas. The simple and unreflective process of examining them brings us into contact with many valuable ideas about leadership. Of itself this has some benefits for a study of leadership 'from the outside'. The study may even permit you to be examined for knowledge of the leadership field. We have indicated, however, that such knowledge stops short of you taking a critical view of the field.

We have begun the process of integration of materials of the two platform of understanding maps and of the contextual maps. Our efforts confirm the increasing difficulties of cross-referencing the materials from five or more different maps. Readers will discover different insights in conducting their own processes of integration.

Trusting your judgement (a dilemma of leadership)

This is why we encourage you to take the journey with us, and develop your own views on the integration of the material. As we have indicated, the most important leader for you is yourself. The more you develop your skills in map-reading or map-testing the better. You are not just testing the map, but testing your own judgement.

Our suggestion is that dilemmas call for careful map-reading, -testing and -making. As you become skilled, you gain confidence as you tackle one of the fundamental dilemmas of leadership: 'Do I trust this "expert" or do I trust my own judgement?' Incidentally, this is one of the dilemmas facing our young aide in the Departure Lounge Dilemma presented at the start of the chapter.

The skills of personal map-making

Reflection and critical thinking processes

What are the ingredients that help leaders to learn from experience *and* from more formal codified knowledge? The question addresses some of the deepest and most important issues in education generally, as well as within business courses. One review has suggested the term 'critical thinking' as capturing the essential features of the process.[4]

Let us be clear. Critical thinking is regarded as something that is of the highest value for the process of individual development. It allows us to explain to ourselves (and to others) why we have arrived at the conclusions we have reached. The process is a universal component of our mental hardware. The bad news is that critical thinking may call for hard mental work, and maybe even the facing of unpleasant realities we would rather not think about. The most widespread conclusion about education is that students are not helped enough in this skill. The good news is that there are a range of ways in which the process can be practised, and probably the skill levels substantially enhanced. Skills of critical thinking can be developed through personal efforts exploring individual experience and secondary knowledge acquired.

Critical thinking seeks to understand the most important (i.e. critical) issues within an area of inquiry. The focus of attention could be a written text such as a business case, or a book, or a business presentation. Critical thinking will be one way that our young executive may be able to approach the Departure Lounge Dilemma regarding the best-seller, *Leadership is for Winners not Whingers*.

Critical thinking relies on prior knowledge ('knowing that') and on higher-level knowledge ('knowing how'). Reasoning of a logical kind comes into the process, but is far from the only mental characteristic. Reflection and judgement (sometimes described as intuition) are also important.

Although there are various versions, the theories can be seen drawing on ideas of experiential learning A time-honoured map is the one developed by David Kolb and colleagues in the 1980s.[5] This map suggests that experiential learning occurs in successive iterations around a learning loop from experience, through reflection, to abstract concept formation, to active experimentation. The experimentation sets up another loop of experiences to learn from, reflection and so on.

This process constitutes a learning loop or cycle so that the learner is actually engaged in a process of repeated learning opportunities. The process also can be seen as associated with more recent theories of knowledge acquisition cycles from 'tacit to explicit' forms.[6]

Kolb describes the connecting process as one of reflective observation. Another deep thinker described it as like having a conversation with the situation.[7] Through reflection, the learner is able to make new sense of experience in terms of codified knowledge, and also to make new sense of codified knowledge in terms of reflection. We become better leaders through reflecting on experience (our own, and that of others) and through linking theory and practice. In our courses for business students and executives, we encourage reflection, which we see as going hand in hand with critique.

We have selected one particular approach which, when applied in a reflective way, can become part of your skill-set when you engage in critical thinking. It is particularly powerful in map-testing and map-making. The approach is one through which a map is tested for unexplained and problematic issues that seem important. We refer to these as dilemmas. Although not the only technique of value, practice in searching for and dealing with dilemmas seems to us to be an excellent all-purpose approach for developing improved skills of critique and personal learning.

Finding and dealing with dilemmas

Because they have not figured prominently outside of specialised studies of logic and research theory, we will spend a little more time looking at dilemmas

Life and death dilemmas

Before considering the dilemmas of modern business leaders, let us briefly look at dilemmas whose resolution may have life and death consequences. The extreme examples are all too familiar. Hostage-takers pose their negotiators with dilemmas through their demands for military concessions. To the outsider, the dilemma presents itself as a struggle between two utterly different ('incommensurate') sets of values each violated by the two obvious sets of actions. To concede to the hostage-takers' demands is ethically dubious, perhaps politically or socially unacceptable. To reject the demands is likely to place in mortal danger the lives of hostages caught up in events. Little wonder that the processes of negotiating are increasingly acknowledged as requiring the most skilful of mediators (who are examples of a special kind of leader).

The Judaic-Christian tradition teaches the dilemmas of leadership through stories and parables. The future King David is said to have been engaged in a fierce battle during which three of his chosen captains dared to break through enemy lines to secure him a pitcher of water. His dilemma: to drink while his warriors remained thirsty, and while such great risks had been taken on his behalf to obtain it?

David carried out a symbolic act of pouring the water on to the sands of the desert, saying it was too precious to drink. We may think of this as a symbolic act of leadership self-denial. The story is backed up by many similar ones in military history. The leader has to find a powerful way of shifting the perspective of the followers, to avoid the most obvious and undesired actions (to accept a gift or refuse it).

In another story, King Solomon was brought a child, with two women each claiming tearfully to be the real mother. King Solomon dealt with the dilemma of the child, by drawing his sword and announcing that he would kill the child so that each of the women could have half of the child. The anguished cries of the real mother resolved the dilemma.

The ancient stories have the power to captivate, bewilder and disturb both emotionally and intellectually. In one sense, this is how leaders are 'supposed to' deal with tough situations, and as we relive in our imaginations these dramatic stories, we may contrast them with our own indecisiveness.

If the actions were decisive, they were also unexpected and unpredictable. As in the account of any heroic story, we may speculate on what 'really' happened at the time, but we can have no doubt that the leader is described as acting in an exceptional and unexpected way. In present-day language we might refer to their actions as being consequential on leaps of lateral thinking,[8] which change the perceptions of those around them.

From heroic prototype to contemporary business leader

It is our contention that organisational leaders also repeatedly face dilemmas, often confronting them with very unpleasant choices. The issues are generally less dramatic than those which require the wisdom of Solomon yet they will still have those aspects of a dilemma described to us by one executive as 'what keeps leaders awake at night'.

Why leaders all face dilemmas

What is a dilemma? The term originally referred to a philosophical position that defeats logical attempts to resolve it. One of two outcomes has to be accepted, yet each contradicts previously held beliefs and their logical consequences. The early philosophers talked of being on the horns of a dilemma – where the choice is to be impaled by one or the other horn of an angry bull. Other powerful metaphors also illustrate what dilemma is like: 'It's being between a rock and a hard place', 'it's a choice between the devil and the deep blue sea' or 'sailing too close to the rocks or the whirlpool' (Scylla and Charybdis were terms used in mythology).

The essence of a dilemma is that there is no satisfactory choice that suggests itself on the evidence available. This is a position leaders find themselves in, all too often. Each action seems to carry with it undesired consequences (including the action of doing nothing, and waiting to see what happens). This can be explained by saying that leadership decisions in general, and strategic decisions in particular, have to be taken under conditions of uncertainty. There is incomplete information about the consequences of the decisions. Even the sophisticated methods of probability and risk analysis are unable to provide more than indications of what might happen, assuming that there are no unexpected surprises concealed in current uncertainties. The uncertainties are obviously worse when the decision addresses outcomes of strategic decisions at some time in the future. It can be seen that all leaders face dilemmas.

When we fail to learn from dilemmas

The bad news is that many of us, including leaders of organisations, often do not deal with dilemmas so as to learn from them. We have identified two quite different ways in which this happens. The first is coping through denying their existence. The second is by being too overwhelmed by them to find even the consolation of denial, and to become powerless to act. The literature of leadership is full of examples of each pattern of behaviour.

Denial of the ambiguities of a situation can be found in leaders who act decisively, but upon wrong decisions, ignoring 'uncomfortable' information that might warn of the dangers of the proposed strategic action (Box 1.4).

At least the strategy of coping through denial is consistent with the image of the leader as being bold and decisive. The leader who is unable to act does not even have that consolation. Inevitably, the blame falls on the hapless leader. Military schools are particularly sensitive to the battles that have been lost through indecision. So much so, that their own leadership training puts at a premium the need to act as swiftly as necessary, accepting the risks involved. The actions, however, follow the best appraisal that can be made under the circumstances, with the best intelligence that can be obtained. Military training has not, however, succeeded in eliminating under battle conditions, either the over-hasty and impulsive action (denial of the complexities of

Box 1.4 When we fail to learn from dilemmas

Example 1: The chief executive officer (CEO) of a company in a price war continues to slash prices, ignoring the evidence that only the most powerful market player can survive such a head-on strategy. The centrality of the dilemma of uncompetitive prices versus long-term survival has been denied.

Example 2: A CEO forces through a large remuneration package at a time when the organisation's performance is weakening, insensitive to the possibility of opposition by large investors. Other organisations have run into difficulties with institutional shareholders when they have attempted to introduce such packages. The consequences of the dilemma of personal gain versus social sanctions against perceived unjust rewards have been ignored.

Example 3: The new image-building campaign claims that the organisation is now listening hard to its customers. To back up the claim, all staff have been issued with a best-practice self-study pack for treating customers well. Some staff have made efforts to respond to the initiative. Others retain their old ways of behaving. This should not have been a surprise, as similar initiatives have failed in the past. The campaign provides opportunities for competitors to draw attention to the continuation of the uncomfortable 'old' realities from which the organisation is trying to escape. The dilemma of image versus reality has been ignored.

the situation) or indecision and hesitancy under pressure (being overwhelmed by the uncertainties). The case is also true in commercial life. Then the accusations appear of a 'rudderless' company, one that is unable to steer a path through its turbulent sea of troubles.

Developing skills in managing dilemmas

We have no 'magic bullet' or technique that guarantees leaders' ways of overcoming their most pressing dilemmas. Almost by definition, dilemmas are not susceptible to formulaic treatments. However, we are able to suggest an approach that has proved itself repeatedly in developing skills so that dilemmas are stripped of their potential of producing over-hasty actions on one hand, or action paralysis on the other.

The process basically is one in which you are trying to become more aware of beliefs and assumptions which shape the maps you are studying (including your beliefs and assumptions shaping your own maps). In keeping with our earlier remarks, we believe it important for you to develop your own 'conversation with the situation', using your own questions. Our own typical questions are of value if they can be taken and reworked.

The dilemmas of leadership in subsequent chapters are examined using questions of the following kind.

Stage 1: Examining a single map

- What's familiar about this map?
- What's new and unexpected?
- Does the new and unexpected present a dilemma (between what we expected and what we found)?

Stage 2: Integrating the information from several maps

- In comparing more than one map, are there contradictions and confusions?
- Do these considerations present dilemmas between views expressed in the different maps?

An example of map-making: a short history of leadership

We have prepared an overview map of leadership for the particular purpose of introducing readers directly to the challenges of map-reading and map-testing. (Personal map-making will become important in subsequent chapters.) A second purpose is to offer maps as ways of approaching the hypothetical Departure Lounge Dilemma posed at the start of the chapter.

The map draws on countless earlier efforts, many being attempts to reproduce or improve on earlier maps. We studied many hundreds of leadership articles and many tens of books, looking for the most widely accepted representations.

We make no attempt at this point to evaluate the map's accuracy or point to inconsistencies or weaknesses (we have already begun these processes as we attempted to test the maps we were studying). All we can say is that the map represents our best efforts at interpreting and redrawing earlier maps as faithfully as we have been able to. Readers who would like to repeat our map-making will find four maps particularly useful starting points. All four are clearly covering similar territory, while offering different emphases and details (Box 1.5).

The map by Alan Bryman helped in the emergence of so-called new leadership maps. It is studied in more detail in Chapters 2 and 4.

The map by Gary Yukl has progressed through many updates over several decades. His historical stages are similar to those identified by the other map-makers. He offers additional ideas regarding leadership as essentially an influence process. Yukl also shows how definitions and treatments of leadership fall into two main categories. The first category of map treats leadership as proper or acceptable influence

Box 1.5 The map of maps: a short history of leadership thinking

Every writer on leadership attempts to understand existing maps and then create a new map from them. Readers can quickly understand the process if they look at a leadership text for their new map. The most important aspects can be found generally in the introductory materials to the book or article. More specific aspects of the map are then dealt with in subsequent sections or chapters. Sometimes the title of the book gives away the most important aspect of the map (*In Search of Excellence, Wealth of Nations, How to Win Friends and Influence People*).

We encourage readers to study leadership texts as maps. Look for the material which indicated the most important messages according to the author as map-maker.

Some texts worth studying for their maps of the history of leadership thought include the following:

- *Leadership in Organizations* by Gary Yukl[9]
- *Leadership: Theory and Practice* by Peter Northouse[10]
- 'Changing theories of leadership and leadership development' by John Storey[11]
- 'Leadership in organizations' by Alan Bryman[12]

You should be able to find a location in each text where the author summarises the key features of the intended map. Are you able to satisfy yourself that you understand the map as intended by its author? Can you find other important earlier maps (mentioned by each map-maker) and which were used in each case to produce the new maps? The 'map of maps' prepared for this chapter was constructed after such a study of these texts. The four texts were selected after a more extended study of many other maps of leadership thought.

processes, *excluding* tyrannical, unethical and inept forms. The second category regards leadership as covering all forms of influence including undesired variants.

The map by Peter Northouse excludes leaders who are extreme and tyrannical. However, he does add leaders who *emerge* under prevailing conditions, as well as those who are *appointed* to leadership posts.

The map by John Storey confirms the main features of these maps, while pointing to the indicators of a new map which goes beyond the features of the new leadership territory (distributed leadership; socially constructed models of leadership).

Leader traits: the philosopher's stone of leadership studies

Our map begins with leader traits, the most studied aspects of leadership in recent times. A trait is a relatively fixed aspect of personality. For many years researchers attempted to find the ultimate essence of leadership. This was considered to be the 'something special' of leadership. As we will see in subsequent chapters, trait theories failed to be confirmed by direct observation. Trait theories were eventually to fall out of favour. With the benefits of hindsight we realise that the search was hindered by the assumption that there was a univeral and unique 'essence of leadership' which characterised the greatest leaders. There is evidence that some trait-like personality aspects are possible predictors of leadership capabilities.

The founding father: Weber and charisma

As we studied these four maps we increasingly found their shared heritage in earlier maps from which they were constructed. One pioneer is widely acknowledged, the great sociologist Max Weber. Among his other contributions in the 1920s was his analysis of forms of authority. Of particular interest to us was his distinction between charismatic authority and other sources of authority arising from ancient traditions, and the more modern rational-legal authority.[13] (His critique of rational authority was an important aspect of his famed theory of bureaucracy.) The charismatic leader exercises authority through the faith of followers in the leader's capacity to create new social arrangements (including the initiation of practices that themselves become established as traditions). The story of charismatic leadership was to be retold in modern forms, as we will see in subsequent chapters in this book.

Stogdill, the handbook and the decline of trait theories

Most bodies of knowledge have a standard text which is deferred to, in an almost obligatory way in later writings, although this is not to say that the book remains directly and thoroughly studied. Ralph Stogdill's *Handbook of Leadership* falls into the category of the ultimate reference text on leadership.[14] Its original impact was the greater because of its encyclopedic scope. Subsequently, however, the handbook became cited primarily for several key conclusions it reaches. The first conclusion is that leadership studies, despite considerable efforts, have resulted in great confusion regarding the nature and definition of leadership. The second conclusion is that much of the work had been directed towards finding the traits associated with leadership. Traits were then, and remain today, fixed and measurable individual personality factors. We might consider trait theorists to have been engaged in a project attempting to map the leadership genome. Stogdill's evidence suggested that the quest was proving fruitless, and the handbook is considered to have been a contributor to a decline in interest and confidence in trait theories of leadership.[15] After Stogdill's death, his collaborator Bernard Bass took over the editorship of the handbook.[16] Bass was to figure subsequently in the story of the rise of transformational leadership research (which we study in Chapter 4).

From traits to skills: from leaders to leadership

The trait era became replaced with a period of growing interest in leadership behaviours and skills. An important implication is that skills are considered to be less inherent and more trainable. That is to say, the possibility opened that leaders could be developed. The change of emphasis also resulted in greater attention being paid to leaders at lower levels in organisational hierarchies, a shift permitting easier access to a far larger population of leaders. (There is a slight complication to our map-making here: the rejection of trait maps was too complete. More recently some traits such as cognitive complexity are being re-examined as predictors of leadership performance, albeit within more complex leadership maps.)

The shift to behavioural maps still failed to show clear links between leader factors and leadership performance. Attempts to do so resulted in a shift towards more complex theories. The focus was no longer the leader, but leadership processes, which included additional variables which attempted to account for different situations ('situational theories') and possible variations in leadership styles 'contingent' on the situation. The efforts failed to resolve the various confusions through identifying the most convincing theoretical framework. By the 1970s, the field of leadership studies, deprived of the dominance of a simple trait theory, was in serious need of a revolutionary new mapping.

Transformational leadership: new territory and a new map

The story took a new turn in the 1980s, under the label of new leadership. The change is widely told as receiving its impetus from a study of great political leaders, by historian James MacGregor Burns, in his book, which was simply entitled *Leadership*.[17] The book contrasted two maps of leadership – the old map which Burns described as *transactional leadership*, and a new map of *transformational leadership*. The new map examined the behaviours of leaders such as President John F. Kennedy. The defining difference between the maps was that the new leaders were the agents of significant (transformational) change. The map had turned interest away from the more widespread organisational leaders of all kinds, back to older tales of heroic leaders, who were creators (or at least purveyors) of compelling visions for change.

Updating and retelling old maps

Transformational leadership became the story of new leadership. Bass, with the authority of the editor of the widely accepted handbook, was to develop measures of transactional and transformational leadership. His story suggested that the behaviours of exceptional transformational leaders could also be found in many leaders, in less spectacular contexts. In so doing he reverted also to an emphasis on leadership as widely distributed across industrial groups. In the process he updated the (old) concept of charismatic leadership within the story of (new) transformational leadership. The story is still unfolding. As was remarked in one of the oldest of stories, there is nothing new under the sun. 'New' stories have a way of connecting up and retelling older ones.

The leader as provider of meaning

The new story also puts considerable emphasis on the management of meaning. This is consistent with the new part played by visionary concepts, whose justification (at least in the period before experience of practical success is available) derives from the relationship between leader and followers. To understand such a leadership style, we have to accept we are entering the world of perceptions, and beliefs, often dismissed as 'soft' and subjective.

On the border of the established maps

Maps used to have unexplored regions where map-makers would indicate dangers and perils. 'Here be dragons' was a popular notation. We became aware of territories that were never easily explored from studies of the most accepted maps. These often become the so-called contested territories for future exploration. Map-makers in general avoid such ambiguities. Map-testing often reveals some of these regions. For our introductory purposes we ignore such complications which become important in subsequent chapters when we are integrating the information from more than one map. One change to the basic maps is awareness of the possibilities of distributed or shared leadership and superleadership (teams operating more powerfully than if led by a traditional leader). Another emerging theme is the serious questioning of the leader-as-hero. These and other newer themes are to be found in the maps in Chapters 5–9 of this book.

Revisiting the Departure Lounge Dilemma

You may well feel you can now carry out the proposed approach on the history of leadership maps of the previous section. By all means do so. If so, you may well be interested to repeat the exercise after working your way through the book, as a means of checking the skills you have developed. A simpler dilemma to begin with is the one presented at the start of the chapter, which we think should now be easier to deal with, and which you should spend a few minutes thinking about again, before reading on. To recapitulate, you have to assess the virtues of a best-selling book, which your boss intends to make an important element in the organisation's future.

Approach A: bluffer's guide approaches

- Take the book at face value: accept the promised benefits from studying it. Suggest a series of leadership development programmes for key executives using the book.

- Hedge your bets (method 1): suggest that a selection of respected senior executives read the book. This to be followed by a meeting to discuss their views on the book and how it should be used.
- Hedge your bets (method 2): request time to check out the views of authorities and reviewers of the book using electronic search engines.

Approach B: a map-testing approach

- Examine the main claims of the book: these are implied in the most clear messages (often in the introduction, summary and the brief descriptions).
- Test the claims for internal consistency: can you think of counter-examples of great coaches or great leaders who do not fit the general model proposed in the book?
- Test the claims for critical reasoning: does the author try to indicate the way in which the main ideas are similar to and different from other 'maps'?
- Test the maps by the comparative approach: apply our map-testing questions (what's familiar, what's unusual, what can be tested against other maps?). What's familiar is the notion of a leader having special traits (of motivation) shared by all leaders. What's unusual is the claim that leadership can be reduced to one universal factor, that of the motivational skills. One dilemma is that the one-factor models of leader traits have all failed. Our expectation is that the book claims too much (when we compare it to other maps). Furthermore, the claim seems to suggest that leaders either have 'the right stuff' (possessed by a few top sports coaches) or they are ineffective. The practical dilemma becomes 'What do we do with the internal people who are not great motivators?' Is it as simple as 'moving people off the team'?
- Look for possible contradictions: the model or map is that of the great sports coach. The book suggests that any leader can benefit by following the principles. The model is of exceptional people based on results. The implication appears to be that anyone can achieve great results following these methods. Is this a dilemma?

There are, of course, other dilemmas intertwined with the general ones outlined. Even if the aide thinks that the book is an unfounded and fad-like tale, how is he or she to present the argument to a boss with other views?

The approaches seem to be of differing levels of complexity. We hope you see the merits of having a wide range of possibilities to select from if faced with such a dilemma. We also hope you see how you will become a more valuable corporate asset if you develop your skills at resolving dilemmas as indicated in Approach B.

We are not offering map-reading, -testing and -making as panaceas guaranteeing leadership success. They are, however, valued skills, the development of which will serve you well in your leadership journeys, and as you construct your own maps for those journeys.

The following chapters offer you opportunities to develop those skills.

Box 1.6 A summary of leadership map-making terms

Critical thinking: a form of consciously controlled thinking directed towards understanding of what to believe and what to do. It involves reflective thought drawing on experience as well as on perception and memory.[18]

Critique: the processes whereby information is studied and judged, applying analytical techniques so as to reveal its implications for specified purposes.

Dilemma: hard-to-resolve but important issues in theory and practice. *Logical dilemmas* arise when formal analysis (including critique) reveals more than one (usually two) possibilities, each of which contradicts a starting contention or proposition. *Action dilemmas* arise when someone (such as a leader) has identified more than one (most often two) courses of action, none of which is acceptable in practice. Dilemmas are discovered in the course of map-testing (critique).

Leadership journey: an expedition into a leadership territory, for purposes of discovery or experience. Journeys are supported by appropriate maps, which may involve personal map-making.

Leadership map: a representation of the territory likely to be covered by a proposed leadership journey.

Metaphoric models: metaphors are ways of expressing concepts so that a less familiar concept is connected to a more familiar one. We have resorted to metaphors of maps and territory, to help us deal with concepts associated with experiential learning, personal development and critical analysis.

Paradigm: a widely held world-view or belief system.

Personal map-making: the creation of personalised maps, based on individual goals and experience, and with specific journeys in mind. Personal maps tend to rely on examination of previously well-established, but general, maps.

Platform of understanding (POU): a standard conceptual map of a body of knowledge. The 'map' is deeply influenced by assumptions about the 'territory', the arbiters of which are authorities or experts. The formation of standard platforms of understanding has been deeply studied in theories of paradigm formation and change.

The basic structure of the book

An overview of 'map-reading' and of the contents of each subsequent chapter is provided in Chapter 1. There is a basic structure repeated throughout its core (Chapters 2–9):

- Orientation
- Overview
- Platforms of understanding
- Contextual materials
- Integration
- Getting personal
- Summary

Each chapter may be seen as a study journey of several related leadership dilemmas. The design encourages leaders to examine the maps provided and then to prepare personal maps around the issues raised.

Chapter 10 links historical materials and emerging issues of potential importance for future leadership journeys.

Orientation introduces the journey to be undertaken, and some of the key issues, often expressed as dilemmas.

Overview is a brief guide to the intended journey and sets out some of the key aspects of the terrain to be covered in the chapter.

Platforms of understanding are explained in Chapter 1. They can be seen as well-accepted descriptions of the topics being studied in the chapter, and the basis from which leadership maps may be constructed, tested and redrawn.

Contextual materials are more specific accounts of aspects of the topics, generally more closely connected with descriptions and prescriptions, and with less critical justification than the platforms of understanding.

Integration: the integration of more general and contextual materials begins the process whereby a reader is able to 'own' the text. We have tried to encourage even more personalised involvement by each reader in this section. In the search for specific leadership challenges, we provide examples of dilemmas we believe are particularly recurrent within the topic under consideration.

Getting personal: this section favours offering 'space to develop' rather than 'prescriptions to follow'. We suggest that the supplied dilemmas and commentary, as well as the 'good practice' ideas to be found in the integration process, are there for critical examination. This seems to us to be the most promising route for each reader/leader to establish how the ideas might have personal application.

Summary: in the final section, each chapter is summarised as an additional guide for readers to compare their understanding of its salient features with that of the authors.

These summaries are closer to the 'obvious' aspects of leadership knowledge to be found – with appropriate digging – in the many publications and textbooks we consulted in preparing the book.

Summary

Dilemmas of Leadership offers a series of leadership development opportunities for the reader. It does so by presenting current and important historical ideas about leaders and leadership as conceptual maps. Readers learn skills at map-reading, map-testing and map-making. *Map-reading* skills involve an appreciation of the stories or *myths* of leadership. One powerful myth is the importance of dominance or power, symbolised by the perceived relevance of the aggressive leadership processes observed in *mandrill* groups.

The metaphors of map-reading, map-testing and map-making are retained throughout the book. Consistent with the metaphor, the book is a support for leadership journeys. The maps are additional supports, and other map-makers (including the authors) are guides for the journey. Ultimately, however, the reader takes responsibility for preparing for a personal leadership journey in the future.

The leadership maps are based on shared belief systems which are described as *platforms of understanding*. A platform of understanding is comprehensively shaped by social beliefs more formally known as the elements of a *paradigm*.

A map is a simplified representation of a territory. It conceals uncertainties. Map-testing involves testing the maps for those concealed uncertainties. The recommended *comparative approach* is to look for unexplained differences between maps. This approach reveals the differences as *dilemmas* which are hard-to-resolve but important issues. Dilemmas by definition have no 'right answer'. Instead, leaders have to make decisions based on personal examination of the dilemmas for specific leadership challenges, drawing on personal mapping processes.

The processes of map-reading, map-testing and map-making are ways of developing a leader's cognitive maps, believed to be an important component in leadership effectiveness.

Notes

1 Boyatzis, R. (2004) 'Sustainable development of cognitive and emotional intelligence competencies through intentional change theory', Academy of Management paper, New Orleans, August; Boyatzis, R., Stubbs, E. and Taylor, S. N. (2002) 'Learning cognitive and emotional intelligence competences through graduate management education', *Academy of Management Learning and Education* 1(2): 150–162.

2 Kuhn, T. (1967) *The Structure of Scientific Revolutions*, Chicago: University of Chicago Press.

3 Stogdill, R. M. (1950) 'Leadership, membership and organization', *Psychological Bulletin* 47: 1–14, at p. 3; Bryman, A. (1996) 'Leadership in organizations', in S. R. Clegg, C. Hardy and W. A. Nord (eds) *Handbook of Organization Studies*, London: Sage, p. 276.

4 Smith, G. F. (2003) 'Beyond critical thinking and decision-making: teaching business students how to think', *Journal of Management Education* 27(1): 24–51.

5 Kolb, D. A. (1985) *Experiential Learning*, Englewood Cliffs, NJ: Prentice-Hall; Kolb, D. A., Rubin, I. M. and McIntyre, J. M. (eds) (1990) *Organizational Psychology: A Book of Readings*, 5th edn, Englewood Cliffs, NJ: Prentice-Hall.

6 Nonaka, I. and Takeuchi, H. (1995) *The Knowledge Creating Company: How Japanese Companies Create the Dynamics of Innovation*, Oxford: Oxford University Press.

7 Schön, D. A. (1983) *The Reflective Practitioner*, New York: Basic Books.

8 De Bono, E. (1992) *Serious Creativity: Using the Power of Lateral Thinking to Create New Ideas*, London: HarperCollins.

9 Yukl, G. A. (2002) *Leadership in Organizations*, 3rd edn, Englewood Cliffs, NJ: Prentice-Hall.

10 Northouse, P. G. (2003) *Leadership: Theory and Practice*, 3rd edn, Thousand Oaks, CA: Sage.

11 Storey, J. (2004) 'Changing theories of leadership and leadership development', in J. Storey (ed.) *Leadership in Organizations: Current Issues and Key Trends*, London: Routledge.

12 Bryman, A. 'Leadership in organizations' [see note 3].

13 Weber, M. (1947[1924]) *The Theory of Social and Economic Organization*, trans. A. M. Henderson and T. Parsons, ed. T. Parsons, New York: Free Press.

14 Stogdill, R. M. (1974) *Stogdill's Handbook of Leadership: A Survey of Theory and Research*, New York: Free Press.

15 Another influence was Mann, R. D. (1959) 'A review of the relationships between personality and performance in small groups', *Psychological Bulletin* 56: 241–270.

16 Bass, B. M. (1990) *Bass and Stogdill's Handbook of Leadership: Theory, Research and Managerial Applications*, 3rd edn, New York: Free Press.

17 Burns, J. M. (1978) *Leadership*, New York: Harper & Row.

18 Smith, G. F. 'Beyond critical thinking and decision-making' [see note 4].

2

Born or made?

Dilemmas of destiny and development

Orientation

The born or made dilemma

Popular accounts from all over the world have promoted stories of natural leaders, who succeeded without evidence of formal training, in business, politics, education, sport, and many other walks of life. Yet, leadership training and development has become a growth industry, and can also be found in all these spheres of activity, evidence of a widely held assumption that large numbers of people can be helped to achieve success in leadership positions. In everyday terms, these suggest a dilemma which may be posed as the question, 'Are leaders "born" or "made"?' In this chapter we investigate the maps of leadership for deeper understanding of such dilemmas involving the identification and development of leadership.

To present this more directly, we invite you to consider two somewhat different maps of leadership. As we will see, each has had considerable support in the leadership literature. The challenge is presented in Box 2.1. You may find it instructive to revisit your initial view on completing the chapter.

Introducing the natural leader

The taken-for-granted belief in the natural born leader was captured in a speech on leadership made in the 1930s at St Andrews University, Scotland, in which the Bishop of Durham, Dr Herbert H. Hensley, noted that:

> It is a fact that some men possess an inbred superiority, which gives them a dominating influence over their contemporaries, and marks them out unmistakeably for leadership . . . [in many walks of life] there are those who with an assured and unquestioned title, take the leading place, and shape the general conduct.[1]

We take the statement as one capturing the essence of beliefs about the natural born leader. We postpone comment on the bishop's insensitivity to the position of women as leaders, beyond noting that in his particular institution (the Church of England) the gender issue (appointment of female bishops) has become a contemporary dilemma threatening a worldwide rift (see also Box 2.2).

Box 2.1 A leadership challenge

Consider the following two leadership maps. Which one makes more sense to you?

Map 1: Each leader has a preferred style of dealing with leadership challenges. The style is largely fixed and permanent. An important factor of style is a motivating preference for relationships with people or a motivation for getting the work tasks done effectively. It is possible to be successful if you find situations in which the style matches the needs of the situation.

Map 2: Leaders find that their situations influence their style. Sometimes a leader is highly task oriented. Sometimes the leader shows concern with relationships. The characteristics of the task (time pressures, uncertainties of means and ends required) and the characteristics of colleagues (maturity, willingness to accept change) contribute to the different styles. The styles may be deliberately assumed, or they may be unconsciously shaped by circumstances.

● What are the implications of your preference for your leadership prospects?

Box 2.2 The little palace

The Indian province of Gujarat was ruled for many years by successive maharajahs. The maharajah reigned from a magnificent palace in the centre of the bustling town of Vadodara. The successor by birth, the eldest son of the maharajah, was prepared from birth to rule. For this to occur, the would-be maharajah was brought up as ruler in the little palace – a sort of maharajah finishing school – a few miles from the main palace, where he became familiar with being the unquestioned leader, to giving unchallenged orders, while being surrounded by servants and wise advisers, in a luxurious environment not too dissimilar to what he would find in his future palatial home. The practice reveals how, even in the most traditional of dynasties, succession went hand in hand with 'leadership schooling'.

Overview

Two platforms of understanding

In this chapter we will look more closely at leadership maps, for understanding the natural leader assumption, and the emergence of beliefs about the possibility of developing leadership capabilities in a wider group of people, less obviously 'natural born leaders'. We start with a platform of understanding of the historical eras of leadership research drawn up by the British leadership theorist Alan Bryman. The map was already incorporated into the 'map of maps' in Chapter 1. Now we look at its finer details.

The map shows how the early trait theories took for granted the existence of natural born leaders. Later theories opened the possibility of 'horses for courses', and the impact of personal development, of self-directed and of externally supported kinds.

Our second platform of understanding deals with the development of leaders and derives from a survey by David Day. The map also helps clarify the region of *leader* development (focus on the individual) and *leadership development* (focus on the leadership processes). The latter is territory less well explored in the mapping of natural born leaders. Day suggests that leader-focused maps deal more with forms of *human capital* and their manifestations, whereas leadership development is more concerned with *social capital*.

Contextual materials

The two platforms of understanding (of eras of leadership thinking, and of leadership development) are augmented with contextual materials providing more specific writings on these two issues. We start with historical and contemporary evidence of the power of natural succession to political and commercial leadership. This is followed with a short case example of someone who believed in natural leaders, while regretting he was not one of them. As a counter to this we outline an approach to personal development suggested and applied in executive education by Richard Boyatzis. Finally, we can compare two of the most influential international approaches to leadership development. The one is European in origin, the other North American.

Map-making for born-again leaders

After studying the materials you will be better placed to consider whether leaders are born or made. This is a major component within your own leadership future, affecting your motivation towards all forms of leadership development (including the one advocated in this book).

Platforms of understanding: leadership research and leadership development

We will look at two platforms of understanding:

- Alan Bryman on leadership in organisations
- David Day's meta-study of leadership development.

Alan Bryman on leadership in organisations

The British researcher Alan Bryman is one of the most respected and cited researchers taking a historical view of leadership. We will concentrate here on his review chapter 'Leadership in organizations', written in the 1990s, and we give particular emphasis to the eras up to that of 'new leadership' which the review helped to popularise.[2] Bryman traces the shifts in leadership thought, presenting a map that provides historical eras from pre-modern times to the rise of trait theories, and the period where trait theories became challenged by more behaviourally oriented ideas. Bryman essentially depicts all these theories as part of a wider 'old leadership' map, and contrasts them with an important map of new leadership which will be important in our subsequent map-reading and map-making activities. Our intention is to take a journey using Bryman's map to understand how trait theories of leadership became dominant, reinforcing beliefs about natural born leaders. We then explore how the decline in perceived significance of trait theories contributed to the eventual rise of interest in leadership developmental possibilities.

Changing eras, changing definitions

Bryman shows how differing views (maps) produce differing definitions of the map's features. We will be encountering this important point throughout our book: definitions of social constructs such as leadership are not absolutes but dependent on context. He indicates that an early definition was repeatedly cited and accepted for three decades, through the dominant influence of Stogdill's *Handbook*:

> Leadership may be considered as the process (act) of influencing the activities of a group in its efforts towards goal setting and goal achievement.[3]

Bryman interprets the definition as indicating how leadership was assumed to operate – through a leader influencing the behaviours of others (particularly followers), particularly where such behaviour influences the achievement of task goals. He notes the definition is not adequate for distinguishing between leadership and management. This lack of differentiation contributes to difficulties of distinguishing leadership and management processes, producing a dilemma to which we will return.

He contrasts this to a 'new leadership' definition dealing with the management of meaning:

> The leader gives a sense of direction and purpose through the articulation of a compelling world-view [the defining characteristic of which is] the active promotion of values which provide shared meanings about the nature of organization.[4]

Bryman's eras of leadership

We have become familiar with the stages of leadership thinking in the materials of Chapter 1. Bryman examined the stages to the 1980s and proposed a change that added to the maps now in common currency. Bryman takes a historian's approach and suggests distinct eras in leadership theory and research. He points out that the eras are indications of periods within which a particular sort of theory ('map') had dominance over other theories. This means that theories were to be found outside their era of dominance, first as faint signals of a theory whose time has not yet arrived; subsequently as vestigial traces of an older theory that has not been completely forgotten, or rejected. As is the case here, such formulations (general maps) conceal deeper issues only revealed by careful map-reading.

The Trait Era (1880s–1940s)

The Trait Era held sway until the 1940s. Emphasis is placed on the essential characteristics of leaders, which were presumed to originate in what would now be called genetically determined traits. The rise of trait theories followed the first attempts to conduct a scientific survey of genius, many years earlier, by Francis Galton.

The Style Era (1940s–1960s)

The Style Era refocused on what leaders did, rather than on their inherent traits. The most influential organisational studies such as the Ohio State investigations set a trend for investigating the reports of followers (a trend followed in the subsequent Contingency Era). Researchers attempted to reduce styles to a few overarching variables, often producing two-dimensional models of *people orientation* and *task orientation*. This conceptual parsimony provided elegance at the expense of excluding other factors that were introduced in the subsequent contingency era.

The Contingency Era (late 1960s to early 1980s)

Contingency theories may be seen as more complex style theories, incorporating situational variables. A contingent variable is one whose significance in a theory is contingent on circumstances. A people-oriented leader style may be more or less effective according to the level of training and education of followers.

The New Leadership Era (1980s to date)

This era is to be covered in subsequent chapters. Its distinguishing features are a move away from the trait, style and contingent modes through focus on leadership as a socially constructed process (management of meaning). A second feature of the new leadership approach was a process of transformational change. This was a clear differentiation from the two earlier eras of style and contingency, although the origins of trait theory could also be regarded as grounded in leader traits associated with major transformations.

The contingency/situational terminology

For an introductory map, Bryman's eras are adequate. However, terms such as contingency theory and situational theory are used in different ways in the leadership literature. Bryman considers situational theories as forms of contingency theory. Gary Yukl suggests that the contingency models are forms of situational theory. Readers will have to study each map they find to establish what the map-maker is implying when using these terms. One of the most widely referenced situational maps emphasises the uniqueness of a leader's style. Contingency maps tend to emphasise the possibility of a leader flexibly shifting style according to environmental context (contingency).

The trait approach: its rise and fall

Traits are fixed characteristics differentiating leaders from non-leaders, including physical traits (physique, height, appearance), abilities (intelligence, communication abilities) and personality characteristics (self-confidence, extraversion, conservatism). We are already familiar with the trait approach, and its dominating effect on leadership research. Bryman indicates that the dominance was challenged since the 1940s by Stogdill's tireless and extensive surveys. Successive editions of Stogdill's *Handbook of Leadership Research* continued to explore the problems associated with the trait approach. In one sense, trait approaches dominated the stage, but were far from being the only show in town. Stogdill had no intention of making an attack on trait theories, when he began his work. However, as is widely known, the search for absolute qualities distinguishing leaders from non-leaders was to prove frustratingly difficult. A major survey of the field at the end of the 1950s had contributed to the growing interest in behavioural approaches.[5] By the 1990s, Stogdill's colleague Bass, in the third edition of the *Handbook*, was wondering whether the accumulated evidence had sounded the death knell for trait theories.[6]

However, when the earlier work was re-examined in the 1980s, using more careful methods, the analysis showed that three traits retained their significance: intelligence, dominance and masculinity. The researchers linked their findings with a reinterpretation of traits as utterly intertwined with perceptions. That is to say, for example, that perceived intelligence is more significant than some absolute measure of intelligence.

The style approach

Bryman considers that the uncontested era for trait theories ended around the 1940s. He points to a shift away from the 'great man' leaders – presidents and founders of organisational dynasties – towards the practical problems of selecting leaders within the tiers of organisational pyramids. Stogdill was at that time at Ohio State University, whose methods and results were also to become highly influential in the field of leadership. The methods were characterised by the design and application of inventories (self-report measures).

The findings from the Ohio studies have become part of common knowledge. In non-technical terms, they found a people-orientation factor and a task-oriented factor. Their more technical terms used were consideration and initiating structures. Practical implications were easy to see: the early data suggested that style influenced performance. Specifically, consideration (as a style) was associated not only with good morale and job satisfaction, but also with lower performance, with the converse true for initiating structure as a style. This anticipates the later research in which leaders with strengths on both factors outperformed single-factor leaders.

The heritage of the Ohio studies can be found in a continued enthusiasm within leadership studies for information derived from self-report and leader-report inventories. As various explanations were examined, a consensus seems to have been reached that trait theory was in need of revision. The early work had offered a theoretical idea in opposition to trait theory, namely that leadership style (behaviours) was the key to understanding leadership impact. The refinement lay in the suggestion that the precise way in which style impacted on group performance was mediated by other factors. This is the central idea of any contingency theory, in which 'causes' are presumed to produce different outcomes according to specific circumstances or contingencies.

Contingency approach and the least preferred co-worker model

According to Bryman, the contingency theories attempted to explain the confusions of early theories by introducing the possibility of 'it all depends' thinking, to overcome the evidence that otherwise refuted the possibility of a general theory relating leadership style to group performance. He identified the model developed by Fred Fiedler and co-workers as the best known of the contingency approaches.

This theory suggests that a leader's disposition to favour task or relationships may be assessed by self-reports by the leader's views of co-workers, and specifically of his or her views of the least preferred co-worker (LPC). A leader who sees good qualities in such co-workers is disposed to relationships. A leader who is unable to see such qualities is likely to be more preoccupied by task accomplishment.

Initial studies went some way to confirm the claims of the LPC model, which has received widespread attention and criticism for several decades. In time, the link between LPC scores and leadership was challenged. Critics wondered why the contingent or situational factor of situational control (meaning favourableness to the leader) was selected as the only situational factor (over alternative contingencies such as stressfulness of the situation, or the possibility that emergent leaders, whose views were not collected, were playing a part in the leadership processes). Unsurprisingly, in light of the complexity of the model, a wider range of empirical results were to prove inconsistent, although under some circumstances, the general theory appears to be supported in practical trials.

As with the still-dominant trait assumptions, the leadership differences were assumed to be fixed, with the implication that an organisation had to be vigilant for changing circumstances calling for a change in leaders of differing LPC characteristics.

David Day's meta-study of leadership development

David Day carried out a thorough examination of leadership development from three interrelated perspectives, of theory, practice and research.[7] One of his broad findings was that the practice of leadership development offered many recipes for conducting programmes for achieving desired goals of leadership development. Unfortunately, he was able to find little substantiation of the connections between the practices and those goals. Although participants and deliverers of such programmes claim success in various ways, the evidence was difficult to assess (see Box 2.3).

Day gives a clear illustration of one of the ways in which leadership research is particularly complex to study and execute. He first differentiates between *leader development* and *leadership development*. The former focuses on the individual leader, and historically was the more important of the two treatments. ('This is what leaders are and do; this is what you need to do to be more like them.') The latter begins from the wider picture of the overall dynamics of organisations within which leaders and others engage in their work.

According to Day, leadership development embraces the individual focus, rather than replaces it. Day complained of the lack of a link between theory and practice. He develops this idea in an examination of six of the most influential techniques for leadership development:

- 360-degree feedback
- coaching

> ## Box 2.3 How a meta-study is carried out
>
> A meta-analysis involves a thorough examination (generally requiring statistical manipulations) through which data from different studies of a subject of shared interest are studied. Specifically, such an analysis often seeks to explain why factors appear to be positive in some circumstances, and negative in others. This is often the case for concepts of a high level of generality, particularly if applied in a range of different contexts.
>
> The power of a meta-analysis lies in its potential for revealing major factors and their interrelationships in a topic of interest. A weakness lies in the need to redefine the original data sets to produce a common standard for statistical manipulation.
>
> In this chapter we see the results of a meta-study on leadership development. Later we will encounter other metastudies, on trust (Chapter 6) and on the differences between genders in studies of leadership styles (Chapter 8).

- mentoring
- networking
- job assignments
- action learning.

360-degree feedback

As shown in Box 2.4, 360-degree feedback involves assessment processes within which executives (leaders) give feedback to and receive feedback from 'significant others', if possible at higher, lower and equivalent levels in the organisation. The 360-degree nomenclature indicates the intention of operating a process that includes as legitimate the views of 'lower downs' and peers, as well as 'higher ups'. The technique reached widespread corporate attention in the 1990s, when a majority of Fortune 500 companies were reporting as using it, or claimed to be planning to use it. Even this, the least embedded of the approaches, has attracted disputes regarding its benefits in leadership development, with supporters claiming it offers competitive advantage, while others see it as yet another management fad.

Coaching

The next two approaches, coaching and mentoring, are two overlapping means of developing leadership competences. Both stretch back to ancient civilisations as educational approaches. Both approaches fit well into the idea of passing on experience through direct encounter between a less experienced (almost always

---

Box 2.4 Why should 360-degree feedback be such a powerful leadership development approach?

David Day's meta-analysis of leadership development identifies 360-degree feedback as the most powerful and widely used leadership development approach. The approach involves assessment processes through which executives (leaders) give feedback to and receive feedback from 'significant others', if possible at higher, lower and equivalent levels in the organisation.

The power and importance of 360-degree feedback is acknowledged by programmes offered by the Center for Creative Leadership, one of the most respected and largest of leadership development institutions (http://www.ccl.org).

● Why might 360-degree feedback have achieved such powerful status as a leadership development approach?
● Can you examine this question using a map-reading and map-testing approach?

---

younger) person, and a more experienced one. Coaching is a term generally associated with the provision of specific sets of behavioural skills (negotiation, communication, presentation skills would be typical leadership examples). The processes tend to assume that codified knowledge is transferred from coach to learner. The term has a particularly wide set of connotations, from developing skills for sporting leaders, to relevant support systems for students of all ages facing examinations and other competitive entry educational requirements.

Mentoring

Mentoring is the classical term for the relationship between a mentor, with deep and relevant knowledge and experience, and a less experienced recipient. Unlike coaching, the knowledge transfer is less concerned with specific skills, and the acquired knowledge more likely to be diffuse. Mentoring is thus more clearly developmental, with vicarious absorption of experiences sometimes called tacit knowledge.[8] This feature opens the possibility of informal mentoring relationships, as well as more institutionally arranged ones.

Evidence on the impact of mentoring suggests that its effectiveness is highly contingent on factors including the formality or informality of arrangements, and gender and ethnic permutations of mentors and recipients. The broad evidence indicates that mentoring schemes rank highly among leadership development initiatives. However, such evaluations remain in need of firmer grounding. For example, more work is needed to identify the characteristics of effective mentors. Such studies would enrich maps of leadership processes.

Networking

Formal programmes have been implemented to encourage business leaders to develop their personal networks in the interests of their organisations. Motorola has focused at the level of vice-presidents in a programme seeking to identify and capitalise on entrepreneurial activities. The programme also seeks to transfer knowledge about the company's heritage and culture (achievements also associated with mentoring).[9]

Networking has been recognised within knowledge management research, as having a connectivist basis. This makes the distinction between theories which consider knowledge as inherent in individuals (cognitivist theories), and those concerned with relationships across individuals (connectivist theories). These theories consider that organisational systems are self-structuring, as a consequence of the information flows through multiple connections (networks) among its individual members. Such processes are increasingly mediated electronically.[10] The networking approach to leadership development is the most obviously connectivist one.

Job assignments

Job assignments have played a part in management development programmes for many years. The simple assumption (not necessarily wrong, therefore!) is that individuals learn by being exposed to varied challenges of relevance to current or future jobs. The argument has been widely applied to justify business exchanges, foreign delegations, even overseas school trips. It will be noted that a job assignment programme will inevitably enhance a change in networking activities of those involved, so that the evaluation of the one technique against the other is a complex matter.

Action learning

Action learning is a term applied to a wide range of experiential learning processes. The processes tend to involve projects as the vehicle for learning, often directed to important business problems.

The term is sometimes used interchangeably with the term 'action research', associated initially with Kurt Lewin and the Group Relations school in the United States, and subsequently with the Tavistock Institute in the United Kingdom. Action research introduced a revolutionary thought into the conduct of organisational research, the notion of deliberate involvement (rather than deliberate detachment) of researchers. Discovery processes occur 'from the inside'. (The notion is new only in context: social anthropologists had long accepted the value of involvement in their investigations of other cultures.) The process comes with a need to work through issues of 'objectivity' and whether findings could be generalised.

A more precise application of the term is to identify it with the work of the British social science innovator Reg Revans. His book *Action Learning* summarises his influential approach.[11] Revans developed a learning methodology involving managers (leaders) from different industries in applying their collective know-how in turn to problems within an action learning group or set. Although such sets are assisted by a facilitator experienced in the action learning approach, the responsibility for learning lies with the participants in the learning set (avoiding the dependency dilemma).

Contextual materials

On being born great

Shakespeare wrote with brilliant insight into leadership, several centuries ago. Nowadays, his words stay with us as we consider the nature of leadership, and his historical dramas are studied within leadership courses. It was Shakespeare who pointed out how some are born great, while others acquire greatness. His plays had powerful messages on issues that were of utmost importance to his audiences, and the exercise of power was a frequent theme. It was a time when the institution of monarchy in England was under threat. There was no serious question that pedigree dictated the right to rule or be ruled. The matter was widely settled by acknowledgement that the birth had been divinely ordained – the divinely given rights of kings. The great debates and wars often occurred around questions of birth, and therefore the legitimacy of kings to rule.

Shakespeare was at one level offering a summary of ways through which power is granted – through birthright, through personal effort, or through being the chosen instrument of some king-making (or queen-making) instrument. He suggests two ways in which a king may be made: he may 'make it', by dint of achieving greatness; he may be 'made king' as the chroniclers put it – that is to say, some may have the job 'thrust on them'. Shakespeare points up the nature of 'bloodline' leadership and the dilemmas posed by such leaders who appear weak (how can the 'one and only sovereign' be deposed?).

History and dynasty

Succession by virtue of bloodline results in the installation of a dynasty, a process explored so deftly by Shakespeare, and much later condemned by Weber as a primitive form of social process. Weber anticipated the replacement of primitive institutional forms of power with more rational forms of succession, particularly in economic organisations. His analysis was in accord with the challenge to 'the divine rights of kings' fought out often in bloody struggles for self-determination and widening of democratic rights (France and the United States being the most quoted examples). Yet, at the start of the twenty-first century, the ancient processes of succession to top leadership position in politics remain far from being fully rational.

Heads of state and prime ministers continue to have an affinity for the old idea of dynastic succession. Winston Churchill was the eighth generation of the aristocratic Marlborough family, and the third generation to enter parliament. The Kennedy 'clan' in the United States was widely regarded as some form of dynasty whose claims on the presidency came almost by birthright. In the 1990s, Lee Kuan Yew of Singapore was widely believed to be grooming his son for ultimate ascent to his rightful position as Lee's heir. It is at least plausible to assume that George W. Bush may have had some benefits from being the son of a former president. Dynastic succession and birthright still mattered in twentieth- and early-twenty-first-century political affairs.

The family firm as dynasty

Dynastic succession is not confined to the political estate. It can be found around the world in organisations, and nowhere more obviously than in the ways of family firms. Even in the United States, proud of its contributions to defining the democratic 'way of life', family firms continue to have dynastic features. Joc Kennedy created a business dynasty before his heirs erected a political one. Three generations of Fords have headed the dynasty founded by Henry Ford. An Wang was creating a dynasty from his electronic calculators and other innovations, before control was passed from his son, as the firm restructured itself. In popular culture, the cult TV series *Dynasty* offered a distorted but recognisable view of a world outside the box. A romanticised view of criminal dynasties has been fictionalised in sagas such as *The Godfather* and *The Sopranos*.

In the United Kingdom, the business empires of William Lever (Unilever), Richard Cadbury (Cadbury Schweppes), Joseph Rowntree and Thomas Cook all flourished down generations of family governance. Meyer Amschel Rothschild founded a banking dynasty which, likewise, prospered for over two centuries under family control. An early TV example of the fictional English dynastic family was John Galsworthy's *Forsyte Saga*.

While other western examples could be found, the locus of family culture in business lies to the east. Increasing interest in the west is being paid the role of the family firm in Asian cultures. Jamsetji Tata founded the Tata dynastic conglomerate based on his original cotton mills. The Chinese family enterprise is of particular importance, as China's economic growth continues. Dynastic succession can be found associated with economic growth in the region, although its interpretation is made more complicated as founding entrepreneurs became engaged in the construction of the mighty state conglomerates (zaibatsu in Japan; chaebôl in South Korea). Eastern dynasties such as the Yi family (Samsung, South Korea), Mitsui and Sumitomo in Japan would be significant examples.

One of Australia's wealthiest tycoons, Rupert Murdoch, appeared to have dynastic aspirations in the 1990s, with both son and daughter encouraged to find high office in his own and other organisations.

Culture theorist Fons Trompenaars suggests that family-style corporate cultures are characterised by a special kind of power, calling for obligations on high-status leaders (usually 'father') of the business towards lower-status 'family' members, and loyalty towards the leader from the employees/followers. The power, as in social family groups, is seen as necessarily pervasive, perhaps strict, but essentially benign. He suggests that many examples of family-style cultures can be found in nations that were late to industrialise. Trompenaars cites Greece, Italy, Japan, Singapore, South Korea and Spain. He also describes the privileges of family over non-family, citing an example of a Brazilian owner arranging for his young and inexperienced nephew to have major responsibility in an international joint venture. The Brazilians saw it as a signal of commitment from the family, while their Dutch partners were puzzled by what must have seemed to be a lightweight choice of leader.[12]

Leadership development

Are leaders made or born? This innocent-sounding question poses a fundamental dilemma facing would-be leaders, concerning their own chances of achieving leadership success. It is also one that successful leaders have to form a view on, in seeking the future leaders of their organisations. If we pose this simple question at the start of executive programmes, we find evidence of a split in opinions: some believe leaders can benefit from training, others take the contrary view (and of course, some say they are there to find answers to just such questions). We have found a similar split among MBA graduates from around the world.

The fixed trait view

The one view is that 'real' leaders have special characteristics, largely fixed and probably genetically determined. Implicitly this is a trait view, and perhaps one which might be described as the 'right stuff' view of leadership. One common line of argument used to support this view is to give examples of well-known leaders from historical or contemporary times. The success of great military leaders such as Napoleon and Alexander 'obviously' had little to do with training programmes. Self-made business tycoons were often considered to be poor learners, by their exasperated teachers. The Edison Museum recounts how the young Thomas Edison was expelled from school as someone unteachable, and unlikely to amount to much in life. Florence Nightingale typifies the outstanding leader who achieved much with little evidence of education preparing her for life as a leader.

The developmental view

The opposing view is implicit in worldwide leadership development programmes. Officer training is in principle a process which both identifies and develops military leaders. Business education implicitly, and sometimes explicitly, has a similar objective.

John Adair's action-centred approach is among the most widely diffused approaches to leadership development, originally provided for military officers, and subsequently across industry.[13] Many of those executives who hold that leaders can be developed have participated in such programmes, or know colleagues who have done so. They share Professor Adair's view that leadership can be developed, a perspective handed down from the times of Socrates and one of his students, the military general Xenophon, who believed that 'the right stuff' (whatever it is) is not universally distributed:

> As Xenophon implied, some degree of leadership potential has to be there in the first place. Many people possess it without being aware of the fact. Given the need or opportunity to lead, some encouragement, and perhaps a leadership course or programme, most people can develop this potential. Those with [more natural potential] can become greater [within their particular circumstances] providing that they are willing to work hard at becoming leaders.[14]

Development programmes: the Center for Creative Leadership

The Center for Creative Leadership (CCL) is regarded as among the foremost and most experienced global leadership development organisations in the world. CCL was founded as a non-profit educational institute in 1970, through the generosity of its initial sponsor, the Richardson Foundation. From its original headquarters in Greensboro, NC, it has developed into a global institution, with other sites in North America, Europe and Asia, as well as contacts with other international locations through networking activities. Its commitment to research and training over the years has resulted in a community of researchers which has produced over a hundred books on leadership development. An estimated 400,000 professionals participated in its programmes in its first thirty years of operations. In the United Kingdom, for example, Ashridge Management College built its extensive leadership programmes in the 1980s and 1990s through a franchise from CCL. Manchester Business School also became involved in its programmes for technical leadership over a period of years, through its Research and Development (R&D) Research Unit.

CCL serves as a valuable example of practices that were to emerge in other leadership development centres. Its flagship open course on leadership development has evolved since 1974, while retaining a coherent educational approach grounded in personal awareness exercises, psychometrics and skilled facilitated feedback. Over time, additional courses were developed for corporate, educational, military, community and volunteer leaders. Some 20,000 participants attend programmes each year.

The CCL philosophy

CCL considers self-knowledge to be the single most important factor in the practice of leadership. Its role is to provide an environment in which self-knowledge and discovery flourishes, permitting personal development. This philosophy explains the emphasis placed on feedback, and the efforts exerted in developing practically powerful instruments such as 360-Degree Assessment, which has probably contributed to its recent worldwide interest and application.

As its name implies, the Center for Creative Leadership has pioneered interest in the link between creativity and leadership, a field in which Stan Gryskiewicz has been active for several decades. Many leading researchers have been attracted as visitors and collaborators, including Don MacKinnon to continue his work into the creative personality, Teresa Amabile at Harvard, who researched intrinsic motivation and creative climate with CCL course participants, and Michael Kirton, who studied adaptive and innovative leadership styles.[15]

Impact studies

Impact studies have been conducted, and CCL now has numerous case studies as well as more formal impact surveys reporting on its findings.[16] Results were obtained from a study out of its European location in Brussels (although based on a limited sample of 84 respondents from 132 participating in programmes over the period April–November 2002). The impact reports were considered to be consistent with assessments of CCL development programmes elsewhere around the world.[17]

The study evaluated the impact of objectives of the leadership development programme. The objectives illustrate the scope of such activities, and are listed here:

- increasing self-awareness
- improving leadership capabilities
- increasing ability to learn from experience
- valuing differences
- building and maintaining relationships
- giving and receiving developmental feedback
- setting and achieving goals
- communicating effectively
- developing others
- building effective teams
- developing strategies for life balance.

Self-report data one month and four months after the programmes gave similar patterns of response. Approximately 75 per cent of the sample reported learning gains around self-awareness, by far the most frequently reported learning gain. More modest proportions (between 19 and 24 per cent) reported learning gains in understanding and valuing others, increased awareness of developmental goals, communicating in a more open fashion and acquiring a more positive view of leadership capabilities. Other learning gains were less frequently mentioned (between 1 and 13 per cent).

Only a minority of respondents reported no (perceived) change in their leadership capacity after one month (11 per cent), with slightly reduced proportions after four months (8 per cent). In contrast, 34 per cent reported significant change and 54 per cent partial enhancement of leadership capabilities after one month. These results changed marginally (47 per cent and 44 per cent respectively) after four months.

Consistent with the evidence of personal development, the most frequently reported organisational gains were of self-improvements (40 per cent), work climate (29 per cent) and direct deliverables (product and process outcomes, 14 per cent). Proportions again increased (to 53, 58 and 45 per cent respectively) after four months.

Action research study

An action research study reported on CCL's website summarised work conducted jointly with CCL in 2003 by Catholic Health Care Partners (CHP). Evidence of behavioural changes associated with the programme was found on all measures examined, using a 360-degree feedback methodology: 18 leaders (69 per cent) and 139 of their respondents participated. In general, the changes were modest but significant, showing a 'rising tide effect' (general overall movement of 20 to 15 per cent in the same direction) for measures such as improving self-awareness, setting and achieving goals, and working across organisational boundaries. Organisational impacts (which we may compare with the direct deliverables of the study above) were assessed as improved for general group effectiveness (64 per cent of respondents), productivity (39 per cent) and efficiency (36 per cent).

More qualitative evidence of impact from the study came from interviews. The leaders had successfully introduced several projects with associated cost benefits of other measurable corporate benefits (for example, in demonstrable improvement to services to patients, working with an associated rehabilitation centre).

Pioneering studies

Our emphasis has been on CCL's contributions to leadership development. Much of leadership development still reveals its 1970s origins, when leadership was still studied according to the contingency models described in this chapter. CCL is also studying and applying the ideas that will be important elements of the newer maps found in subsequent chapters: project leadership (Chapter 3), transformational and relational leadership (Chapter 4), and of the diversity and ethical issues, and prospects for the leader of the future (Chapters 8–10).

Developing a personal view on leadership development

The Center for Creative Leadership, Greensboro, NC, has had considerable experience in training and in researching leadership development. It suggests three important ways in which leadership development programmes may have value, namely assessment, challenge and support.[18] We have already come across these factors in Day's meta-analysis of leadership development practices. These factors provide a framework for analysis and critique, although they permit the examination of programmes from both trait and developmental perspectives. Assessment is perhaps more obviously linked with a trait approach for identifying 'real' leaders, although it may also identify potential for development. Challenge and support may be seen as more obviously linked with developing leadership skills, although it may also serve as an identifier of 'real' leadership talent.

John Adair and action-centred leadership

It is hard to overestimate the contributions of John Adair on leadership education in the United Kingdom and beyond. Adair's contributions to leadership courses at the prestigious military college at Sandhurst in the 1960s gave him unrivalled access to the military commanders and heroes of the Second World War. His unusual career (adjutant to a Bedouin regiment in the Arab Legion, deckhand on an Arctic trawler, military historian) gave his writings a combination of insights from wide experience and great scholarship. Estimates of participants at subsequent programmes around the world, based on his action-centred leadership approach, have been set at approximately 1 million. To understand the intentions of his approach, we have to examine the deeper ethical and conceptual grounding which he tried to retain within his development programmes.

The European cultural tradition

As a historian, Adair regards leadership as drawing on three sources, which have become particularly integrated within the European culture of leadership. First, a *tribal tradition* treats a leader as 'first among equals', anticipating a more egalitarian and democratic society. Second, an *eastern tradition* has provided us with the view of the leader as the cultural transmitter of moral values. According to this tradition, the leader has to avoid the (all too human) trait of arrogance. The links with ethical leadership (Chapter 9) are clear. The approach also reduces the dilemma of the tyrannical leader ('the Hitler problem'). Third, the *western tradition* derives from the teachings and philosophy stretching back as least as far as two and a half millennia, to Socrates and his group in Athens. The key concept is that authority flows from knowledge. Furthermore, this tradition has become associated with democratic beliefs, that the knowledge is not an inherited gift, but rather something that may be cultivated through education. Through this long tradition, the country's innovations in parliamentary democracy took shape as the notions of democracy and freedom were worked out. These are values that require active leadership for their preservation.

Functional leadership

At Sandhurst, Adair worked on an approach to military leadership development, which he saw as drawing on the motivational theories of Abraham Maslow and Frederick Hertzberg, and the classical managerial theories (more influenced by Henri Fayol than Frederick Taylor).[19] Adair described his work as a functional model, and the functional elements were only marginally modified over many years of use in and beyond their original military setting:

- planning
- initiating
- controlling
- supporting
- informing
- evaluating.

Adair captured the essential components of leadership in a model of three regions represented as three overlapping circles, each with a single word label:

- task
- team
- individual.

The leadership functions were enacted across these three interacting regions of achieving the task, building and maintaining the team, and developing the individual.

Origins of action-centred leadership

John Adair moved to the Industrial Society, and his functional leadership model acquired the name it retained thereafter, action-centred leadership (ACL), developing away from the earlier military context and course contents. Participants in the courses shifted towards supervisory organisational levels. The Industrial Society was renamed the Work Foundation in 2002 and has continued to develop its leadership contributions within a framework of improving the quality of British working life.

Adair considered the three overlapping circles a powerful learning and communications device, although he regretted a tendency for it to have lost much of its conceptual grounding when replicated in many leadership books and courses.[20] His own courses would always indicate the deeper aspects of the map of ACL. Specifically, he claimed to have retained what he called the qualities approach, which had diminished with the decline of trait theories of leadership. Adair remained constant to the view that leaders had exceptional qualities (even if they had not been easy to pin down in rigorous research). He suspected that ideas about the exceptional leader had become unfashionable as in some way anti-democratic and elitist. This encouraged him to resist the rejection of individual traits ('qualities') in understanding leadership. His view anticipated a revival in interest in personal qualities, with the so-called new leadership ideas of the 1980s, which we examine in Chapter 4.

Interestingly, Adair did not consider the qualities of an exceptional leader in what were to be known as essentialist terms. Rather, he considered them qualities expected of the leader by their colleagues and work groups. In this he anticipated the remapping of leadership, away from what was later to be called *essentialist* theories, to *constitutive* ones (in which the 'specialness' derives from the perceptions of the social group).[21]

Situational leadership, participation and motivation

Adair introduced aspects of situational leadership within his ACL courses, giving particular acknowledgement to the well-known representation by Tannenbaum and Schmidt.[22] This suggested that leaders could effectively deploy approaches in which decisions were shared with others, as the group developed its own maturity. For immature groups the leader may have no better option than to 'tell or sell'; for more mature and development groups, the leader is able to involve and delegate. Adair argued (following Maslow) that involvement and participation supported individual (and team) motivation. In ACL, situational leadership is presented for its insights into functional components (leader actions in practice) of motivating leadership. Adair notes (but sees no serious dilemma in) a group's need for consistency in a leader, and yet for the situational needs of a leader to enact various decision styles over a short space of time.

I know I'm not a born leader

Our story is one we could repeat from many personal accounts of would-be leaders. It concerns Alan, who had left his employment as a professional in a financial institution and was studying for his Master in Business Studies: 'I just wanted out of banking. I hoped maybe I could learn more about being a leader, although I know for sure I'm not a natural leader.'

How had Alan arrived at that conclusion? Mainly from his work experiences. In group work, he felt most comfortable as a loyal follower, finding a niche, and generally supporting the ideas and proposals of more dominant group members. He recalled what happened on his leaving party. His boss read out the conclusions of some personal inventory Alan had been assessed through.

> He probably meant it as a joke. It more or less said I was not cut out for being a leader. I have had other tests, and they all seem to be saying pretty much the same thing. My preferred style at work is to be a team player. I suppose my boss was telling me I shouldn't bother going to business school. I don't have what it takes to become a leader.

Alan went on to describe how the decision to go back to 'school' had turned out to be a good one for him. He found that he was accepted by his new colleagues from various parts of the world, who sought him out as a team colleague. Although some were more obvious leaders than he was, in their various group activities, he developed such a newly found confidence that at times he could take the lead.

Alan says that he knows 'for sure' that he is not a natural leader. But his action in studying leadership within a formal course of business studies suggests that he believes (or maybe desperately wants to believe) that he can become some kind of leader. He went out to search for what he wanted, and found confirmation of his hopes. Other would-be leaders respected him (in considerable contrast to his boss at the bank). He did not make the connection directly in his story, but he talked not of his leadership traits, but of his leadership style. Style is something that can be worked on and developed; traits are more persistent psychological features of one's make-up.

The story also says something about the leadership and organisational culture. Alan does not state that the behaviours at the leaving party were particularly out of the ordinary. If so, the culture seems one of insensitive banter. How pathetic, the boss suggested, that someone as ill-equipped as Alan was leaving, to become a *leader*. Alan's view was that the boss 'probably meant it as a joke'.

Richard Boyatzis and intentional change theory

One of the most vociferous advocates of the merits of leadership development is Richard Boyatzis. He began a long and fruitful collaboration with David Kolb on the nature of experiential learning ('learning through doing') and then became interested in personal competencies. This led to work with David Goleman on emotional intelligence (EI), and a formal leadership development programme within the Weatherhead School of Management at Case Western Research University.[23]

Competencies are capabilities of individuals for effective action. According to Boyatzis, there are three clusters of competencies germane to leadership:

- cognitive abilities
- self-management skills
- social skills.

Most management programmes (and particularly MBA programmes) are mostly concerned with the first cluster of cognitive abilities (use of concepts, quantitative analysis, written communications, and so on). The other two clusters are more closely associated with EI, which has gained considerable research interest (and controversy) following claims in the 1990s that EI is a stronger indicator of leadership effectiveness, than cognitive skills as measured by classical intelligence quotient (IQ) measures. Boyatzis bases his work on careful measures of performance of executives undertaking executive education programmes. He offers evidence that performance on the emotional intelligence factors increases, as the programme is geared more towards social skills and self-management.

Intentional change theory model

Intentional change theory proposes that leader development programmes support personal change through offering ways in which intentional change strategies are organised. The principles behind this model are shared with the ideas of other personal development practitioners.[24]

This model encourages focus on perceptions of *actual* and *ideal* self-images for moving towards achieving individual leadership goals. The focus is enhanced through experimentation in a climate of trust, augmented by coaching (one of the six developmental systems noted above in Day's meta-study). For Boyatzis, coaching is a means of helping others in their intentional change efforts. Under such conditions, the individual seeks (and is more likely to find) understanding of gaps between actual and ideal self (image) and also acknowledgement of strengths (when ideal and actual perceptions are similar).

The theory further suggests that positive emotional experiences (claimed as a left-prefrontal cortical bias) are more promising for developmental change than negative ones (claimed as a right-prefrontal cortical bias). Thus, the attention should be more on finding future possibilities, building on strengths, rather than on coping with weaknesses through gap-filling remedies.

As self-directed and intentional change develops, the individual is better able to cope with unexpected changes and shocks. Such experiences become less threatening, disorienting, and less likely to be assessed as potentially catastrophic. A benign personal development process has been established.

Integration

The eras of leadership map gives us a simple picture of changing views of leadership. We learn from it that for many years leaders were assumed to be born. The assumption is central to traditional, bloodline succession (e.g. 'divine rights of kings'). It is now time for us to apply a closer critique to these ideas, to reveal their dilemmas, and relevance for personal development.

We noted how such successions accepted that the young heir required wise advisers to prepare them for a life as a leader. The trait era thus can be seen to hold to two assumptions: first, that the 'best leader' is dictated by bloodline, so there are no questions of identifying and selecting from a wide range of pretenders. (We noted, in passing, that the legitimacy of a leader may also exclude female heirs.) The second assumption is that the young leader benefits from development (sometimes difficult to disentangle from notions of education and training). These assumptions carried over from succession in traditional cultures to the governance of family firms, where it is still often taken for granted that there is a succession 'right' for the eldest son to ascend to leadership of the firm.

The assumption persists when someone rates himself or herself as not being a 'real leader' (as illustrated in the case of Alan, described above). Training is presumed to create a Pygmalion surrogate or phoney leader, perhaps able to bluff through many leadership challenges, but always risking being found out as a phoney. Unlike the young maharajah (Box 2.2), development was not believed to be a substitute for being of the 'right stuff' in the first place.

The development dilemma of embeddedness

Trait theories were largely replaced by leadership behaviour theories. Yet the trait theories did not completely die away. If we look closely we see the dilemma that persists and which helps explain why the behaviour theories never completely succeeded. This is the dilemma of *embeddedness* of developmental programmes. To study and gain convincing information about programme influence on leadership, you need simple programmes, with one or two defining operational characteristics. The 360-degree feedback programmes would be a good example.

According to Day in his meta-analysis of leadership, development programmes that are simple to study are relatively simple and disconnected from other necessary factors that would promote leader behaviour change. He terms this the degree of embeddedness of the programme. The dilemma is that the study of simple programmes is the study of incomplete programmes of development – while the study of richer and core complex programmes ('embedded' in organisational practices) finds difficulty in 'disembedding' the elements of the programme that are making a difference to leadership performance.

The consequence of the dilemma is that researchers of simple programmes such as 360-degree feedback can make statements only about simple empirical relationships (at a time where leadership theories have become more aware of multifactorial nature of change, including intervening and contingent factors). Conversely, researchers deploying complex designs such as action learning may acquire evidence that 'something seems to be working' through their use, although the mechanisms (revealed in the simpler programmes) have become lost in a complex 'black box' of activities.

Getting personal

Do I have the 'right stuff' of leadership?

Few people have unswerving belief in their own leadership potential, so such doubts need not disqualify you as a wannabe leader. Perhaps you may now be reflecting on the question, taking the information above into account. Alan found himself in an environment which reinforced his doubts about his leadership capabilities. How have your views been influenced? Have you been sustained by an encouraging mentor or family member? Or have you been more influenced in environments closer to the one that Alan experienced? Many leaders spent their early days with their leadership potential unnoticed. One of many examples befell the young Thomas Edison, a giant of technological discovery, and ultimately founder of a great industry (electric power) and a mighty organisation. Edison was sent home from school with a note from a teacher saying that he was unteachable, and that he probably would never account for much in life.

We have seen that leadership is, in any case, no longer assumed to be a special set of attributes which you are born with. With the more systematic examination of leader characteristics (fixed traits), the bloodline assumption became increasingly open to question, particularly in firms, where the assumption was not backed up by recourse to a divine right to rule. In the absence of identifiable sets of traits, the leadership dilemma of selection or development emerged.

It now becomes more appropriate to ask the developmental questions suggested by Boyatzis, for those in search of intentional personal change. One of the intentional change theory elements is the benefits accruing from a positive orientation. Can you think of strengths that will help you achieve those leadership goals? Look back at people who had a deep and long-term constructive influence on you. What did they say and do, and how did it make you feel: enthused? motivated? See also Box 2.5.

Box 2.5 Positivity and Pollyanna: a leadership challenge

There are various arguments in favour of an optimistic orientation by a leader. We have touched on one theoretical justification in the intentional change theory of Richard Boyatzis. Another related view can be found in many writings on stimulating creativity in individuals and teams.[25] Yet another justification has been made that positivity arouses positive emotions and supports willingness to accept change.

However, we would not wish the view to be offered without some reflective effort on the part of the reader. We have many experiences of executives who associate a positive orientation with naïve, impulsive and unconditional positivity towards all ideas and suggestions. This is sometimes referred to as a Pollyanna outlook. Therefore, we would ask you to give some thought to what might be framed as a dilemma:

● Does positivity in a leader risk blindness towards real dangers and difficulties?

Even more importantly, we suggest you pose the matter as personally as possible:

● Has positivity risked me being blind towards real dangers and difficulties in my past experience?
● Is positivity likely to do so in the future?
● On balance, should I make it part of my leadership strategy to present a positive attitude?

Summary

This chapter confines itself to two main maps of leadership, one covering eras of thought about leadership, the other dealing with the territory of leadership development.

We took as our journeys an interest in a fundamental dilemma, whether leaders are born or whether they can be developed. The earlier eras favoured the idea of leaders born to greatness. Even now, we have the unthinking acceptance of the 'bloodline' in leader succession, for example in family firms all over the world.

When scientific studies failed to locate the ingredients that made up the right stuff of leaders, traits theories fell out of favour among researchers. They were replaced by increasingly complex theories, shifting emphasis from leaders (the person) to leadership (leaders, followers and their interactions and consequences in context). Studies refocused on leaders at supervisory and project team levels, as well as on the more exceptional person. This opened up the possibility for leadership development.

Leadership development programmes have become a ubiquitous part of life for people in many professions, including business. Evidence of success of such programmes is extensive, but difficult to evaluate, partly through the vested interests of those involved in them. In addition, the dilemma of embeddedness adds to the difficulties of evaluating specific programmes in a thorough-going critical fashion.

We indicated that the first map covered territory adjacent to additional theories (the so-called new leadership theories) to be covered later, and which will offer new dilemmas, and reinterpretation of older ones.

(Note: The shift in emphasis from traits to behavioural theories is far from the end of the story. Traits were discarded too comprehensively, and a mixed trait/behavioural 'map' is becoming more important than the earlier maps which kept the processes separate.)

The leadership challenge

At the start of the chapter we set you a leadership challenge. It amounted to asking your view on two popular and conflicting views of leadership. The first view or map takes a rather fixed view of human preferences and behaviours. Each leader has a preferred style of dealing with leadership challenges. The style is largely fixed and permanent. Our preference for people over tasks (or vice versa) is hardly influenced by circumstances. Leadership success depends on identifying the appropriate niche.

The second map takes a more fluid view of human behaviours. (Note that it may not take a more fluid view regarding human preferences.) As a leader you may find yourself being directive or supportive. You may be autocratic or participative. The factors influencing behaviour will arise from the situation.

The maps capture one aspect of the born or made dilemma. The first map was popularised by Fred Fiedler's work in the 1960s and 1970s initially with sports teams and military units. These groups had clear objectives and easy-to-assess performance criteria. According to Fiedler, the preferred style was relatively fixed. This permitted identification and selection of appropriate leaders for a given situation. Sometimes this would be a more supportive leader, sometimes a more directive one. It did not consider that development training would change the leader's basic orientation. The results eventually proved inconclusive and were unable to sustain a fixed-behaviour theory. Nevertheless, it offers further evidence that there is no 'one right way' of leading. A modification to the map is provided by Elliott Jaques, who proposed a stratified set of capabilities.[26] Each individual is assumed to develop through experience, but always within a predetermined band. Individuals with greatest potential had greatest cognitive complexity.

The second map offers the possibility of a leader who deliberately changes style according to circumstances. Several very influential development models present this map for leaders to follow. Among them are the path-goal theory of Robert House and co-workers and the approach of Hersey and Blanchard (see Chapter 4). These approaches are particularly strong on diagnosing leaders' preferred styles. These views are more compatible with leadership development programmes.

Notes

1 Quoted in Adair, J. (1989) *Great Leaders*, Guildford, Surrey: Talbot Adair Press, p. 13.
2 Bryman, A. (1996) 'Leadership in organizations', in S. R. Clegg, C. Hardy and W. A. Nord (eds) *Handbook of Organization Studies*, London: Sage.
3 Stogdill, R. M. (1950) 'Leadership, membership and organization', *Psychological Bulletin* 47: 1–14; Bryman, 'Leadership in organizations', p. 276.
4 Bryman, 'Leadership in organizations', p. 276.
5 Mann, R. D. (1959) 'A review of the relationships between personality and performance in small groups', *Psychological Bulletin* 56: 241–270.
6 Bass, B. M. (1990) *Bass and Stogdill's Handbook of Leadership: Theory, Research and Managerial Applications*, 3rd edn, New York: Free Press. Cited in Bryman, 'Leadership in organizations', p. 277.
7 Day, D. V. (2001) 'Leadership development: a review in context', *Leadership Quarterly* 11(4): 581–613.
8 Polanyi, M. (1967) *The Tacit Dimension*, New York: Anchor.
9 Day, 'Leadership development', p. 596.
10 Von Krogh, G., Roos, J. and Kleine, D. (eds) (1998) *Knowing in Firms: Understanding, Managing and Measuring Knowledge*, London: Sage.
11 Revans, R. (1980) *Action Learning: New Techniques for Management*, London: Blond & Briggs.
12 Trompenaars, F. (1993) *Riding the Waves of Culture: Understanding Cultural Diversity in Business*, London: Economist Books, pp. 141–145.

13 Adair, J. *Great Leaders* [see note 1].

14 Ibid., p. 37.

15 McCauley, C. D. and Van Velsor, E. (eds) (2003) *The Center for Creative Leadership Handbook of Leadership Development*, 2nd edn, San Francisco, CA: Jossey-Bass.

16 Hernez-Broome, G. and Hughes, R. L. (2004) 'Leadership development: past, present and future', *Human Resource Planning* 27(1): 24–32.

17 Ascalon, M. E., Van Velsor, E. and Wilson, M. (1994) *LPD Europe Impact Study*, Greensboro, NC: Center for Creative Leadership.

18 Van Velsor, E., McCauley, C. D. and Moxley, R. S. (1998) 'Our view of leadership development', in C. D. McCauley, R. S. Moxley and E. Van Velsor (eds) *The Center for Creative Leadership Handbook of Leadership Development*s, 1st edn, San Francisco, CA: Jossey-Bass.

19 Adair, J. (1979) *Action Centred Leadership*, Epping, Essex: Gower.

20 Adair, J. (1990) *Understanding Motivation*, Guildford, Surrey: Talbot Adair Press.

21 Grint, K. (1997) *Leadership: Classic, Contemporary and Critical Approaches*, Oxford: Oxford University Press.

22 Tannenbaum, R. and Schmidt, W. H. (1973) 'How to choose a leadership pattern', *Harvard Business Review* 51 (May–June): 162–175, 178–180 (reprinted from 1958, *Harvard Business Review* 36 (March–April): 95–101.

23 Boyatzis, R. E. (1982) *The Competent Manager: A Model for Effective Performance*, New York: Wiley; Boyatzis, R. E., Stubbs, E. and Taylor, S. N. (2002) 'Learning cognitive and emotional intelligence competences through graduate management education', *Academy of Management Learning and Education* 1(2): 150–162.

24 Pedler, M., Burgoyne, J. and Boydell, T. (2001) *A Manager's Guide to Self-Development*, 4th edn, London: McGraw-Hill.

25 Parnes, S. J. (ed.) (1992) *Sourcebook for Creative Problem-solving*, Buffalo, NY: Creative Education Foundation Press.

26 Jaques, E. (1989) *Requisite Organization: The CEO's Guide to Creative Structure and Leadership*, Arlington, VA: Cason Hall/Gower.

3

Dilemmas of coordination and boundaries in project team leadership

Orientation

In Chapters 1 and 2, the focus of the maps was very much on the leader – either as a special person, or as someone from whom special behaviours and results arise, through a process of leadership development. In this chapter we will look at a special form of organisational structuring which sets the context for many leadership efforts. The form is the team project, and the dilemmas are those facing the project team leader.

Many readers will be familiar with projects, either through direct experience, or perhaps through what you have learned from business courses. However, both sources of knowledge tend to gloss over aspects of project leadership, which we will approach in this chapter. The direct leadership objective of the chapter can be summed up as indicating ways in which project leaders can understand and deal with the dilemmas of leading their projects in practice.

The project leader challenge

Take a few minutes to reflect on your current understanding of organisational projects (Box 3.1). You may already feel comfortable making your map using the approaches found in Chapters 1 and 2.

The importance of the project team structure

Project teams have been acknowledged as the organisational structure of choice for conducting a specified organisational task, in many different contexts. In the second half of the twentieth century, technological projects around the world grew in complexity. The achievements of the NASA space programmes were one of the high-profile boosts for such project teams, followed by endorsements from teams shaping the innovation goals of emerging high-technology global firms, as well as the quality goals of firms in more mature industries. Nowadays, the project team has received attention as the structure of choice for innovation and technological development

---

Box 3.1 Your current map of project leadership

What do you think are the necessary aspects that would be needed for an organisational process to be described as a team project? What do you consider are the circumstances that would suit such projects? What might the special challenges be for project leaders? You may wish to start with a summary of your ideas before giving the matter critical thought. This tests what you believe, and in that sense there is no right or wrong answer. If you then examine these ideas following the critical approach outlined in Chapter 1, you have a basis for reassessing your earlier ideas.

● What are the necessary aspects that would be needed for an organisational process to be described as a team project?
● What sort of situations may be particularly suited for team projects?
● What special challenges might face project team leaders?

---

projects, and a well-respected means of structuring organisational tasks more generally where the task involves the creation and implementation of change. More broadly, the creativity industries including the performing arts are widely dependent on project teams in artistic productions. The leadership of such teams, in all their diverse forms, is an important issue.

The nature of project teams

One essential feature of project teams is the primacy of the project task. Regardless of leadership influences, team members are 'led' by their commitment to the task – be it 'to design a global tsunami detection and protection system', 'to recreate *Hamlet* in modern dress for an open-air performance' or 'to develop a sugar-free chocolate bar'.

Why project teams face dilemmas

Any organisational form exists as a means of dealing with uncertainties. In the project team format, the uncertainties are largely concealed in the clarity of the major goal, and the explicitly defined constraints, roles, criteria of success and so on. However, the structure and functioning of teams create often unnoticed dilemmas for team leaders that we reveal in this chapter. We have described them as dilemmas of coordination and of boundary management.

Dilemmas of coordination arise because the nature of the project goal is essentially holistic, and has nothing to say about whether sub-tasks and individual differences may require reconciliation, for effective achievement of the primary goal. As a diversity of skills and knowledge may be required, the team leader has to find ways of aligning the needs of project team members, perhaps from different professions and cultures.

A related dilemma arises because a project simplifies its primary task and conditions by clearly defining the boundaries of the team and its responsibilities. This process inevitably sets up boundary spanning dilemmas. The leader protects the team from the complications of the world outside the defined boundaries of team responsibilities. So processes have to be set in place to permit communication across those boundaries – perhaps with markets, or with other people in the wider organisation. If the communication is totally unfettered, the benefits of the team structure are lost; if the boundaries are completely closed, the communications suffer, and in many instances, the achievement of the project's primary goal is compromised.

Overview

Two platforms of understanding

In this chapter we examine the processes of leadership of such teams, selecting two major international reviews for our platforms of understanding (maps). The first is a survey of the contemporary literature of teams and team leadership from an American perspective. The authors prefer the term 'action teams', but suggest how this terminology is close to the more generic term 'project team'. The map provides us with an interpretation of integrative team processes as a form of *social problem-solving*. Team leadership is a means of supporting the team's problem-solving efforts. This approach indicates the lack of attention to the process of integrating individual efforts (a signal of a coordination dilemma) and proposes that group problem-solving is a powerful means of setting up integration mechanisms *within* project teams.

Our second map provides a European perspective of the team leadership territory. It traces team leadership roles from the original concept of the entrepreneurial leader, to a range of roles which were to spring up subsequently. This map shows how there are coordination dilemmas connected with knowledge transfer *across* the boundary of team and its environment. It also provides a different means of dealing with the integration challenge through a more distributed approach, involving several kinds of leadership role within a single project.

Contextual materials

To help us appreciate the dilemmas, we then examine a range of contexts. The first contextual map explores the idea of self-managed work teams, which leads to the new idea of shared (distributed) or even invisible leadership. The second map introduces a more dynamic element to team processes. In practice teams develop and change and learning takes place. We look at Bruce Tuckman's well-known group development model and a more recent remapping which explains failing and exceptional team performances. Next we take a look at sporting teams as examples of simple goal-oriented groups. Finally, we touch on the emotional life of groups as interpreted by psychodynamic theorists.

Integration and personal mapping

The new mapping found in the materials of this chapter presents us with the issues of project coordination and boundaries. We hope to recognise the potential and limitations of the project approach in organisational innovation and change. We may also see ways of revising our map of leadership itself through the possibilities of more distributed or shared leadership roles.

Platforms of understanding: project leadership

We will first look at the work of Stephen Zaccaro and colleagues, and then at some European studies.

The team, the project and the leader: a functional approach

We have already seen how early leadership studies focused on what leaders *are* (traits) and later studies focused on what leaders *do* (or get done through others). Stephen Zaccaro and Andrea Rittman of George Mason University, and co-worker Michelle Marks of Florida International University, conducted a survey of team leadership, taking the second approach.[1] They refer to this as a functionalist or action approach, thus implying its defining characteristics as observable and plannable activities.

Action teams

Zaccaro and Rittman take as a definition of an action team:

> a distinguishable set of two or more people who interact dynamically, interdependently, and adaptively toward a common and valued goal/objective/mission who have been assigned specific roles or functions to perform and who have a limited lifespan of membership.[2]

The researchers identify what they call action teams as a covering term for functional teams including performing and production teams. They see this as a subset of all possible teams, citing also project teams, service teams and parallel teams. Thus, their work spans the complexities of leading a team with members working around the world (Boeing and Airbus projects), to the challenges of a local community trying to fund-raise for facilities for a local community centre, to the team assembled to create an advertising campaign.

Team leadership and social problem-solving

Zaccaro and colleagues regard the activities of an action team as being directed towards a process of *social problem-solving*. This distinction acknowledges that the processes are essentially social, rather than individual. As implied in the definition, the model places rather less emphasis on the efforts of isolated individuals, and more emphasis on the *interdependencies* of those individuals. It furthermore brings the activities of teams into the territory of problem-solving in general, and team problem-solving in particular. The researchers suggest that in a great deal of the extensive literature on teams, the emphasis has been on the *differentiation* of roles, rather than on the way in which the activities (functions) of differing roles require *integration* or *coordination*.

A three-stage sequence of functional activities in social problem-solving is presented as:

- solution finding (generation)
- solution selection
- solution implementation.

Four main dimensions are associated with the stages: there are two information dimensions:

- search for information
- structuring of information

and two resource dimensions:

- personnel
- material resources.

Other researchers have proposed differing numbers of stages in problem-solving, and have offered different labels to the stages.[3] We will therefore take this classification as being specifically constructed from studies of leadership, giving it particular authority in that respect. In our subsequent critique, we consider other 'maps' of the territory offering somewhat differing perspectives.

Internal coordination processes

The model implies differing responsibilities allocated to individuals as team roles. This is a modern version of Adam Smith's principle of division of labour, originally recognised as the key to economic efficiency. Associated with division of roles is the leadership issue of coordination *within* a team across these role boundaries.

(The boundary spanning questions of coordination issues between a team and its organisational and market environments is considered later.)

Three management features are identified as relevant to internal leadership coordination processes:

- shared mental models
- collective information processing
- team metacognition.

One of the three features, the development of shared mental models, occurs internally, rather than through observable processes necessary for a functional approach. We will also be revisiting this territory in subsequent chapters.

Collective information-processing is often well codified, incorporating structured group techniques such as brainstorming, stage-gate sequencing and decision-matrices. Thus, collective information processing has become strongly connected with a participative leadership style, and with attempts to encourage 'empowered' behaviours of team members.

Metacognition is a term generally referring to 'knowing about knowing' processes such as personal or group discovery processes. Structures and actions associated with such discovery learning, creativity, self-insight and development all help in a functionalist way in enhancing a team's metacognitive processes and outcomes.[4]

Performance feedback

Zaccaro and colleagues' article strongly couples metacognition with performance feedback, suggesting that the discovery of shared mental maps is enhanced through deliberate discussions of team actions. As was suggested in Day's list of development processes (Chapter 2) team leaders can help, by providing performance feedback to team members, and by encouraging collective reflection.

Team cohesion, task orientation and the efficacy effect

The functional analysis of team integration has to borrow from less functional social science theories to address the question of *how* mental models become shared, of *how* information is collectively gathered, of *how* individual metacognition becomes a team's metacognition. In other words, functionalism has particular trouble with the coordination of individual perceptions.

Managing non-cognitive processes

The functional approach tends to emphasise observable and rational behaviours. Such an approach differentiates between cognitive and non-cognitive procedures.

Broadly speaking, cognitive conflict, once resolved, is regarded as more likely to result in enriched outcomes, whereas affective (emotional) conflict (worsened under operational crises and high stress) is difficult to resolve, and largely undesirable. Resolution involves (or is consistent with) the rational problem-solving which we have seen lies at the core of the functionalist approach. Clear shared goals, role assignments and performance strategies are believed to reduce 'unhelpful' emotional reactions, particularly under stressful circumstances.

From such a perspective, emotional reactions are regarded as potentially unhelpful for team effectiveness. As such they offer opportunities for leadership interventions, and for establishing 'leader-shaped control norms'. By encouraging or discouraging specific emotional responses, the leader indicates the appropriateness or otherwise of displays of emotion in the working patterns of the team.

Implications of a functionalist approach

The functional model of team leadership suggests how a thoroughgoing rational approach leads to effective project work, and the alignment of individual and task requirement. The allocation of roles, and leader-shaped behaviours, succeed in the processes of solution search, selection and implementation. Zaccaro and co-researchers are aware of significant assumptions implicit in the majority of writings on the subject. The team operates with an initial problem which is adequately defined and stable enough to permit rational search, selection and implementation processes. If conditions are unclear (or even worse, unstable and turbulent) the team risks an inappropriate focus for action ('solving the wrong problem').

There is increasing recognition of widespread turbulence in project environments. In principle, the development of the metacognitive skills discussed above goes some way to dealing with this issue. A second implication of turbulent environments is a shift towards more distributed leadership as projects teams are forced to become more sophisticated, and to confront more ambiguous and complex challenges both internal to the team, and in the team environment.

Innovation leadership

This map takes a closer look at leadership within innovation processes. The author, Jürgen Hauschildt, has been a pioneering influence in this area, and specifically in studies into the different roles of influential players in the innovation business. In a book on the dynamics of innovation, he reviews the field.[5]

Product champions and other project leadership roles

Professor Hauschildt identifies the seminal influence of Josef Schumpeter on the theory of innovation leadership. Schumpeter identifies the innovation leader as a descendant of the entrepreneurial leader, who re-emerged within the emerging industrial organisations, and particularly within technological departments. In the 1960s, Donald Schön introduced a new term for this type of leader, the *product champion*, a term later popularised after NASA's adoption of the term.

In Germany, the concepts of entrepreneurial leader and project champion were reinterpreted as three leadership roles, providing different contributions to the group's performance:

● The *power promoter* contributes resources and hierarchical potential, and is generally in a high-status position within the organisation.
● The *technology promoter* contributes specific technical knowledge to the innovation process, and influences through know-how, rather than high status.
● The *process promoter* catalyses or supports the processes of change, and may be seen as a form of team facilitator, whose role is to enable rather than to direct change.

Boundary spanning roles

A series of studies by Ancona and Caldwell offered further clarification. Their work showed the importance of boundary spanning roles in innovation research. They suggested four kinds of activity: ambassadorial, task coordinating, scouting and guarding activities.[6] Hauschildt considers that the work, as well as pointing to boundary spanning, also may be taken in support of a model of innovation promoters as essentially managers of conflict and of cognitive activities.

Complexity and division of labour

System complexity and division of labour offer challenges contributing to the nature and number of kinds of innovation champion in a specific project.[7] It has been suggested that the early prototypic project champion was a technological professional, and was the focus of relatively simple project tasks. As complexity and division of labour increased, other 'forms' of leadership emerged, as entrepreneurs and product champions. Yet more complexity and executive champion roles developed. The overall map here implies that the more complex environments incorporated the earlier forms of leadership – rather than substituting them. That is to say, complexity has resulted in leadership activities distributed across more roles, and different types of leader within one project.

The promoter model summarised

Early research identified a committed champion as the most important role for success in project management. Subsequent work identified other individuals with other sets of skills dealing with conflicts constructively, and handling information creatively. Hauschildt identified a dilemma facing the innovation leader. The literature of project management emphasises formal organisational tools such as matrix management, Gantt charts and stage-gate procedures at the expense of behavioural principles. Those approaches emphasising behavioural principles (such as creative or facilitative leadership) conversely pay limited attention to structures and tools for project management.

Contextual materials

Self-managing work teams

Manz and Sims contributed to the popularisation of self-managed work teams, through empirical observations and theory development reported in an article in *Administrative Science Quarterly*, in 1987. They later popularised their theory through a successful book in 1989 on *Superleadership*, and reworked it a decade later.[8]

At the core of their work is an important idea, namely that many of the responsibilities assumed by traditional leaders have been handed over, thus empowering the wider team. Empowerment has overcome the absence of a direction-giving leader. The superleader is effectively the total team; leadership may be thought of as *distributed* among the team members. The leader is not so much a hero as a maker of heroes.

Superleaders

Manz and Sims contrast limitations of three conventional leadership types, before turning to their new leadership form. They classify these as the strong man, the transactor and the visionary leader.

- *The strong man* style is portrayed as the bullying and uncaring leader. They suggest that the style is commoner than is generally admitted, even in successful and highly regarded organisations. They cite a president of the Kellogg organisation who had been ousted for grounds materially around his ultra-abrasive style. They list other examples, such as Pepsico's culture, which *Fortune* described as being like a boot camp, rewarding the survivors, and making it easy for those not comfortable with the arrangements to drop out. Those who are comfortable and effective in this culture receive the spoils. Those who are not comfortable tend to leave early in their career.
- *Transactors* are similar to the task-oriented leaders modelled in Chapter 2. Their influence style is based on the exercise of direct transactional rewards and punishments to subordinates. The style is particularly inappropriate for situations calling for radical or transformational change.

- *Visionary leaders*, while recognised as often engaged in radical change processes, are described as vulnerable to ignoring succession dilemmas, and failing to develop others. As a consequence, visionary leaders may only be succeeding in developing dependency.

Superleadership, participation and involvement

Although only one organisational production unit was studied, Manz and Sims provided evidence of a carefully developed statistical kind to illustrate perceptions of teams on their self-appointed internal leaders, and also on the external facilitators. In addition, careful observational studies and interviews were carried out.[9]

The impetus for the work is presented as a perceived weakness in American work practices in the 1980s, associated with decreased quality of production, absenteeism, high labour turnover and disruptive behaviours. These weaknesses are associated with the most common organisational cultures and leadership styles. The premise for change is that such styles alicnate the workforce, through failing to provide a genuine sense of involvement in and commitment to corporate goals. The basic challenge, then, is to find ways of 'power sharing' in the interests of productivity gains. The proposed approach is through participation and involvement.

At the time of the articles, involvement and participation in work design had appeared to have come and gone. A particularly innovative approach by the Volvo car company in Sweden had been discontinued. Although a gross simplification of the issues, the failure of a single experiment was taken as evidence of the refutation of an entire innovative approach to work design. Furthermore, what was believed to have failed in a car manufacturing context was assumed to be unworkable in any organisation whatsoever. Under such circumstances, leaders of organisations in the 1980s were not inclined to consider participative methods as their vision for the future.

They faced the challenge of many innovators: how to present the basic idea as appealing and worthy of support. However, there were examples of self-managed work teams succeeding, in Europe and even in corporate America, where some middle managers, often at plant level, had been conducting their own experiments in work design. These believed from experience that a participative approach could achieve substantial results. These results had often been found in plants physically remote from the scrutiny of a head office.

Manz and Sims reported in detail as an illustration of what could happen through such an approach. The team system was found in what the researchers described as a small-parts plant. The site had been set up some years earlier, as a potential experiment in innovative work practices, and had been located in the southern United States. At the time of the research, the evidence collected suggested that the plant was believed to be running at a 20 per cent gain in productivity over what might be expected from traditional work design systems. The local workforce was non-unionised and approximately 320 employees worked at the plant. The ultimate owner is described as a large corporation.

The degree of autonomy of the teams in this particular example was actually found at a rather modest level. The increased ownership of the self-managed teams over their roles was confined to discretion over in-group methods of work. It did not provide for discretion over work targets as such. It included the right to allocate differential payment levels to group members, yet not discretion over the overall size of the group salary budget. The more strategic levels of decision remained the province of others at a different (higher) level in an organisation, which still had distinct layers of management if not a traditional pyramid of control.

The upper level is the classical executive level, dealing with the overall planning and client interface responsibilities. The middle layer included the people who were regarded as the external coordinators of the self-managed teams. It is this level at which we find the innovation in project leadership. The role of *team coordinator* had emerged as the plant developed its self-managing team approach. It was a role that had considerable ambiguities – for example, was it a leadership role? If so, it had different kinds of leadership responsibilities than any experienced before. Manz and Sims took the coordinator to be a new form of external leader, and examined the characteristics and context of the role.

The teams ranged from three to nineteen in size, with the majority having eight to twelve members. Each team elected a team leader. Teams were trained in ways that enhanced their skills, for example in problem-solving and in communicating in supportive ways. They were also trained in more task-specific areas, linked with remuneration levels. Overall, the training was reported as enhancing the self-efficacy of the workforce.

The teams would sometimes invite their coordinators to join them for specific problems, although the whole approach sought to avoid the natural deference towards his or her status or expertise. One way this had developed was through a culture in which the coordinators would operate in an opening-up or questioning style. This style avoids reinforcing the pattern of seeking answers outside the team, rather than attempting to work them out at an individual or team level.

The researchers concluded that the leadership functions of the coordinator and team-selected internal leader were significantly different from leader roles to be found according to prevailing 'top-down' leadership theory.

In their subsequent work, Manz and Sims collected and described numerous examples of such leadership roles and practices both from their own experience and from other sources. They suggest that the original idea has become aligned with a wider range of innovative approaches concerned with achieving high performance through high commitment teams.

The concept of self-managed teams remains a promising means of dealing with the dilemma of coordination of interests.

Team development processes

Much of the work on project teams and team leadership makes the assumption that the team is able to execute its required team goal or objective. While this may be the case for well-established teams, leaders also have to work with newly constituted teams. As such, a map of team development processes is of value.

Bruce Tuckman's stage model of team development

In the 1960s, an American educationalist, Bruce Tuckman, proposed a synthesis of existing research of groups and group development. He suggested that team processes passed through the stages of

- forming
- storming
- norming
- performing.[10]

With the subsequent addition of the unsurprising termination stage, the Tuckman model remains widely accepted.[11] It has the considerable merit of face-validity for the majority of team members and leaders. That characteristic requires that the different terms make sense to people, who are able to recognise and discriminate each stage from the others.

Appeal to common-sense is (unfortunately) not enough. In practice, attempts to define the stages accurately within the activities of real-life teams have largely failed. Some teams seem able to operate at a high level of performance, immediately after their formation. An interesting suggestion is that such teams carry with them a pre-existing 'shell' providing a set of expectations, and from which collaborative and competent team actions spring.[12]

Other teams have been found to cycle through successive iterations of storming and performing, or show sequences of stages unpredicted in the simple Tuckman model.

Such considerations have led researchers to challenge the basic precepts of the Tuckman model, and raise questions relating to what may be seen as the storming and outperforming dilemmas respectively:[13]

- What happens when a team fails to pass the storm stage?
- What happens when a team outperforms expectations?

One suggestion is that the model conceals two different kinds of barrier. Some teams, even with adequate resources for the task, seem to spend far too long in a storming mode. These are unkindly called teams from hell, and have been found in project-based organisations as well as in student assignments.[14]

Furthermore, a minority of teams do exceed expectations. These two refinements to Tuckman's map have been linked to the possibility that a facilitative or creative

Box 3.2 Boundary management and self-managed teams

Another explanation of the leadership of self-managed teams (SMTs) is offered in a study by Druskat and Wheeler.[15] These researchers looked at a large consumer goods manufacturing plant in the Midwestern United States, which had moved to self-managing work teams. The plant had some 3500 employees, many organised into work teams. There were 66 external 'advisers', each with responsibilities for five to eight teams.

The inside/outside dilemma   Druskat and Wheeler point to the well-reported importance of managing the boundary of work teams and the increased importance placed on the role of boundary management in SMTs. The literature presents the role with the metaphor of someone at a boundary, or in a related term, as a *gatekeeper* between two otherwise separated territories, or an *ambassador*.[16] The occupant risks been regarded as an outsider in both territories. How, then, might such a leader operate? A careful qualitative analysis revealed evidence of a cluster of high-performing leaders and another cluster of moderate-performing leaders. The superior leaders in general showed greater tendency towards various practices, manifest both outside and inside the team boundaries.

> Our data suggest that for an external leader, spanning boundaries and shifting attention and allegiance back and forth from a team to an organization requires conscious strategic manoeuvring . . . Team members' and managers' poor understanding of the leadership tasks required on the *other* side of the boundary contributed to the ambiguity around boundary spanning.[17]

leadership style may be particularly suited to achieve progress. A facilitative style encourages openness among team members, thus reducing the barrier often found at the storm stage. The style is also effective in encouraging teams to challenge their own mental maps and thus discovering unexpected and innovative possibilities for change (see Boxes 3.2 and 3.3).

Sporting teams and their dilemmas

The effectiveness of sports teams has been a matter of direct interest for sporting managers, and specifically the special roles of front-line manager or the performance coach, and the on-field captain. Both kinds of team leaders have become popular additions to the executive lecture circuit. Their relevance to more general leadership issues is a beguiling possibility, although specific contextual features (as so often) must not be ignored.

Box 3.3 Team development and creative leadership

One approach to team development has been provided by practitioners of techniques for stimulating creativity at the level of the team. The approach has been variously described as facilitation, team process leadership and creative leadership. It has found particular attention within the so-called creative problem-solving methodologies associated with Alex Osborn, pioneer of the brainstorming approach. The approaches were extensively researched and refined, initially at the Creative Education Foundation, Buffalo, NY, and subsequently in a multitude of centres around the world.

The style of a brainstorming leader is marked by efforts to concentrate on team processes – encouraging all other members of the team, at the expense of avoiding contributing his or her own (task-related) ideas. Osborn's original concept of brainstorming was a means of overcoming the tongue-tied junior members of work groups in meetings. Later work suggested that his basic principle of deferral of judgement generally had a positive effect on productivity of idea-generation groups.[18]

Other related approaches include the synectics method of creative problem-solving.[19] Pioneers George Prince and Bill Gordon and subsequent co-workers developed procedures for the creative leader in idea-seeking and problem-solving sessions to include ways of encouraging team-building, idea generation and idea support. They also initiated ways of triggering powerful metaphoric images.

Some researchers regard the leadership style and formalised structures of techniques for stimulating creativity as particularly appropriate for innovation-seeking teams, supporting the relevant creative climate, and even enhancing boundary-spanning processes (e.g. by involving the outside sponsor or client in the team activities).[20]

A distributed leadership system

For example, in team sports like football, the coach remains isolated from the team when it is in operation, acting as non-playing leader. There is an on-field captain, who may be able to provide direct leadership instructions during periods of 'time out' (rugby, football of various kinds, and so on). The coach may have a similar opportunity during a half-time break. In less professional codes, coaches are often former players with no specific technical training. Prior reputation may help establish their credentials as coach, and many leadership principles with which we have become familiar come into play – charismatic coaches are common.

A sporting leadership dilemma: who is in charge?

In sport, various such distributed leadership systems are commonplace. They offer the first sporting dilemma: 'Who is in charge?' From time to time, the on-field captain and non-playing coach disagree. In one infamous incident, the captain of a World Cup football team, en route to the championship finals in 2002, attacked the lack of training facilities and the general leadership failures of the coach in a dressing-room confrontation. The matter could not be resolved to everyone's satisfaction: the captain was sent home and was not selected again, even though rated the best player in the team. The remaining members of the team rose to the challenge they were facing, and performed as well as might be expected. However, the coach did not survive the captain in his post for much longer after the competition ended. The handling of the critical incident is worthy of further consideration by any team leader.

Distributed leaders: the theory of sporting architects and performance anxiety

A conceptual approach to football coaching has been introduced by Sven-Göran Eriksson, the Swedish coach of the England football team. The team had, arguably, under-performed for many years, often when coached by charismatic former players. Reluctantly, the Football Association of England opted for Eriksson, the first ever non-English manager of the team. The team qualified against the odds, and lost a close game to the eventual winners (Brazil) in 2002. Despite continued media opposition and nationalistic antagonisms, Eriksson had consolidated his leadership position.

Eriksson's style was in contrast to the more uncomplicated and experience-based style of many English coaches. He was evidentially more articulate (he communicated well and in an engaging way with the sporting media in several different languages). He even brought with him a developed theory of on-field leadership in association with Swedish psychologist Willi Railo, drawing on visualisation, positive thinking and cognitive reframing.[21]

According to this theory, a successful football team of eleven requires about three leaders – one of whom is a designated captain. These form a core demonstrating the required leadership behaviours that work to promote necessary behaviours from others. The performance in the teams is then sustained by the behaviours and influence of the core leaders, which are effective in countering reactions from less positive players, which could spread rapidly and negatively, particularly after setbacks in play. The outcome is a culture in which *performance anxiety* is reduced. This adds to more familiar team characteristics (visionary thinking, mutual respect and support of all team members, ambitious goals, concern for quality).

Treatments for team pathologies

There is a large body of work referring to the weaknesses of teams as a special kind of working group. We will take a look at the theories of team dysfunction here. We leave the equally interesting issue of the dysfunctional leader to Chapter 4.

One of the most comprehensive approaches to examining and seeking to deal with various team weaknesses of this kind has emerged from the Group Relations movement in the United States. A related approach drawing on various psychodynamic influences was developed from workers associated with the Tavistock Institute in Europe.[22] Among these figures, one pioneer, Wilfred Bion, is widely acknowledged as drawing attention to the displacement of the planned and rational activities of groups by largely unconscious influences.

One of Bion's distinctions extends the intra-personal concepts of Freudian psychology to intra-group concepts. Bion considered that some groups retain a strong grounding in the reality of the present. Other groups were more influenced by unconscious and emotionally charged forces. He described the former as task groups and the latter as basic assumption groups.

Specifically Bion identified three forms of basic assumption: dependency, fight-flight and pairing. He suggested that the basic assumption provided the group with its reality, a world *as if* the hate object was an enemy to be defeated or *as if* the leader is the all-providing and all-knowing saviour who may also become another hate object. The conceptual grounding of basic assumption theory remains a matter of the deepest debate within the psychoanalytical community.

Social groups offer protection from anxiety, although the means may be through a distortion or denial of the direct evidence of their working experiences. In extreme cases (maybe not even extreme cases) the work of the group becomes filled with fantasies of what might be happening and what might happen in the future.

The fundamental principles of group dynamics have been integral to the design and implementation of project-based experiential learning in many institutions internally including schools of business in Australia, Canada, India, the Netherlands, Switzerland, United Kingdom and United States.

Understanding the principles and applications of group psychodymanics requires many years of study and learning from involvement in practical work. For our purposes we may simplify the discipline as involving the exploration of patterns of group behaviour through which groups avoid becoming prey to deep emotional beliefs. The exploration is conducted in ways that help the group members develop towards more fully functioning collaborative relationships.

Integration

Our maps of the project leadership terrain have been rich in detail and depth. The map-makers have gone some way to pointing to some of the core dilemmas.

The coordination dilemma

Our first map provided by Zaccaro and colleagues explores the functionalist perspective – of what leaders of action teams do. As the researchers defined them, we may take action teams as close enough to project teams for us to consider them together.

We saw that the great corpus of knowledge on project teams has tended to ignore the processes through which individual efforts are channelled into a group purpose. This gave us our first dilemma of project teams, the dilemma of coordination. Zaccaro's proposition is that the lack of coordination can be resolved by a process of social or group problem-solving.

This process was claimed as a means to achieving shared mental models, collective information processing and team metacognition, all of which would support a transition to a less fragmented and individualist team performance.

A recurrent example from our own experience comes from experience with project teams within business school projects. Teams of MBA students working on a project for an external company sponsor will almost always divide up the tasks required at the outset. The final report, usually completed under intense deadline pressures, typically reads as if it had been assembled from four or five individual contributions with inadequate coordination, revealed by comparing the central sections with the project objective(s) and conclusions of the report.

In this example, the dilemma is a relatively simple one to understand. The overall task can be split into a set of sub-tasks for individuals by a team leader. The practical difficulties arise primarily at the level of checking for inconsistencies, overlaps and gaps in the individual summaries. The more successful teams are able to do this with processes of information management and critique not unlike those we recommend for exploring the dilemmas of leadership. The individual contributions are discussed collectively until their 'maps' become more aligned. We can also see how the processes are akin to Zaccaro's 'social problem-solving'. Some of the MBA project teams achieve this after recalling advice and applying problem-solving techniques suggested earlier on their course. Other teams take a more informal approach.

The team almost always follows a functionalist approach, putting great emphasis on identifying individual task responsibilities. The harder challenge is to refine the individual outputs so that they are aligned with the overall project objective.

These findings relate to realistic business school team projects. Real-world project teams will have more complex dilemmas of coordination. There are well-known dilemmas between managerial and professional values (for example in health teams, 'juggling' budgets and medical imperatives). There are dilemmas of coordination between creative designers and accountants in design project teams. There are dilemmas of time, cost and quality trade-offs. Later in the book we consider dilemmas of gender, and cultural differences and their reconciliation. These differences arise from deeply held and diverse individual value systems which occur within teams, as well as more generally.

Distributed leadership and boundary management

In our second map, the challenges of integrating individual requirements through project leadership were approached in a different way. Jürgen Hauschildt reports on a widely accepted European view that innovation (an important form of project work) requires not one but three leadership roles. The map implies that the roles are likely to be occupied by different individuals. This introduces us into a formalised enactment of the principle that leadership may be shared around. We begin to see a map that changes from the earlier ones where the leader had one role and followers had others.

We saw how leadership could be *distributed* across several different leadership roles, each offering a means of promoting the primary project goal. Increasing project complexity and uncertainties were suggested as factors leading to more distributed leadership. Included in these roles is the process-oriented leader, whose description is close to that of the facilitative problem-solving leader in Zaccaro's map. It is also similar to the creative problem-solving team leader described in the contextual materials.

The distribution of leadership roles was extended in the maps found within the contextual readings. Manz and Sims saw distributed leadership as a means of overcoming the central problems of unempowered workers. This is a concept of reframing our understanding leadership as a collective rather than individual activity.

The concept of distributed leadership re-emerged in our examples of sporting teams, in which the captain acted as the leader in action, and the coach as a kind of boundary-spanning leader. Also in sports teams we had the concept of a coach assembling a subgroup of leaders in action (captain and other influential players as 'social architects').

This analysis of leaders of innovation teams connected the roles to the information flows across the boundaries of teams. This implies dilemmas concerned with coordination *between* a team and its environment, and the role of boundary spanning *within* project team work.

Beyond the functionalist maps

The project team finds its most common expression as a rational and structured way of achieving a desired and specified goal. Our maps show how far this goes to make an accepted platform of understanding. Through critique, we are able to assess what may lie beyond the most widely accepted maps.

The materials in this chapter provide indications for us to consider. The functionalist approach is acknowledged as less able to deal with contexts of complexity and ambiguity, although these are also acknowledged as becoming more critical to present-day project leaders.

At the level of the team we have to look for understanding of deeper forces at work. One direction is to acknowledge that teams have a developmental trajectory. At the outset there may be emotional barriers between individuals. Tuckman's model of group stages still has face-validity for many actually engaged in project work, warning project leaders that 'hitting the floor running' may not always be possible for behavioural reasons.

However, we should remember the difficulties of accurately locating Tuckman's stages of forming, storming, norming and performing, in the life of actual teams. The issues of permanently under-performing teams, and the possibilities of outperforming and norm-busting teams, are worth considering. This approach takes us away from the cognitive towards processes of conflict and conflict resolution. Bion's legacy exploring fantasies as an explanation of team pathologies is another promising approach.

Getting personal

Most readers engaged in current work environments will have experience of project teams of some sort or another. More will become part of such teams, and eventually will occupy a role as a team leader.

This chapter has offered some maps to help you on the journey. We have seen how the most widespread accounts of projects tend to emphasise the tools and structures of a project in a 'one-size-suits-all' kind of way. The accounts also tend to focus on the project leader as the person who sees that a project is clearly specified and understood by the project team members according to preordained criteria of success, and resources constraints.

Experienced project leaders will have their unique experiences to reflect upon. Perhaps you have followed a highly structured and codified stage-gate approach, or perhaps you have developed your own approach, without a great deal of contribution from textbooks or from consultants. In either case, you may now wish to consider whether you have placed too great an emphasis on the functionalist approach (putting emphasis on those aspects of project work that can be precisely specified and monitored). If so, you may now consider how increasingly complex projects may require strategies for more distributed leadership and social problem-solving. You may also wish to review the outbursts and more emotional aspects of project life. Might this indicate a group which had engaged in the sort of dependency fantasies mapped by Bion and subsequent psychodynamic researchers?

'Wannabe' leaders are also advised to consider the kinds of leadership context they aspire to, before reflecting on the limits of a functionalist approach. Are you hoping to work in a team in which innovation, change and uncertainties are central? If so, you should be more willing to review the ideas of distributed leadership. These views also may help you take a more focused view on what kind of leader you see yourself becoming: an entrepreneurial leader, a change-centred process leader or a technological product champion?

Whether experienced or wannabe leader, the maps and your examination of them should help you approach the subject of project leadership in a way that takes more account of its generally ignored dilemmas of coordination and boundary management.

Summary

This chapter explores how project leaders deal with the dilemmas of leading projects in practice. The dominant maps emphasise project structures and stages which reflect what is essentially a rational and functionalist approach. Our concern has been with the consequential unnoticed dilemmas of coordination and boundary management, which themselves cannot be disentangled from the complexity of individual interests, emotions and capabilities within project teams.

Zaccaro and colleagues noted how such a functionalist approach presents project leadership as those efforts by a leader directed towards achievement of a stated project goal. Leadership is observable and primarily concerned with what leaders do to ensure team members direct efforts to achieving the goal. The approach takes for granted the legitimacy of the goal. Typically the team behaviours are prescribed and understood in rational terms. The procedures may be codified into project stages with subdivided goals or objectives, with identified individual and shared responsibilities. Most project team members accept the functional arrangements without questioning them. The essentials of the map of project management is that of a world of rational decision-making in which problems are dealt with rationally. Leadership is reminiscent of the task-focused kind of transactional leadership of maps that were popular prior to the introduction of contingency theories (which suggested alternative relationship-oriented leadership as the preferred styles for some work contexts).

The approach works well if the broad project task is unchallenged, and is easily divided into simpler and *non-interacting* tasks. These conditions apply only for simple projects. However, the principle of *interdependence in action* of team members is a characteristic of project teams whose work involves uncertainties of resource management (who should do what, when and how). This is where the leader faces the dilemma of coordination. The greater the need for handling unexpected deviations from the project plans, the greater the need for a response to the dilemma.

Zaccaro and colleagues argued that *team problem-solving efforts* are a powerful means of developing the *integration* mechanisms required within teams. This implies the resolution of human and emotional issues as well as functional problems. It suggests that the leader needs to be able to deal with emotional reactions constructively, rather than seeing conflict as a rare occurrence that could be removed through appropriate leader action, drawing on formal management techniques. One well-established version of such leadership is to be found in the approaches to creative problem-solving. Such approaches have also been suggested as a means of dealing with teams which have difficulty in developing into fully functioning groups.

Hauschildt's map of the team project terrain identifies a shift from the notion of a simple leadership role to a distribution of roles, which are most likely performed by different individuals. This is a shift from earlier maps where leadership is assumed to belong to one individual who influences others. The map introduces the possibility of distributed leadership, which was also seen in the arrangements of sporting operations. Here the pattern of coaches, team leaders and managers is widespread. Even within teams, the idea of social architects or multiple leaders has been advanced.

The boundary-spanning role since the work of Ancona and Caldwell has helped redefine important aspects of leadership in which the team members are to a degree protected from ambiguities and uncertainties emerging both from outside the team, and within the team boundaries.

Manz and Sims extend the concept of distributed leadership to their idea of a team as its collective leader. Distributed leadership is offered as a practical way of dealing with the dilemmas of resource management and coordination of conflicting individual interests within teams.

The broad shift in the leadership maps for project leaders is towards acknowledging that non-rational and individual behaviours are common occurrences rather than rare abnormalities of problem teams. The proposals for distributed roles and especially distributed leadership roles address the issues of coordination and integration. Some maps would consider these approaches to be ignoring deeper psychodynamic processes of fantasy formation and projection which require more complex modes of resolution.

Notes

1 Zaccaro, S. J., Rittman, A. L. and Marks, M. A. (2001) 'Team leadership', *Leadership Quarterly* 12: 451–483.
2 Citing: Salas, T., Dickinson, T. L., Converse, S. and Tannenbaum, S. I. (1992) 'Towards an understanding of team performance and training', in R. W. Swezey and T. Salas (eds) *Teams, their Training and Performance*, Norwood, NJ: Ablex.
3 Kaufmann, G. (1988) 'Problem-solving and creativity', in K. Grönhaug and G. Kaufmann, *Innovation: A Cross-disciplinary Perspective*, Oslo: Norwegian University Press.
4 Metcalfe, J. and Shimamura, A. P. (eds) (1994) *Metacognition: Knowing about Knowing*, Cambridge, MA: MIT Press.
5 Hauschildt, J. (1999) 'Promotors and champions of innovation: development of a research paradigm', in K. Brockhoff, A. K. Chakrabarti and J. Hauschildt (eds) *The Dynamics of Innovation: Strategic and Managerial Implications*, Berlin: Springer.
6 Ibid., p. 172, citing Ancona, D. G. and Caldwell, D. (1992) 'Bridging the boundary: external activity and performance in organizational teams', *Administrative Science Quarterly* 37: 634–665.
7 Maidique, M. A. (1980) 'Entrepreneurs, champions and technological innovation', *Sloan Management Review* 2: 59–76.

8 Manz, C. C. and Sims, H. P., Jr (1987) 'Leading workers to lead themselves: the external leadership of self-managing work teams', *Administrative Science Quarterly* 32: 106–128; Manz and Sims (1989) *Superleadership: Leading Others to Lead Themselves*, New York: Prentice-Hall; Manz and Sims (2001) *The New Superleadership: Leading Others to Lead Themselves*, 2nd edn, San Francisco, CA: Berrett-Koehler.

9 Manz and Sims (1987) 'Leading workers to lead themselves'; Manz and Sims (1991) 'Superleadership: beyond the myth of heroic leadership', *Organizational Dynamics* 19: 18–35.

10 Tuckman, B. W. (1965) 'Development sequence in small groups', *Psychological Bulletin* 63(6): 384–399.

11 Tuckman, B. W. and Jensen, M. C. (1977) 'Stages of small group development revisited', *Group and Organisational Studies* 2: 419–427.

12 Ginnett, R. C. (1993) 'Crews as groups: their formation and their leadership', in E. L. Wiener, B. G. Kanki and R. L. Helmreich (eds) *Cockpit Resource Management*, San Diego, CA: Academic Press.

13 Rickards, T. and Moger, S. T. (2000) 'Creative leadership processes in project team development: an alternative to Tuckman's stage model', *British Journal of Management* 4: 273–283.

14 Rickards, T. and Moger, S. T. (1999) *Handbook for Creative Team Leaders*, Aldershot, Hants: Gower.

15 Druskat, V. U. and Wheeler, J. V. (2003) 'Managing from the boundary: the effective leadership of self-managing work teams', *Academy of Management Journal* 46: 435–457.

16 Ancona, D. G. and Caldwell, D., 'Bridging the boundary' [see note 6].

17 Druskat, Y. U. and Wheeler, J. V., 'Managing from the boundary', p. 453 [see note 15].

18 Rickards, T. (1999) 'Brainstorming revisited: a question of context', *International Journal of Management Reviews* 1(1): 91–110.

19 Nolan, V. (2003) 'Whatever happened to synectics?', *Creativity and Innovation Management* 12(1): 24–27.

20 Sutton, R. I. and Hargadon, A. (1996) 'Brainstorming groups in context: effectiveness in a product design firm', *Administrative Science Quarterly* 41: 685–718.

21 For an insightful popular view, see Eriksson, S-G., Railo, W. and Matson, H. (2001) *Sven-Göran Eriksson on Football*, English translation, London: Carlton.

22 Trist, E., Emery, F. and Murray, H. (1997) *The Social Engagement of Social Science*, vol. 3, *The Socio-ecological Perspective*, Philadelphia, PA: University of Pennsylvania Press.

4 The magic of leadership
Charisma and its redress

Orientation

Charismatic leadership

Leadership has for centuries been associated with heroes and myths. In the earliest myths, the great leaders were gods, or blessed by gods with superhuman characteristics. These special properties were examined extensively by the great sociologist Weber. He retained the ancient term charisma (blessed by the gods) for the special property possessed by great leaders, and he labelled the leaders as *charismatics*. Weber considered that charismatic leaders had unshakable power over followers, and saw the phenomenon as a primitive form of leadership that would be replaced by a more modern and rational form in the emerging industrial organisations of the nineteenth century.

The early charismatic form did not completely disappear, despite the rise of modern business studies and more scientific managerial approaches. Even now, many books about leaders tell stories giving an emphasis to the uniqueness of the great leader, and in so doing, separating them from the more humble capabilities of ordinary people. These books mostly take for granted the fundamental premise of charismatic leadership: the uniqueness of the individual leader and the special properties associated with that uniqueness.

A charismatic leadership challenge

Charisma clearly has the appearance of a leadership trait. Take a little time to reflect on your own understanding of the term (Box 4.1). Have you ever met a charismatic leader? How about a charismatic teacher?

From charismatic to transformational leadership

As we learned in Chapter 2, the British researcher, Alan Bryman, suggested that since the 1980s, the field was entering a period of *new leadership* theories.[1] The term

Box 4.1 A charismatic leadership challenge

- My understanding of a charismatic leader is . . .
- My understanding of a successful leader is . . .

Now use the matrix below to identify a set of leaders of differing levels of charisma and of success. A starting list is provided. Any leaders you are not sure of can be found using simple web-scanning searches. For simplicity concentrate on the leaders when they were at the peak of their achievements. If possible you should add to the list of names, especially if you have had direct experience of a charismatic leader.

	Charismatic leaders (list by name)	*Non-charismatic leaders (list by name)*
Successful leaders		
Unsuccessful leaders		

The candidates are:

- David Beckham
- Richard Branson
- Barbara Cassani
- Carly Fiorina
- Bill Gates
- Roberto C. Goizueta

- Nelson Mandela
- Richard Nixon
- Mary Robinson
- Jeff Skilling
- Margaret Thatcher

became reported in numerous reviews, and in general, the distinctive difference between it and older forms was mentioned as transformational leadership.

The contemporary use of the term 'transformational leadership' can be traced to an influential book published in 1978 by James MacGregor Burns.[2] Burns, a historian, studied the characteristics of great political figures, such as John F. Kennedy. One of his most significant observations was that of leadership behaviours which *transformed* situations, in contrast with *transactional* behaviours which were more closely associated with the classical contractual role of ensuring that employees conduct their work to required standards in order to achieve identified goals or targets.

The concept was taken up and studied deeply by Bernard Bass and co-workers, who developed a 'full range' model of leadership comprising transformational and transactional components, and who developed an instrument for its quantitative study. They suggested that each leader displayed the full range of leadership factors, and that the more effective leaders (who were also in general more acceptable to their followers) had higher proportions of transformational behaviours.[3]

Overview

In this chapter, we examine the ancient leadership property of charisma, and its relationship to a more modern concept of transformational leadership. Our platform of understanding draws on reviews by leading researchers into transformational leadership.

The platform of understanding is actually a 'map of maps' of new leadership ideas. A leadership scholar examines the maps of three other leading researchers.

The contextual materials take us into more specific aspects of empowerment, and to the dark side of charismatic leadership processes. A theory of fifth level leaders is also provided, helping us challenge stereotypic notions associating excellence with charismatic leadership.

The integration of these materials reveals how a shift of emphasis towards transformational leadership has had an impact on the way we understand charismatic leadership, and also on our understanding of 'transactional leadership'. Each is now treated as illustrative of 'old leadership' approaches and ideas. We show how this change produces dilemmas of the ego-driven transformational leader, and of the alignment between organisational and individual goals.

Platforms of understanding: transformational leadership

We have suggested that map-testing is better conducted with more than one platform of understanding. This adds to the complexity of the chapters, but allows us to employ the comparative method of map-testing. This chapter has three platforms of understanding, each covering the work of a pioneering map-maker concerned with transformational leadership. However, the three maps have already been extensively examined by a fourth researcher, a bonus for the map-testing process.

The three platforms of understanding are:

- Robert House and his path-goal theories of leader influence
- Bernard Bass and his full-range model of leadership
- Jay Conger and the dilemmas of charismatic leadership.

The three maps were reviewed by James G. (Jerry) Hunt, who has played a major role in leadership research as author, editor and director of the Texas Tech University's programme in leadership.

These three 'new leadership' pioneers all emphasised the visionary aspects of transformational/charismatic leadership, which extended the traditional leader's role into that of a manager of meaning, and established a strong link with literature of organisational culture and symbolic aspects of organisations. It also shifted attention away from the leadership at the level of production and operations management towards upper-level leadership.

Hunt concluded that changes in the way researchers viewed the social world in the mid-1980s created the force for change in the leadership field from a wider range of academic disciplines.

Robert House and path-goal theory

One of the best known theories of leadership was developed by Robert House of Wharton Business School. Its prominence follows a particularly influential article published in 1971, in which House revealed his path-goal theory of leadership.

Origins of path-goal theory

The theory originated with the essential claim that leadership impact is influenced by the ways in which the leader behaves towards the paths and the goals of the employees.[4] The nature of the task is introduced as a situational variable. The early theory shared the popular mapping at the time of leadership effectiveness being influenced by circumstances. House followed the general mapping of the two areas calling for leader attention: the initiation of orienting structures and a demonstrated consideration of follower needs.

The orienting structures were indicated to be ways of clarifying expectations of employees through the way their work requirements were described. The emphasis is on structuring the psychological frames (or 'maps') of the followers. A general principle was that uncertainties or ambiguities of roles and role expectations would have a negative effect on a person's motivation and work productivity. The situational component of path-goal theory suggested that differing levels of initiating structure would be required according to job conditions (this is the typical feature of situational leadership theories). For a well-routinised job there is little role ambiguity, and few benefits from a leader who introduces new structural guidelines. In contrast, the provision of psychological reassurance through clarifying objectives and expectations is recommended where there are considerable ambiguities ('No one tells us what's going on around here').

Path-goal theory drew on the motivational approach known as valance theory. This proposed that individuals were motivated to act through a kind of rational calculation of outcomes of actions according to self-interest. Thus a leader is advised to attend to the perceptions of followers and to indicate how efforts directed towards wider organisational goals could align with calculations of self-interest. Readers will find rather similar patterns of advice for leaders in other situational theories, for example, that of Hersey and Blanchard.[5] Typically, situations of ambiguity require more directional leadership; situations of repetitive work require more encouragement and consideration.

Path-goal theory transformed

These considerations demonstrate the transactional nature of House's early work. According to Jerry Hunt, House was subsequently provoked by a question from a member of a lecture audience to consider the lack of progress in leadership studies. This contributed to a shift of emphasis so that by the late 1970s, House and colleagues had become more interested in the potential of a new mapping of charisma for encouraging employee motivation. By the 1990s, House had reformulated path-goal theory so that it was far more aligned with what by then had become known as new leadership ideas.

He had concluded that the valance-expectancy theory of motivation (prevailing in the 1970s) had assumed people to be primarily rational and calculative in their decisions and behaviours. It had underestimated the importance of emotional and non-conscious efforts of members of social groups and the symbolic significance of leader behaviours.

Bernard Bass and the full-range leadership model

A 1999 article by Bernard Bass offered a useful and insightful review of the previous two decades of research on transformational leadership and its contrast with transactional leadership.[6] He highlighted the important contributions from empirical studies of the 1980s and 1990s and offered a commentary on areas where work is still needed.

The core assumptions: self-interest and personal development

Bass summarised transactional and transformational leadership as based on different core assumptions. Transactional leaders essentially respond to their followers' immediate self-interests. This contrasts with the transformational approach, which he described as uplifting the morale, motivation and morals of their followers. For Bass, transformational leadership is thus strongly connected with attempts to provide an empowering environment, where autonomy, job satisfaction and commitment flourish under challenging and motivating work conditions.

Transactional leadership involves exchanges rooted in self-interest. Transformational leadership involves a form of influence that moves followers to accomplish more than is usually expected of them. Leaders influence workforces to go beyond simple self-interests. The process is seen as one in which participants are enriched in ways that also enrich the wider group. The transformational business leader is assumed to promote the achievement of economic goals of the organisation, and the development of socially desirable 'elevating' behaviours among its followers.

The full-range model of leadership: transactional styles

Bass and co-workers have developed a model, addressing what has been termed the full range of transactional and transformational leadership styles. Transactional leadership refers to the exchange relationship between leader and follower to accommodate their own self-interests. In factor analyses, two transactional factors consistently emerge: contingent rewards and management by exception.

Contingent rewards

This style rewards followers for conforming to performance targets. The key responsibilities of the leader are the clarification through direction or participation what the follower needs to do, and how he or she will be rewarded for achieving what is required.

Management by exception

In this style, the leader takes action when task-related activities are found to be failing, so that procedural or task goals are not being achieved. The style may be further split to contrast *active management by exception* in which the leader constantly monitors the follower's performance and takes corrective action when necessary, *passive leadership*, where the leader waits for problems to arise before taking corrective action, and *laissez-faire leadership*, through which the leader makes no further interventions, having set the required performance procedures and goals. Recent studies have supported the factorisation into active and passive forms of management by exception. However, such extended studies have cast doubt on the precise formulation of the sub-factors.

The full-range model of leadership: transformational styles

Transformational leadership refers to the leader moving the follower beyond immediate self-interests and elevates the follower's level of maturity and ideals as well as concerns for achievement, self-actualisation, and the well-being of others. The transformational leader achieves this through the 'Four Is' of

- idealised influence (charisma)
- inspirational motivation
- intellectual stimulation
- individualised consideration.

Idealised influence is displayed when the leader envisions a desirable future, articulates how it can be achieved, and engenders pride, respect and trust.

Inspirational motivation is associated with leaders who motivate by creating high expectations, set an example to be followed through setting high standards of performance and who show determination and confidence by modelling appropriate behaviour and using symbols to fuse the effort. Followers want to identify with such leadership.

Intellectual stimulation is displayed when the leader helps followers to become more creative and innovative, continually challenging followers with new ideas and approaches.

Individualised consideration is displayed when leaders pay personal attention to the developmental needs of followers, giving them respect and consideration.

Bass has reported that transactional leadership may induce more stress, and that transformational leadership enhances commitment, involvement and performance of followers and also helps to deal with stress.[7]

Personal development and transformational leadership

Bass has also examined how transformational and transactional leadership may be affected by moral and personal development, training and education. Mature moral development is required of the transformational leader, although there is still a need to learn more about the ethical factors that distinguish transformational leaders.

A critique of the Multifactor Leadership Questionnaire

The full-range model of leadership proposed by Bass has been most widely examined using the Multifactor Leadership Questionnaire (MLQ).[8] Over time, claims have been made that the model has wide applicability across different contexts including national cultures. This has led to a vigorous debate among leadership researchers.

Charisma and transformational leadership

In the full-range model, two of the four Is of transformational leadership, idealised influence and inspirational motivation, have been treated as factors offering 'new leadership' insights into the older concept of charismatic leadership. Charisma in leadership studies has often been associated with flamboyant and magnetic personalities, and pseudo-transformational leaders (e.g. Hitler).[9] Some researchers see it as an all-inclusive term for transformational leadership.

However, the construction of the MLQ provides a means of distinguishing whether there were two similar, yet differentiable, leadership styles in contemporary organisations, the one more connected with the idealisation of the individual leader (idealised influence), the other more associated with the inspirational content of the leader's words or vision (inspirational leadership). The factorisation has not been adequately resolved. In particular, researchers remain unconvinced that the idealised influence and inspirational leadership scales are representing two distinct factors. Together, these scales may be the closest we are able to get with the MLQ to a measure of a charismatic leadership style. Furthermore, factor does establish that this style is distinct from the two associated with the factors of intellectual stimulation and individualised consideration.

To summarise, the MLQ is advancing our understanding of the new leadership concept of transformational leadership. Through it, we are discovering the potential benefits to leaders of offering various ways of winning the support of followers. These include intellectual stimulation and individualised consideration. In addition, one style has been more closely identified to notions of charismatic leadership. The style may be a single factor, or may comprise idealised influence and inspirational leadership. However, further work is required before we can conclude we understand the precise nature of the sub-factors within the full-range leadership model.

Transformational and transactional styles: a common misunderstanding

Popular articles tend to focus on the differences between transformational and transactional leaders (an analytical device employed by Burns in his pioneering work). This leads to the classification of leaders as *either* transactional *or* transformational. However, Bass and co-workers have consistently indicated that leaders exhibit a mix of styles. Research using the MLQ has shown that transformational leadership adds to the effectiveness of transactional leadership, yet does not substitute for it. The best leaders are both transformational and transactional. It would be more accurate to consider transformational leaders as showing more transformational behaviours (rather than manifesting a 'pure' transformational style).

Jay Conger's work on empowerment

Jay Conger helps us appreciate not only the importance of empowerment, but also the dilemmas associated with the concept. For example, he acknowledges that empowerment contradicts the stereotype of a leader as having to demonstrate an omniscience, which includes a sort of all-powerful influence over the followers.

He illustrates this in a study of leaders of major business organisations, nominated for their exceptional qualities.[10] He observes the growing emphasis in writings on change on the importance of instilling people with a sense of power. Put crudely, the theory suggests that the first step is to establish self-fulfilling mindsets: 'you can if you think you can'. Conversely, 'and if you think you can't, you probably can't'.

Conger offers a theoretical rationale from work on social learning theory, predicting that individuals feel more self-determined where they encounter four kinds of experience:

● *Evidence (feedback) that they are actually being successful:* this justifies the emphasis placed by many effective leaders on breaking down large goals into achievable smaller tasks. This is the most significant of the four kinds of personal experience
● *Recognition of progress, by words of encouragement.*
● *General emotional support:* this becomes particularly important under conditions of high stress.
● *Powerful role models.*

Creative jolts to expectations

At times the leaders jolted their followers out of a debilitating sense of negativity and behavioural impotence.

The leadership jolts are highly specific to the situation, so that attempts to follow the examples blindly may be utterly counter-productive. For example, Conger tells of a newly installed leader facing a demoralised young group of employees. Shortly after being appointed, the leader took part in a miserable meeting with sullen indications of low morale from the participants. There seemed to be widespread disbelief that the new leader would be able to change anything. The leader, in what was described as a playful manner, pulled out a squirt-gun (water pistol) and squirted its contents over one of the employees. This served to shock them into realising that the new leader was not just another boss expected to be the same as all the others. The shock appeared to work.

Conger's point is subtle. Each situation will call for an act of leadership that works for those people in that situation. The water-squirting showed the new boss was someone who was prepared to 'play around with the gang'. The leader had found a powerful way of achieving something symbolic that most words alone would not achieve. The UK hit television series *The Office* introduced us to David Brent, who is quite inept at winning over his people. It would have been in character for him to have wielded the squirt-gun, which we can imagine would only have reinforced his image as an incompetent and out-of-touch leader. The US version of the show continued the theme of the inept leader.

Conger considers that the impact is likely to have been high at least in part because it was an action so different from those associated with the (disliked) previous leader, who kept a psychological distance from his employees. He is particularly insistent that an autocratic leadership style is widespread, pernicious and damaging.

Conger's work on the dark side of leadership

Conger has tended to take the gadfly role, making painful attacks on the exposed parts of cherished bodies of knowledge. In particular he is one of a small group of leadership scholars who warn of the dangers associated with high-profile leadership practices.

Be careful, he warns. We are beginning to understand these skills, and how they work. They may earn our admiration as part of an ethically grounded programme of change. Or they may reveal how the leaders have distorted a vision in order to meet personal and egocentric ambitions. They may work on the frailties of others through great communication and impression management skills.

In one way it is the ancient Greek warning against *hubris* (what happens to someone who forgets the human condition in striving to become more like the gods). It is the mythology of the Faustian pact – the promise of anything you desire, at the cost of a deal with the devil. Most specifically, it introduces the importance of ethics in leadership by showing it to be lacking in the patterns of behaviour most frequently associated with the dark side of leadership.

Conger suggested that the charismatic leader has unusual, exceptional capabilities. In the 'heroic' case study, these exceptional capabilities are associated with the achievements valued by society, and which are attributed to some significant degree to the leader's behaviours. Conger looks at such leaders, who were at first hailed as exemplary and charismatic and later decried as misguided, unbalanced and perhaps morally suspect or worse.

Some of the examples are historical, although others are still fresh to the memory. He indicated that the very same capabilities make the very same leaders vulnerable to failure. Conger takes Steve Jobs, the mercurial co-founder of Apple computers, as one illustration, and Lee Iacocca, of Chrysler, as another. He suggested that these leaders, in common with Ross Perot and John DeLorean, had the exceptional skills of anticipating a future opportunity, and articulating in a way that convinced and inspired others. He also cited one of the United States' successful female corporate founders, Mary Kay Ash, without elaborating on a subsequent manifestation of her 'dark side'. Among the others, however, he paints a common pattern of an increasing sense of invulnerability. DeLorean, perhaps one of the more extreme cases, was reported as firing those who disagreed with him.

Conger believes the process to be that of cognitive dissonance. This is a theoretical model of behaviour which considers it to be a common defence mechanism for people to deny facts that challenge a cherished aspect of self-image. Better to deny the facts, than to shatter the self-image. For successful leaders, the social construction of hero-worship, adulation and unconditional respect goes a long way to reinforcing what may be a driven personality, and that personality's belief in the rightness of their 'vision'. In time the vision becomes distorted by the leader's needs.

Thomas Edison, for example, pioneered direct electrical current (DC) for urban power grids and was blind to the benefits of alternating power (AC) systems. Identification with the vision will influence the manner in which the leader communicates the 'real' picture.

Three aligned and mutually reinforcing factors are described as contributing to the seeds of destruction, and the ultimate failure of the charismatic leader. The first is the leader's relationship with the vision. Conger takes for granted that the process of charismatic leadership is necessarily bound up in the vision and impact it has within the organisation. The second is the manner in which the leader communicates, including communications connecting with the vision and its corporate impact. Finally, there are aspects of the style of charismatic leaders.

The leader's utter commitment to the vision (which he or she may have created) risks the shift from single-mindedness to obsessiveness. The single-minded leader is capable of combining this with sensitivity to the need for flexibility – flexibility in reviewing the situation, and expectations, for example, partly due to an openness to fresh information. The obsessive leader becomes trapped by the original vision. Conger refers to the ancient tale of Pyrrhus, the King of Epirus who remained true to his military objective, eventually winning a victory over the Romans at a devastating ultimate cost to his cause. The term 'pyrrhic victory' captures the outcome of obsessive pursuit of a visionary goal.

The communication skills of the visionary leader are widely acknowledged. As the vision becomes less grounded in available evidence, and more an extension of the leader's personality needs, the communications become less authentic. Techniques that gain commitment and dependence become exaggerated. They may depend increasingly on distortions of the evidence and use of stereotyping the enemy (within, or without). The process is one that is often accepted as necessary and legitimate for leaders whose progress remains acceptable. For example, it is common for a charismatic leader to pour scorn on outsiders to increase the bonding of insiders. At work the outsiders may be 'the dinosaurs', or 'the bean counters', or 'the suits'. The insiders are the 'people like us' (as Margaret Thatcher was fond of saying). At Apple, Steve Jobs enthused the team working on his own special projects, and belittled other groups, who were actually contributing more to the financial well-being of the company. It was the sort of practice that contributed to his downfall and ousting.

The processes of exclusion and stereotyping will recur in the book, particularly in Chapter 8 on the dilemmas of diversity. These two interrelated factors are made worse by tendencies or characteristics often accompanying a charismatic leader's style. The leader tends to be unusual and unorthodox. Other behaviours may single out individuals in a belittling way. Symbolic acts demonstrating closeness to the employees may reduce the contributions and credibility of middle-level executives. It is a very crude change strategy to suggest that there are tiers in the organisation that are worthless, and can be removed to the benefit of the whole. To suggest the recurrent problems of a department are due to some 'worthless' individual is always likely to be a simplification.

In the 1980s there were some pretty crude attempts by organisations to 'slim down'. Many organisations now believe the approach ignored the unintended consequences of such corporate axe-wielding. More thoughtful leaders treated those who lost their jobs with respect and dignity, and did what was possible to care for the casualties. The general thrust of Conger's analysis is that the features associated with visionary leadership may always be potentially associated with a dark side. Some leaders may remain vigilant to deal with their potential weaknesses – of self-aggrandisement for example. Others may have their egotistical style reinforced by the adulation from and dependence among their followers.

Contextual materials

We consider two contextual readings in this chapter:

- James MacGregor Burns on empowerment
- Jim Collins on the fifth level leader: beyond charisma.

James MacGregor Burns on empowerment

As an unchallenged pioneer of transformational leadership, James MacGregor Burns deserves attention when he reflects on empowerment, and the consequences of two decades of research into the subject. In a review prepared under the Kellogg Leadership Studies Project, he returns to his understanding of the transforming nature of a leadership act.[11] Burns describes the initiation of a change process as through the unexpected and individualistic action of an individual. Many such acts have transient impact. A few deeply touch and lead to the mobilisation of others. The most famed acts are of political or military bravery: the unarmed student against the advancing tank, Nelson's 'blind eye' to orders. Burns further suggests that the consequences of the act rely on an intimate 'we' of future acts and relationships.

The acts involve so-called leaders and so-called followers. The manner in which each influences the others is problematic. He suggests that we reconceptualise the actors in such change processes. As well as the person identified as the transforming leader, there will be other actors. The action will reveal *opponents* to the change being initiated. There will be *passives*, a large group whose members are difficult to rouse, and the *isolates*. He further suggests that we think of leadership as 'made by the system' in ways comparable to parents being 'made' by their social circumstances – not least of which are their children. Here, Burns is arguing for a view of leadership roles as existing in a web of relationships.

The ethical dimension

If we take the perspective of a web of relationships, Burns argues, we find new insights into the way values impact on leadership. He reiterates his own understanding of values as being of three kinds. The first is of an ethical kind, for example chastity, sobriety, abstention and kindness to the poor; the second is social values, such as honesty, trustworthiness, reliability, reciprocity and accountability. The third kind is of normative or socially desired goals such as order, liberty, equality, justice and community (fellowship). These are the elements from which a socially negotiated order emerges through acts of transformational leadership.

Burns points out that an initiating act triggers value-laden reactions from the people acting out the three kinds of role. The initiator triggers reactions from supporters and opponents. These reactions contribute to what may be called a first-order calculus of the trustworthiness of the initiator and his cause. But the reactions themselves become triggers for scrutiny and second-order assessments of trustworthiness. Are the opponents trustworthy? He suggests that a dilemma in leadership studies has been recognised for some decades. Leadership-influencing processes appear to reduce freedom of choice in followers, regardless whether the leadership is coercive or more positive in style. The argument that the leader is obliged to exercise awareness and self-restraint seems to Burns to be 'a weak reed'. However, if leadership is regarded as a social process, outcomes of change are better regarded as the outcome of a social calculus: the outcomes are defined by the wider set of relationships.

The dilemmas of empowerment

Burns develops a similar argument in dealing with a well-known criticism of the vocabulary of empowerment. As Burns points out, the term invites the questions 'who empowers who[m]?' and 'to whose purpose?' Parents lead their children to greater levels of development, in what is a process of benign empowerment. However benign the intent, as Burns points out, this is a top-down process. How should we regard similarly well-intentioned efforts of empowerment from leaders in the workplace? Burns considers that the conventional two-way relationship between a powerful leader and less powerful followers inevitably sets up a possibly irresolvable ethical dilemma.

Here Burns makes an interesting comment. Twenty years earlier, he resolved ethically acceptable from unacceptable behaviour, by distinguishing between power brokers and 'real' leaders. The essential difference was that power brokers mobilised their powerful resources regardless of the needs and values of the followers. In contrast, 'real' leaders mobilise resources in order to achieve mutually desired goals.

Burns suggested several weaknesses in the formulation. In particular he notes that there is still a top-down sense to it. He also concedes that he underestimated some of what he refers to here as other roles, particularly that of the 'passives', in holding back changes. Although he does not take the point further, we are left with the

Box 4.2 Explanations of charisma

Charisma has been associated with the greatest of human achievements. In his book on charisma, Alan Bryman suggests that Weber failed to provide an unambiguous critique of charisma.[12] The outcome of charisma was uncritical devotion to someone perceived as having outstanding personal properties. These could be the sanctity of a priest or heroism of a military leader. As we have seen, the exceptional properties could be inherited through a bloodline or through edict. Manifestations of that uniqueness could also be diverse. Weber suggests that charisma serves to relieve the distress of a group under conditions of crisis. He considered that the primitive modes of charismatic influence were diluted but not eliminated in modern societies. The power of the leader often involves appeal to a mission revealed to the leader as the way forward. As such, charisma tends to be associated with a promise or vision for the future. He illustrated the way in which charismatic personalities were accepted as natural born leaders. As such they were contrary to formal structures and organisational forms. However, Weber also indicated that the charismatic personality could well survive in and influence managerial bureaucracies.

Later researchers considered explanations for the charismatic power a few people exercise over others. One group has followed the psychoanalytical tradition of personal projection of fantasies. The most obvious examples come from the great social reformers with their dreams of a better world. The controversy in a general psychoanalytic explanation of charisma is that we still have to explain the visions of a Martin Luther King or a Nelson Mandela with the visions of a Hitler or a Charles Manson. Weber had no problem with this, as he seemed to imply a universal reaction towards a great cause or mission under appropriate conditions. The ethical intention or consequences of the charismatic leader was not salient. Present-day organisational and political leaders are equally aware of the potential for a great idea to win acceptance. The complicating issue is the intermediary forces in communication and in particular the media and the leader's media experts.

Its almost unconditional acceptance as a social good has contributed to attempts to find an alternative mapping. The process of map-testing (Chapter 1) involves a search for dilemmas. These are not difficult to find. Closer examination of the consequences of charismatic leadership reveals frequent abuses of the rights of individuals in the interests of a greater good as perceived by the charismatic leader. The dilemma is present enough if the lofty cause is universally agreed upon. Often the causes are highly contested.

The dark side of charismatic leadership As well as Conger's work, additional interesting studies of the dark side of charismatic leadership have been made by the Dutch social scientist Manfred Kets de Vries,[13] and by Barbara Kellerman.[14]

Kets de Vries points to the psychological weaknesses that often accompany enormous energy, ingenuity and commitment. One psychological type that often succeeds is the narcissistic personality. Driven by a sense to prove their self-worth, the charismatic leader may create innovative products and organisations to the benefit of society. Kets de Vries mentions Ingmar Kamprad of IKEA and Mads Ovlisen of NovoNordisk in this respect. The same drive may flow from a more destructive kind of narcissism. Some of the most powerful leaders of all time seem to fit into this category. For reasons we leave our readers to explain, a disproportionate number seem to be found at the top of media organisations.

Kellerman goes further than Kets de Vries and claims to have found a spectrum of dysfunctional leadership from the milder forms of narcissism to the pathologically disturbed.

impression that Burns now feels that such a view of leadership and power is inadequate for dealing with the dilemmas posed by the models he helped to popularise. He concludes that our treatments of leadership render the concept too focused on the individual, ignoring the evidence that transformation occurs through a far more collective process. He believes that the term 'leadership' has become so intimately connected with an individual rather than a collective process, that he would welcome the dropping from the vocabulary the term 'the leader' if the concept were not so thoroughly embedded in social discourse.

Jim Collins on the fifth level leader: beyond charisma

The charismatic business leader continues to hold considerable sway in the beliefs and assumptions of many people (see Box 4.2). The charismatic story, briefly, holds that great changes are achieved by exceptional people. More careful studies are beginning to reveal that the story is at best partial. At very least, our image of the exceptional leader has been shown to ignore the contributions of people with characteristics of style and behaviours that are in many ways the mirror image of the larger-than-life charismatic.

This particular dilemma seems to be on the way to being resolved, at least in respect of the founders and leaders of the great American companies, thanks to research conducted by Jim Collins. Collins was a respected academic who subsequently turned thought leader and guru, publicising his ideas around the world. His work is a nice combination of well-grounded research and well-rounded stories easily communicated to a wider audience. His earlier work with Jerry Porras had revealed the secrets of exceptional companies, ones that survived and prospered. Collins and Porras called the companies those that were *built to last*.[15] Now with teams of experienced researchers, he has gone more deeply into the features of such companies. Although he wished to avoid the risks of over-celebrating the great leader, the results were unavoidable.

From over fourteen hundred companies studied, eleven achieved the kind of sustained excellence he was looking for. In the eleven companies, the strongest differentiating factor was what Collins called *level five leadership*. The various levels were summarised as follows:

- *Level one leadership* is that of individual talent individually applied; in teams and groups, the individual may be an isolated but valued technical or professional expert.
- *Level two leadership* is leadership in the sense of collaborative team efforts, and may include specialised professional or personal talents.
- *Level three leadership* is the competent manager, effectively organising people towards predetermined goals.
- *Level four leadership* is the effective leader, who promotes commitment to and pursuit of a compelling vision together with high performance standards.
- *Level five leadership* is the executive who builds great companies through exercise of personal humility and great will power.

The level five leader

Collins compares level five leaders with those at other levels, particularly those who had been hailed as 'the greatest' in recent times, and yet, on their departures from organisations they had 'transformed', were subsequently found to have left no lasting legacies. Level five leadership implies the acquisition of capabilities found in the other four levels.

In vivid and at times in harshly judgemental tones, Collins lists the might-have-beens. His point is that cultural stereotyping of leaders permits the continued elevation of 'non-level fives' to top positions. And the characteristics of level four leaders are too often incompatible with his recipe of *humility with strong will*. The descriptions of modest leaders of steely resolve help us understand some of the features that were previously concealed. Interestingly, as he points out, the leaders were never celebrated in the media in the way which some of their level four counterparts were.

Collins takes the case of Darwin E. Smith of Kimberly-Clark as having many characteristics of all his level five leaders. A spartan upbringing reinforced no-nonsense attitudes to life's problems (including a battle against a life-threatening illness). For Collins, this is the modest yet iron-willed characteristics of an Abe Lincoln. Smith saw the necessity for Kimberly-Clark to get out from its core business of coated paper. The implication was entry into the highly competitive consumer products markets, against such big hitters as Procter & Gamble. The consequence was the painful closure of paper mills and a risky repositioning of the company. The financial institutions reviled the strategy and the share price plummeted. The strategy eventually succeeded. Inevitably, the company rather than the leader became the hero of the tale.

Similar stories were told of the other relatively unheralded level five leaders. Colman M. Mockler, CEO of Gillette from 1975 to 1991, was 'a reserved, gracious man with a gentle almost patrician manner . . . who fought off three bitter take-over attempts'. George Cain of Abbott laboratories did not have an inspiring personality, but he had 'inspired standards' which led him to deal ruthlessly with nepotism in his family business, resulting in ultimate transformation. Charles Walgreen was another quiet but strong-willed leader, whose gentle 'invitations to act' were as effective as more strident approaches. Again, through his leadership, unwelcomed transformation occurred taking a food service company into convenience drugs.

The pseudo level five leader?

With some enthusiasm, Collins contrasts Darwin E. Smith of Kimberly-Clark with Al Dunlap of Scott Paper. 'Chain Saw Al' had become a business celebrity for his exploits in companies, primarily through ruthless downsizing. After less than two years at Scott Paper, Dunlap (not known for his modesty) announced that he was leading what would be one of the greatest and fastest corporate turnarounds. In his autobiography at the time, he described himself as a corporate Rambo. This particular morality tale ends with Dunlap's Scott Paper collapsing, and eventually being taken over by Smith's Kimberly-Clark.

According to Collins, in roughly two-thirds of the comparison companies, continued mediocrity of performance was associated with leaders whom he described as having 'gargantuan egos'. That is not say these leaders were unsuccessful. On the contrary, many were lauded for their instant success and dynamism. The same leaders perpetrated the myth through their enthusiasm for self-publicity ('in the interests of their company', they might have believed). The fifth level leader is offering insights (and perhaps not a little comfort) to many leaders and researchers into leadership.

Integration

The significance of transactional leadership

The fundamental story told in this chapter is that of charismatic leadership, and its re-emergence within new leadership thinking. Charismatic leadership, and its newer form transformational leadership, regardless of differences, stand in contrast with transactional forms of leadership. The fundamental difference is that transactional leadership is essentially a means of economic exchange. It supports the economic world-view of barter, and is consistent with contemporary ('neo-classical') economic theories. One feature of such theory is the ultimate rationality of the combination of transactional exchanges. It is possible to conceive of the system without the intervention of leaders who 'make a difference'. Indeed, the basic economic principles taught in business schools remain wedded to transactional neo-classical processes, and leadership is largely confined to case illustrations within strategy courses.

The limits to transactionalism

Under such circumstances, it is hardly surprising that for some years, there has been a debate regarding the differences between leaders and managers. According to transactional theories, managers are intermediaries ensuring the smooth running of economic and socio-economic institutions, and offer no theoretical place for leaders. Such a place arises outside the theories in what are called exogenous variables, to explain economic growth spurts. Leadership, along with technological change, is such a variable. Thus, leadership becomes important if we wish to understand substantial change. Transactional leadership, essentially coupled with the models of smooth economic change, remains inadequate. Thus, transformational theories may be seen as arising through inabilities of transactional models to explain substantial organisational changes.

The differences in transformational and charismatic modes

Charisma in its earlier form was prior to economic theories. It was rooted in ideas of mystical and even religious 'super-heroes', with magical powers. Such ideas had pre-scientific 'explanations' for change which persisted, although they became increasingly examined in search of more modern and scientific principles they may be concealing. This seems to have been one motivation for the shift to transformational leadership, with its preference for accurate measurement of leadership features. With new leadership, attention was paid to 'new charisma'. These studies are ongoing, but the core of the research is becoming clear: to understand better the manner in which leaders bring about transformation changes.

In comparison with transactional theories, attention shifts towards ways of moving social actors ('followers') beyond simple transactional relationships. The old-styled charismatic leader was able to do so by a system of institutional reinforcements of authority and legitimisation. The new leadership studies have begun to propose and explore the mechanisms through which changes become accepted and enacted. We have seen the significance of shared acceptance of a vision, in this respect.

Dilemmas of charisma and transformational leadership

Dilemmas of charisma and transformation confronting researchers of leadership have been identified in the platform of understanding and contextual materials.

We will examine them, and introduce additional dilemmas suggested by leaders themselves.

- *The extrapolation dilemma:* our models of leadership began with the studies of political leaders. How far can we extrapolate our understanding of President John F. Kennedy or Prime Minister Margaret Thatcher to gain insights of leaders in business organisations similar to our own? Within this dilemma we may also note the unresolved issue of contextual extrapolation. In what ways might different cultures and contexts influence the manifestation of transformational leadership?
- *The inclusion dilemma:* charisma and transformational leadership are top-down theories. What 'space' do they leave for leaders at other organisational levels? Does this imply 'transformation at the top, transaction below'?
- *The maverick dilemma:* to whom is the 'pure' charismatic leader accountable? Is it to the proposed 'vision'? If so, how does the leader remain accountable within complex constituencies (for example in public service organisations)?
- *The tyrant dilemma:* Conger and others warn of the consequences of a charismatic style as reinforcing leader feelings of invincibility. Petty tyrants as well as dictators are vulnerable to a belief in their own invulnerability. Yet Burns, Bass and others emphasise how transformational leadership shifts followers from narrow self-interest to wider ('loftier') and more socially coherent perspectives.

The broad issue is the shift of attention from transactional to transformational leadership, a move associated with new leadership studies in the 1980s. The extrapolation dilemma should be considered in light of the antecedents of charisma, and the impact of Burns' book on transformational leaders. These antecedents offer a 'story' of the exceptional transformational leader, and his or her differences from 'ordinary' leaders. However, the story is at odds with the full-range model of Bass, which consistently locates leaders as displaying a *range* of transactional and transformational characteristics. Even the most charismatic leader will exhibit some transactional behaviours. In this treatment, we find ourselves again accepting the situational nature of leadership. This is in accord with Bass's transformational leader as someone who has developed a performance repertoire strong on the various elements of transformational leadership (idealised influence and so on). From time to time, the transformational leader will also present elements of a transactional style (according to the mainly follower-based reports with the full-range leadership inventory). The transactional leader is reported as mainly exercising the transactional style elements.

Such empirical results point to transformational leadership as a style that develops as an add-on to transactional skills, rather than as a replacement for them. More work is required before the issue can be said to have been resolved, with increased attention needed to be paid to longitudinal studies.

The extrapolation dilemma

We have arrived at a view of charismatic leaders, including those within the modern transformational treatment, which suggests that assessment by followers goes beyond rational or experienced-based grounds. This explains *why* extrapolation remains a dilemma unresolved through direct evidence. We have to rely on judgement based on more theoretical considerations. However, the theory of charismatic leaders, as we have seen, draws strongly on Weber's conceptualisation of pre-modern societies, whereas the theory of transformational leaders relies on empirical evidence from mostly less senior modern leaders.

The inclusion dilemma

Bass reports results showing the presence of transformational leadership at all organisational levels studied, and interprets this as a mimesis or imitation effect, for example strengthened by social identification and role modelling. Transformational behaviours and values cascade (or perhaps trickle) down from the top echelons of an organisation. This is an old idea, earlier suggested by Likert in his linking-pin model of integration of organisations operating a top-down management by objectives approach.[16] For success, communications and, indeed, influence have to operate in both upward and downward directions; subordinates have to believe that they have some scope for influencing up and down. This proposal is consistent with Bass's idea of cascading transformational leadership. It also indicates that the inclusion dilemma may require some sort of distributed influence model of transformational leadership.

The maverick and tyrant dilemmas

Absence of leadership accountability points directly towards the reinforcement of the excesses of a charismatic style, as noted by Conger and others. The magic of charisma remains untamed. At the level of individual followers, the influence of the leader may appear limitless and irresistible. The emerging ('new') theory of transformational leadership is unable to resolve the dilemma, partly because it is, in Yukl's terms, a one-way and relatively incomplete model, and in Burns' term a web of relationships.[17] When additional factors are brought into the picture, we see that even the most charismatic business leader has to deal with powerful external influences. (This would include negotiations with one or more business and political figures, themselves with charismatic features to their interpersonal styles.)

The related dilemmas remain: the emergence (or appointment) of a powerful charismatic leader always leaves open the possibility that the leader will operate in an uncontrollable fashion, and for egotistical rather than more general socio-economic goals.

Getting personal

A question of culture

> In my culture it is impolite to be a certain kind of leader. It is difficult for me to speak up loudly in teams, even in my own culture. I want a career in an international organisation. What can I do to become a transformational leader?

It is true that cultures differ, and that some cultures are more collectivist, so that their leaders appear relatively quiet. Yet every culture has its examples of transformational leaders in its organisations. Also, you will know of famous charismatic leaders who founded some of those organisations. Study their stories, and try to find ways in which you can follow their examples. This will help you find a preferred style which you know can work in your culture.

Can you become too involved with your team?

> I have been a successful leader in several different jobs, and have worked hard at my career. Now I am in charge of a large national institution. I know that I am good at influencing my people, and gaining their loyalty and motivation. In most of the jobs, I have found politics and opposition to my ideas, and I have even been accused of being too loyal to my own department or team.

Can you become too involved with your own team?

Charismatic leadership doesn't work in my group

> I am in charge of a group of highly qualified scientific professionals. They are motivated to succeed scientifically, but only respond to scientific logic. They are particularly resistant to any attempt to play on their emotions. Transformational leadership, and particularly a charismatic style, does not seem appropriate in my role.

Can you be transformational without empowering your people?

> If your main responsibility is transforming your organisation, why should you have to worry about transforming the people in it? Why not concentrate on expressing your strategy clearly and communicating it? You can still draw on the factors for achieving transformation, and for generating and communicating a vision of the strategic goal.

Box 4.3 is an exercise on evaluating charismatic behaviour.

Box 4.3 Evaluating charismatic behaviour

- How would you explain the processes of charismatic leadership using the metaphor of map-making?
- What does the charismatic leader do in constructing the map for the wider group?
- What part may other group members play in making the map?
- How might a lack of map-testing contribute to the process?

Summary

In this chapter we looked at the most mysterious kind of leader, the charismatic. We have seen how the early explanations of charisma were pre-modern, and invoked primitive origins of a mythological nature. Although charisma was somewhat ignored in the modern theories of scientific management, it was to be rediscovered and modified during the rise of new leadership theories in the 1980s.

These theories picked up on studies of charismatic political leaders, and reinvestigated charisma as related to transformational leadership. A clear distinction was made between charisma (in old or revised forms) and transactional leadership. The latter was more closely allied to economic models of exchange. The modified charismatic modes of leadership now provided *mechanisms* through which leaders mediated organisational change, and which were unavailable to the transactional models. The mechanisms were more open to empirical study than the mysterious functioning of charisma according to earlier beliefs.

One extensively investigated model of transformational leadership developed by Bass and co-workers provided a full-range model of leadership. The model was supported with methodologically sound inventories which could be factor analysed into leadership styles. This work presents leaders as having a range of styles, with transformational modes being an *addition* to transactional ones, rather than a replacement.

The results show that followers report a proportion of leaders *at all levels in organisations* as having transformational styles. We interpret this as evidence of perceived influence through such styles as *distributed*, rather than located in an individual top-level leader. This gives encouragement to leadership development programmes directed at lower as well as higher echelons.

The new leadership theories have tended to associate transformational leadership ('new charisma') with follower empowerment. Such a view has to explain the processes of leaders who show little concern for empowerment. Other workers have examined a more widespread tendency among charismatic leaders to becoming isolated from criticism of their beliefs and actions. This is a likely consequence of a style that does not rely primarily on rational arguments, and may produce increasingly egocentric behaviours. Taking an extreme version, this has been described as the Hitler problem, and the leaders as pseudo-charismatic. The so-called dark side of leadership poses particular problems to the new leadership position of moral rectitude and ethical values. These issues seem to have been ignored in biographies and autobiographies of leaders, which have tended to emphasise the virtues of transformational leaders in achieving change. As we have shown, the approach throws up challenging dilemmas of theory and action. The evidence of modest yet deeply committed fifth level leaders helps us broaden our understanding of leadership excellence.

Notes

1 Bryman, A. (1992) *Charisma and Leadership in Organizations*, Newbury Park, CA: Sage; Bryman, A. (1996) 'Leadership in organizations', in S. R. Clegg, C. Hardy and W. A. Nord (eds) *Handbook of Organization Studies*, London: Sage.

2 Burns, J. M. (1978) *Leadership*, New York: Harper & Row.

3 Avolio, B. J. and Bass, B. M. (1991) *The Full Range of Leadership Development: Basic and Advanced Manuals*, Binghampton, NY: Bass, Avolio and Associates.

4 House, R. J. (1971) 'A path-goal theory of leader effectiveness', *Administrative Science Leadership Review* 16: 321–339.

5 Hersey, P. and Blanchard, K. (1988) *Management of Organizational Behavior*, 4th edn, Englewood Cliffs, NJ: Prentice-Hall.

6 Bass, B. M. (1999) 'Two decades of research and development in transformational leadership', *European Journal of Work and Organizational Psychology* 8(1): 9–32.

7 Bass, B. M. (1998) *Transformational Leadership: Industrial, Military, and Educational Impact*. Mahwah, NJ: Lawrence Erlbaum.

8 Avolio, B. J. and Bass, B. M., *The Full Range of Leadership Development* [see note 3].

9 Bass, B. M., 'Two decades of research and development', p. 18 [see note 6].

10 Conger, J. A. and Kanungo, R. N. (eds) (1998) *Charismatic Leadership in Organizations*, Thousand Oaks, CA: Sage.

11 Burns, J. M. (1998) 'Empowerment for change', in *Rethinking Leadership Working Papers*, College Park, MD: Academy of Leadership, University of Maryland.

12 Bryman, A., *Charisma and Leadership in Organizations* [see note 1].

13 Kets de Vries, M. F. R. (1994) 'The leadership mystique', *Academy of Management Executive* 8(3): 73–93.

14 Kellerman, B. (2004) *Bad Leadership: What It Is, How It Happens, Why It Matters*, Cambridge, MA: Harvard University Press.

15 Collins, J. C. and Porras, J. I. (1994) *Built to Last: Successful Habits of Visionary Companies*, New York: Random House.

16 Likert, R. (1961) 'An integrating principle and an overview', in Likert, *New Patterns of Management*, New York: McGraw-Hill.

17 Yukl, G. A. (1981, 2002) *Leadership in Organizations*, Englewood Cliffs, NJ: Prentice-Hall; Burns, 'Empowerment for change'.

Shared meanings and why myths matter
The power of the symbolic

Orientation

An existential dilemma of leadership. Why can't they understand the situation? In countless businesses, leaders have attempted to introduce changes in what they believe to be a legitimate way. Within the process, a trigger point seems to result in a catastrophic breakdown of relationships, with accusations of bad faith from all 'sides'. The vocabulary remains that of confrontation and class conflict. The leader may well think, 'Why can't they understand the situation?'

For many years the conflicts developed a story line. The British version reported the employee representatives as accusing 'the bosses' of ignoring previously negotiated arrangements: 'By its unilateral action, the management has ignored the legitimate demands of the work force.'

The leadership of the organisation responds in similarly outraged tones: 'The union's actions show how it is trying to take away the right of my managers to manage.'

Much is spoken of shared cultures, but what if there is a difference in views and beliefs?

> I listen to what my staff say, but at the end of the day I have to take the hard decisions. Anyone who wants to go in a different direction had better find a different ship.

Overview

In this chapter we move into territory hardly indicated to exist in our earlier maps. The shift is to new kinds of maps which address issues of the making of meaning, and of culture change. They take us beyond the assertion that shared visions are important, to explanations of the power of visions and how they become shared (or not). They explain why a remark or an incident can trigger off significant (and sometimes unpredicted) changes for better or for worse. These are all elements which have symbolic or mythic power. The maps present organisational reality as an invented world, or map which arises through the actions (including communicative actions) of those most closely connected. The formal terminology is that the map of organisational reality is socially constituted or socially constructed.[1]

For readers with a technical or professional training, this may appear both new and perhaps highly suspect. We suggest only that you postpone such map-testing until you have studied the maps in this chapter, after which you may feel that the approach has value in your leadership journeys. By then you may see how the maps explain the example above, in which an encounter judged by management to be a trivial incident, appears to have triggered a highly significant reaction. You may also find yourself shifting understanding of leadership, away from a property of the leader, and more the property of a reality constructed by the words and actions of the leader, and the wider group involved in the situation.

Most maps are influenced by earlier map-making processes. In a very important sense the maps are based on similar assumptions. Map-reading has been relatively straightforward, partly because their assumptions, when we do go in for map-testing, are in accord with our own map-making assumptions. Such modern maps claim their accuracy through empirical studies and carefully constructed measures of personality, behaviours and achievements. They place emphasis on that which can be observed and if at all possible measured.

Although we have examined maps of the so-called *new leadership* territory, those assumptions have been mostly retained. As a consequence, new leadership has not appeared all that new. In this chapter, we come across more radical maps, which are grounded on quite different assumptions. The map-makers come from the social sciences; emphasis shifts from a belief in a scientific and observable reality, to a socially constructed reality, with emphasis on meanings and symbolism. We also see how such maps revive those ancient ideas of realities that transcend the observable and tangible aspects of the workplace. They help us understand how visions may arise, and what might be the basis of their significance for organisations, and leadership.

A symbolic challenge

You can test your personal map for its symbolic content by spending a few minutes thinking about the realistic situation in Box 5.1.

Two platforms of understanding

Symbolism explores the production of meaning through the use of symbols, and its map-makers draw attention to the interrelationships between social actions and social communications. Whereas a modernist approach would emphasise the observable

---

Box 5.1 Introducing your restructuring plans

You have reached one of your great ambitions, through appointment as chief executive officer of a construction and manufacturing organisation Bulner Gates. You have deep knowledge of the company, as you have been recruited from a leading consultancy, where your last assignment had been to restructure the finances on Bulner Gates, in face of declining orders and profitability. Your restructuring plan calls for across-the-board cost controls. Discussions regarding the viability of two (out of ten) divisions have been going on, and your plan indicates that the preferred option is that of phasing out the two divisions quickly. The plan has been reluctantly accepted, and resulted in the resignation of the chief executive. Your nomination as replacement CEO was supported by a major institutional shareholder.

What do you see as your first actions facing this situation? To keep your memory honest, jot down the key considerations for you in reaching your decision. We will look more deeply at the case, drawing on maps of symbolic leadership, later in the chapter.

---

signals of communication, symbolists are sensitised to the meanings carried by behaviours. Our first map, that of Smircich and Morgan, presents leadership as the management of meaning. Their work furthers our understanding of the nature of leadership as a social process developed through shared forms of understanding, shaped through the meaning structures and symbolism of leaders and followers. For a general survey of symbolism, we draw on the work of the English sociologist Barry Turner.

Contextual materials

The more context-specific materials include contributions from organisational leaders we invited to address our leadership courses. Requested to share their experiences, yet otherwise unprompted, they repeatedly revealed the symbolism that they considered gave potency to their leadership actions.

The work departs from earlier maps in its interest in possibilities derived from acknowledging more than one cultural perspective (the so-called multiple and contested belief systems). We look at Will McWhinney's map in which he suggests that symbolic leadership or myth-making is one of the most powerful of the general paths taken by leaders to bring about change. We also consider Edgar Schein's contributions on organisational culture and leadership. Karl Weick's much cited work offers sense-making as the process that shapes reality.

Platforms of understanding: symbolic leadership

We will look at two platforms of understanding:

- Smircich and Morgan's map of the management of meaning
- Barry Turner's treatment of symbolism.

Smircich and Morgan's map of the management of meaning

Emergence of leadership

Linda Smircich and Gareth Morgan wrote an influential article at around the time that interest was growing in mapping new leadership ideas.[2] They did so as part of a growing network of researchers who considered that symbolism could be a powerful means of understanding organisational life. They were advocating a fundamental shift of mapping, or organisations, and of leaders as participating agents in organisational life.

The shift was towards a view that the most important aspects of organisations – such as the stability of beliefs, acceptance of authority of leaders to lead, commitment to, or resistance to change – cannot be effectively understood through the prevailing maps. The dominant maps of the 1970s retained a confidence in rationality. Organisations were understood as examples of rationality, and management as a rational and scientific occupation.

We read such maps with confidence bred through familiarity, and our map-testing tends to focus on assessing evidence offered through empirical studies, and through the rigour with which the various elements are measured. The maps place emphasis on that which can be observed and, if at all possible, accurately measured.

Smircich and Morgan brought to a wider audience a quite different conception of organisations as socially constructed systems. In doing so they provide an approach to understanding something that is taken for granted by practical managers. Organisational symbolism became a focus of interest in the 1970s, where it was applied to understanding the increasingly important issue of organisational culture.[3] Organisational symbolists often acknowledged the earlier influence of Peter Berger and Thomas Luckmann, and their book, *The Social Construction of Reality*.[4]

Smircich and Morgan departed from sociological terminology in their encapsulation of symbolic processes as the *management of meaning*. They argue that dominant beliefs about organisation have simplified the more general processes through which groups make their world of work meaningful. They compare the processes of leadership *emergence* in unstructured groups, and from this compare formal with informal leadership patterns.

From studies of unstructured and apparently leaderless group situations, they suggest that individuals find themselves in the role of an emergent leader as they engage in the situation, and because of their role in framing (mapping) and changing the situation for the group. As such a map is developed it forms a basis for organised action. Leadership depends on followers being willing to allow the leader to shape their reality maps. When the group is being influenced by strong and competing maps, there will be a struggle for formal leadership to evolve.

The authors suggest that in such situations,

- leadership is a social process defined through interaction
- leadership involves defining reality in ways that make sense to followers
- leadership inevitably requires that some individuals give up their power to interpret and define reality to others
- formal leadership roles emerge, and with them the rights and obligations of the leaders to define the system of shared meanings are recognised.

Leadership in formalised settings

According to Smircich and Morgan, within the business organisation the social processes of unstructured groups are simplified. Most employees much of the time accept the set of rules and procedures provided. The authority patterns and work practices provide the means through which an individual makes sense of working life. A pattern of dependency relationships is thus established. In particular, this *institutionalisation* specifies that organisational reality is defined by your boss/manager/leader, acting on behalf of 'the organisation'. Leaders who act according to this map are primarily concerned that their actions and the reactions of others sustain the unchallengeable order of things, that leaders set and direct the rules, and followers comply with them. Non-compliance is unacceptable. Leadership is essentially depersonalised.

This approach to *imposing* reality is inadequate to provide the sense that emerges in informal groups. As leaders know from experience, the right to lead has in some way to be earned. There is therefore a need for leaders to offer a compromise between the formalised leadership requirements of the organisation, and the more emergent needs of the individuals within it. An effective leader transcends the specification of formal structure to provide members of the organisation with a map of how they are organised. This is the way in which leaders are believed to provide meaning or sense for those whom they lead. Smircich and Morgan are suggesting that leadership in a formal setting has two critical aspects:

- the leadership process is institutionalised through formalised roles and authority relationships, often leading to a dehumanising sense of meaning
- mediating or interpersonal leadership (operating within the context of the formal structure) is necessary for effective action and it is this interpersonal process which operationalises the principles of leadership; the process is an emergent one, that is to say it emerges from the interactions of the members of a particular group.

Leadership as the management of meaning

Leadership actions may be seen as (more or less conscious) attempts to shape and interpret situations, influencing a common interpretation of reality for followers. Smircich and Morgan conceptualise the leadership process in terms of a relationship between what they term *figure* and *ground* – the person and the context, with leadership seen as a form of action that seeks to shape its context.

This occurs through the symbolic significance attributed to a leader's words and actions. This explanation of leadership goes beyond an emphasis on formal responsibilities of management, direction and control. It is based strongly on the sense made within the working group. In the example they cite, a leader believes he or she has set up a process for overcoming a business problem (work backlog). The leader believes this will provide a meaningful way for the company to make progress. Staff members interpreted the initiative as a futile act, *symbolic* of the leader's failure to understand the organisational realities of the workforce.

Leadership is analysed by Smircich and Morgan as a distinctive kind of social practice in a case study of leadership. An ethnographic ('fly on the wall') study was carried out of executive staff at a large insurance company. The focal project may be seen as an attempt by the president to respond to evidence of poor back-up support for sales agents, and slow processing of orders. The goal was to eliminate a backlog of orders. The authors analysed how the project led to different and competing interpretations of reality.

The leader's map was one of refocusing the organisation's staff towards a future state in which the orders backlog had been eliminated, through a joint effort in the interests of future success. As the initiative started, the president, Mr Hall, was impressed by the efforts he became aware of, as he involved himself in the short-term activities arising. He saw his plan as working.

The senior staff saw things very differently. They made sense of the initiative not in terms of a desired level of task performance, but against what they felt were the inadequacies of their existing organisation, in terms of a fragmented culture and of individuals not dealing with problems in a team spirit. They doubted whether the plan would succeed in addressing either the short-term or longer-term issues. They were to be proved more accurate in their predictions.

The case serves to demonstrate how even if the leadership is perceived as inappropriate or ineffective, the leader's actions still involve the defining and framing of organisational situations. Unfortunately, the reframing results in the group reading from a different map than the leader intended.

A focus on leadership as the management of meaning, stems from the notion that leaders symbolise the organised situation which they lead. Leaders are seen as shaping imagery in the minds of the followers, through the articulation of their vision and through the actions they take to initiate their views of desired future states. In so doing, they attempt to define the experience of those led through symbolic and instrumental modes of action, and hence to influence the actions in the context as a whole. Sense-making activities initiated in the followers are, of course, voluntary activities, although the nature of the leadership role provides 'non-symmetrical' opportunities to influence the sense-making of others.

Barry Turner's treatment of symbolism

Symbolism: culture, codes and meaning

Barry Turner, in his work on the symbolic understanding of organisations, has acknowledged his debt to Jungian concept of archetypes, as culturally embedded symbol systems.[5] He regards Jung's emphasis on the ancient and mythic as challenging to the modernist perspective and suggests that new organisational forms (virtual organisations, temporary teams) are becoming less amenable to a 'rational mechanical' perspective. This is the start of a justification of analysis of the symbolic in organisations.

Turner examines attempts to address the nature and significance of symbolism in organisational studies. He indicates the contribution of cultural theorists who have raised the profile of symbolism, largely outside organisational theory. If leaders are engaged in the management of meaning, these ideas have considerable significance. He is aware that for organisational leaders and employees alike, considerations of the nature of reality do not intrude directly into their daily work or thoughts. However, the nature of reality has been a concern of philosophers down the centuries, through to a generation of contemporary social theorists. If we wish to associate leadership with the management of meaning (cf. Smircich and Morgan), we need some indications of what is meaning.

Turner suggests that the organisational culture movement has largely ignored the wider debate, which he refers to as the structural allegory. This is a shorthand expression to indicate the schools of cultural thought whose work has disputed the notion that the social world is best explained as having a reality which can be established beyond doubt. This movement includes those who have been labelled postmodernists, structuralists and poststructuralists.[6] The movement has vigorously explored the nature of reality – at times helpfully demonstrating the limitations of conventional beliefs in scientifically or rationally grounded evidence. The work has also been replete with internal contradictions and inconsistencies.[7]

The production of meaning

Maybe we should be aware of the elements which differentiate the 'allegory'. Structuralists placed great importance on interpretation of the codes within cultural life. Thus they are said to be concerned not so much with meaning, but with the way in which meaning is produced. From them, we have the notions of signs and signifiers which are to be found within language. The combination of a word (a signifier) and a concept (the signified) become unified as a sign in a conceptual act of meaning-making. Of pertinence within the theory is that words and signs are of themselves arbitrary. However, there are structures (linguistic and grammatical) which permit coherence and consistency while permitting linguistic development and change.

Poststructuralists, simulation and meaning

Structuralist ideas indicated a form of indeterminacy. This was taken further by poststructuralists who denied any form of meaningfulness to be found in texts. This was to become one of the self-limiting aspects of the so-called postmodern movement. Jean Baudrillard, one often-cited social theorist, suggests that meanings are created, but that they have the nature of illusions. Their reality lies in the beliefs of people in the sign. He presents us with the concept of a simulacrum – that which is believed in, a replication in culture of what never existed. In such a treatment, concern for 'what is real' is replaced by awareness that cultural life is moving to a hyper-reality utterly dominated by symbols.

Is there another show in town?

Turner rejects the view that poststructuralism 'exhausts our options' in trying to understand organisational culture and symbolism. He is unable to accept in its entirety the implications of work which connects cultural interpretations with an otherwise concealed component. Such approaches suggest that there is a definable essence, which somehow becomes revealed to the seeker. This is his objection to theories such as Jung's, which present universalistic explanations making no concession to the possibility of variations in the theory over time and space. He sees merits where such work encourages a reassessment of the orthodoxies of industrial thought, which focus primarily on what can be directly observed and accurately measured.

Turner suggests that treatments of the symbolic need not inevitably produce the mythic and mystical. This brings him to the view that culture arises as people engage and develop skills, including skills about skills. These higher-order skills have been a matter of interest in organisational learning writings. This is a treatment of an optimistic kind. He speculates that understanding culture offers escape from cultures threatened by the dominance of powerful but mythological symbols. He is suggesting that the escape is likely to come from participatory cultural forms. Leaders may wish to exploit followers through the potency of symbolism, or develop partnerships through the development of more participative modes.

The message is not one of complete comfort for those offering current programmes of leadership development. The approach seeks to warn against remystifying power. Turner poses the matter as a dilemma of the myth-maker and the leader as manager

Box 5.2 Mandrill management: examining its symbolic significance

Recent work has suggested that animals offer rich insights into the nature of dominance, cooperation and conflict. Specifically, the mandrill has been identified as exhibiting behaviours associated with tyrannical human leaders. Before examining the evidence, we consider how and when it may be appropriate to rely on animal metaphors for insights into human leadership.

Avoiding the anthropomorphic assumption Animals have been worshipped within many religious traditions, and leaders have been long associated with the courage and strength of a lion, or fleetness of foot of a cheetah, or the great vision of an eagle, surveying the world coolly from a lofty vantage point. We think of foxes as 'cunning', and perhaps 'cruel' if they break into a hen house. We also often describe humans in terms of animals (which may in a complicated way be no more than projecting back on to humans, those human properties used to describe animals).

However, socio-biologists warn us of attributing human characteristics to animals (the anthropomorphic assumption). They point out that the term leader is used to refer to the dominance achieved by animals within species-specific groups, identifying behaviour patterns which secure for the leader more privileges than non-leaders. The most important privileges are those permitting transmission of the leader's genes to future generations. According to this theory, animal behaviours are determined by the environmental conditions, and therefore it is a gross error to pass judgements on the cruelty of the predator, based on human values and ethical standards.

Social identity and sense-making approaches Leadership ideas since the 1980s have made us aware of the processes of sense-making, including the power of symbolic and metaphoric thinking. Animals, as indicated above, have long been powerful symbolic stimuli for sense-making about leadership.

Identity theorists like to ask corporate executives to agree which animal best describes their organisation, and which animal best describes its ideal future form. In this approach, animals are assumed to have powerful symbolic significance for the group, and its search for social identity. In one of our courses, we learned of an organisation which believed it to be most like a mole, unable to sense much that was going on in the world above its subterranean home. In some contrast, the same executives nominated a hawk as the creature they would most prefer to identify their company with!

The symbolism of the mandrill A visit to the zoo reveals different leader behaviours in different species. Some species, such as chimpanzees, engage in a complex mix of violence and collaboration, with the leader appearing to display both kinds of behaviour. One animal, the mandrill, captures the imagination of visitors in a particularly powerful way. Regardless of the sophistication of the observers, their discussion quickly reveals the powerful symbolic impact of the experience.

The leader of a troupe of mandrills demonstrates dominance through highly confrontational and physical means. The leader is the physically strongest animal, and has the brightest displayed colouring, in particular its vivid scarlet nose. Under natural conditions, the leaders of two competing groups easily identify one another. Mating is also a violent, non-consensual process.

One feature of the behaviour of mandrill leaders leaves a particular impression. It takes a great deal of effort to retain leadership. Each encounter with a troupe member is a potential power-struggle, calling for energy that cannot be directed elsewhere. The consequence is that the leader's rule does not last long (typically around two years). The battle for leadership, once lost to a younger contender, is rarely regained. As another symbolic consequence, the deposed leader loses its status. It even loses its colouring – the bright scarlet nose was biologically linked to testosterone levels.

The story of the mandrill leads to considerable discussion among managers. Some say they 'know leaders like that'. Further discussion makes it clear that 'mandrill-type leaders' channel so much energy towards 'being in charge' that they are unable to find time to devote to influencing the achievement of goals of the organisation. It is also assumed that the mandrill manager exercises influence through a kind of violent style identified with the mandrill leader.

The psychopathic leader   The story has further credibility in its implication that such behaviours are ultimately self-defeating. In mandrill groups, this has a kind of Darwinian fatalism about it – a *Just So* story. The mandrill has little choice of style, in its struggles for survival.

For human leaders, the mandrill style seems to be more open to the criticism that it contributes to a violent, competitive, and bullying environment, likely to end in a confrontational deposing of the leader. Unlike the mandrill, human groups and leaders have choices regarding leaders, and leader styles. Psychopathic leadership, although far from uncommon, is not 'the only show in town'.

What can we learn from the mandrill leader?   The power of the symbolism hints that there are some deeper learning points to be gained here. We would expect readers to recognise the benefits from a map-testing and map-making approach. The mandrill story (or map) can be tested for its dilemmas. An immediate dilemma is faced by the leader spending too much time 'being in charge' and too little time in trying to make a significant positive contribution to task or to team development. Followers of such a leader may find themselves preoccupied in surviving, or in scheming to depose the leader. Their dilemma is whether to confront the situation, or 'sit it out' until the leader is deposed.

of meaning. If we set reason and myth-making as alternatives, we may be trapped because of the limitations of each approach. An approach premised totally on rationality and logic misses the power of the symbolic; to assume that symbolic processes are irrational, and perhaps resistant to rational investigation or deliberate application, is to place symbolic leadership alongside discarded superstitions of the inspired charismatic leader. See Box 5.2.

Contextual materials

We consider three contextual readings in this chapter:

- Will McWhinney's paths of change: mythic and other leadership realities
- Edgar Schein on organisational culture and leadership
- Karl Weick on sense-making in organisations.

Will McWhinney's paths of change: mythic and other leadership realities

We have discussed, through the first platform of understanding, the notion of the leader being considered as a manager of meaning. The vocabulary of visions also indicates the importance of the symbolic. The notion of vision is perhaps dangerously close to becoming a cliché, or an element within a training or corporate rhetoric. We need guidance to go more deeply. One such guide is Will McWhinney, academic, designer and systems theorist, who has developed a conceptually rich approach to understanding and shaping change.[8]

McWhinney developed a view that change requires a shift in beliefs about reality. If he were to borrow our metaphor, he would say that change requires those involved to shift from putting confidence in one map to confidence in another map. Furthermore, conflict arises where such a shift is opposed by some and supported by others. He concluded that he needed to understand the styles which were chosen by people to negotiate their way through their realities (maps) in attempts to achieve their goals.

He constructed a theory of four types of leadership maps, indicating four archetypal leaders:

- idealists
- realists
- mythics
- social relativists.

Idealists hold *unitary beliefs* and are guided by notions that the world is of a single preordained nature; the future can be predicted from understanding of the 'true' nature of the past, and (logically) cannot be influenced by human intervention. These leaders believe in the ultimate guidance offered by a unified philosophy of leadership.

Realists hold *sensory beliefs* and put their faith in elements which can be empirically observed. The observable elements have been analysed or decomposed ('scientifically'). Sensory leaders put their faith in dealing as well as possible with the observable 'facts'.

Mythics combine a perspective that a 'one true view' exists, with a belief that a reality is what you choose to make of it ('*My* way is *the* way').

Social relativists, who hold *social* beliefs, combine belief in the possibilities of more than one 'truth' ('My way is my way not the way').

We will concentrate on the mythic mode of leadership, paying particular attention to the significance of visions and symbolism.

The mythic explanation of leadership

McWhinney considers the mythic reality the most mysterious for those grounded in the western traditions of unitary and sensory realities. He points to the way in which Churchill created his view of an idealised people that became the wider shared view of the reality of the British will to win against all odds.

We may find some value in considering the extreme mythic leaders who founded religious or social movements. They turn out to be profoundly influential, and also often utterly impossible in their disregard for convention and social conditioning.

McWhinney uses the two-dimensional frame to locate leadership styles and to predict more about their functioning. He unambiguously places the charismatic leader in the mythic reality. However, he suggests that charismatics may be distinguished by their impact on the realities of the other domains, under which circumstances he considers them the most powerful agents of change. More directly relevant for business leaders is the leader whose mythic beliefs become mixed with other realities. Of three variants, he points to the *prophetic charismatic* (Churchill, Ronald Reagan, Mary Baker Eddy, founder of Christian Science, even Michael Eisner in his style of promoting the Walt Disney tradition). The *entrepreneurial charismatic*, and related forms of impresarios and innovators, bring into traditional organisational realities products from their ethereal ideas. The *facilitative entrepreneur* charms the members (of a team or group) into a feeling of co-ownership in the symbol's creation and propagation (Richard Branson appears to act in this way).

In recent times, the power of the sensory (and unitary) belief systems runs through social and organisational life. Charismatics are as suspect as they always have been, yet with new 'rational' beliefs to counter their potential for change. It follows that cultures are more prone to espousing charismatic realities when conditions become unclear and threatening, and when willingness to hate and attack 'the other' becomes easier. It may also be seen that the cultural perils of the charismatic approach are likely to be recognised and resisted, even in milder versions of entrepreneurial and facilitative modes.

Edgar Schein on organisational culture and leadership

Edgar Schein has written about culture and leadership in as lucid a way as any writer. His capacity to communicate ideas simply has made him one of the most influential writers, and almost unique among academics in the influence he has had on practitioners as well as on other managers. His text *Organizational Culture and Leadership* stands as one of the most influential management books.[9] In it, he provided a frequently cited definition of culture:

> A pattern of shared basic assumptions that the group learned as it solved its problems of external adaptation and internal integration, that has worked well enough to be considered valid and, therefore, to be taught to new members as the correct way you perceive, think, and feel in relation to those problems.[10]

Schein summarises his view of corporate culture as an all-embracing phenomenon, which reveals itself in terms of how it is created, embedded, developed, manipulated, managed and changed. He considers that culture is at least partly determined through leadership, and indeed he states that culture defines leadership. Culture is for Schein the royal road to understanding leadership and the organisation.

Schein's map treats culture as the secret to understanding leadership and organisation. The culture view suggests that the situation (context) is an essential part of leadership, which has become a *relationship in a social system*, rather than a *property* of an individual. Indeed, Schein urged those who would understand and influence change to take an anthropological approach. This implies there to be important, perhaps unique, aspects of each organisational culture that have to be considered and discovered by any outsider ('anthropologist') or indeed by any insider seeking deeper understanding. Such an approach involves attention to the customs and rites of the organisation. It is almost by definition the study of individuals as social groupings; it is interested in the way in which regularities of human interaction arise and persist. Culture is very much a way in which shared meanings are established, negotiated and retained or suppressed. Metaphors, myths and stories have all been deeply studied in this respect. The approach sits well with the view of the leader as manager of meaning. At the very least, leaders should be conscious of culture and its consequences.

Organisational symbolists Joanne Martin and Peter Frost described Schein as among those for whom culture is 'an internally consistent package of cultural manifestations that generates organisation-wide consensus, usually around some set of shared values. Subcultures are noted only as a secondary consideration, if at all.'[11] In this he is seen as part of the movement that praised the power of a strong culture, for example in Tom Peters and Robert Waterman's book *In Search of Excellence*.[12]

Karl Weick on sense-making in organisations

Karl Weick may be regarded as one of the main protagonists in introducing sense-making as a key issue in the field of work and organisation.[13] He argues that people are constantly trying to make senses of the contexts in which they find themselves. Thus an understanding of leadership from the sense-making perspective requires us to examine how individuals see things rather than seek explanations for organisational issues in terms of structures or systems (e.g. initiating structure and consideration for people). Weick is keen to differentiate sense-making from interpretation, arguing that sense-making is clearly about an activity or process, that is it is about how individuals generate that which they interpret.

The phenomenon of sense-making

Among Weick's most cited concepts is the notion of sense-making. According to Weick, there are at least seven characteristics that distinguish sense-making from other explanatory processes such as understanding and interpretation. Sense-making is:

- *Grounded in identity construction:* an important part of making sense of a situation concerns a person's sense of who he or she is in a setting; what threats (to this sense of self) the setting contains; and what is available to enhance, continue and render efficacious that sense of who one is. These considerations all provide the basis for judgements of relevance.
- *Retrospective:* the perceived world is actually a past world in the sense that things are visualised and seen before they are conceptualised. Sense-making is influenced by what people notice in elapsed events, how far they look back and how well they remember what they were doing.
- *Enactive of sensible environments:* sense-makers create their own environments for future action.
- *Social context:* sense-making is influenced by the presence of others. Sensible meanings tend to be those for which there is social support, shared relevance and consensus.
- *Ongoing:* the experience of sense-making is constrained not only by the past, but also by the speed at which interpretations become outdated. It is one in which people are thrown into the middle of things, and forced to act.
- *Focused on and by extracted cues:* sense-making is about the resourcefulness with which people elaborate cues into stories that selectively support initial views.
- *Driven by plausibility rather than accuracy:* sense-making is about coherence, how events hang together with a certainty that is sufficient for present purposes and credibility.

These properties of sense-making, Weick argues, have an effect on the willingness of people to disengage from, discard or walk away from their initial story and adopt a newer story that is more sensitive to the particulars of the present context.

Linking this to the process of leadership, sense-making might seem to follow a sequence. People concerned with identity in the social context of others (e.g. the leader and others in the situation) engage with ongoing events, extracting salient cues to make plausible sense of the situation, taking into account their actions past and present. The sense-making also directs future actions.

The processes of sense-making are distinguished from interpretation and problem-solving. Weick considers interpretation more a matter of unfolding and revealing, whereas sense-making deals with the ways in which people achieve their interpretations (Box 5.3). Problem-solving provides specific episodes within which sense-making occurs. Weick offers sense-making as influenced by theories of symbolism and meanings attached to objects. However, he does not consider prevailing theories to capture the essence of sense-making, which we offer as an emerging and promising set of ideas. Where he is quite emphatic is that sense-making differs from taking a metaphoric frame to stand for a deeper reality. The reality exists of itself. This position rescues him from the dangers of irreconcilability of different beliefs arising from sense-making (which is a danger in work on metaphors as maps of reality).

Box 5.3 An old story about sense-making

When you are lost, any map will do. There is a famous story of Hungarian troops lost in the Alps. After a fatiguing march, they finally reach safety. Only later do they discover they had been following the wrong map . . . Efforts at sense-making eventually . . . make sense!

Maps animate and orient people. Once people begin to act (enactment), they generate tangible outcomes (cues) in some context (social), and this helps them discover (retrospect) what is occurring (ongoing), what needs to be explained (plausibility) and what should be done next (identity enhancement). It is what managers do – not what they plan – that explains their success. Weick makes the point that in terms of leadership, followers often need direction. There is a strong chance that the strategic plan (or map) that the leader has might not be sufficient for success. However, in terms of sense-making, the leader must instil confidence in people, get them moving in some general direction and be sure that the followers look closely at clues generated by their actions, such they learn where they were and get a stronger idea of where they are and where they want to be. The leader needs to set sense-making in progress.

Case example of a symbolic leader

To begin to look at symbolic leadership and to envision the notion of sense-making in practice we now look at the experience of a leader invited to speak to the students on one of our courses on his views on leadership. His presentation reveals the significance of the symbolic side of leadership.

Peter describes his life as 'a career in leadership'. He was a popular presenter at our leadership electives for his capacity to bring back to life his experiences. His career path had been one of seeking and taking on challenging jobs that increasingly involved him as a general manager. He had few formal qualifications, relying on experiences gained from a family firm background which gave him considerable technical know-how in the printing field. In his last career move he had been an international manager with responsibilities in eight countries.

Peter presents a commanding physical figure. He attached considerable importance to the symbolic impact he has as a leader on followers. He was alert to signals of weakness and untrustworthiness in others and worked hard at presenting a self that was strong, decisive, physically imposing, reliable and honest. He believed he moved in a world in which such attributes were presented both to impress and deceive.

He had recently left a major job, and had found considerable self-learning in the reflective process of writing his first CV at the age of 55. He showed a capacity for deep personal reflection on the various formative incidents in his leadership career, often expressing experiences as leadership 'tips'. The views tend to be expressed as certainties 'Never ask for more money because you have just done a good job', rather than the more cautious academic 'Be careful you do not lose more than you gain by the way you seek to capitalise on doing a good job'.

Peter's tips are accompanied by vivid specific examples, which are evidently significant episodes in his work life. For example, he conveys a view that leaders tread a path beset with dangers. These can be triggered by failure to follow those leadership beliefs captured in his tips. Here are some of the stories.

'Don't attempt a rebellion'

Once, faced with a headstrong CEO whom he believed was following a faulty policy, Peter set about launching a challenge to the CEO and his views.

> I had found the main spokesman who would start the attack. I was to follow him. Other directors were then to speak, or indicate their intention to vote down the chairman. After the first rebel had his say, the chairman asked if anyone else agreed. Somewhat nervously, I said I had some similar misgivings. The chairman then played his next card. 'Does any one else agree? This is a resignation matter.' But no one else stepped forward although I had their agreement in advance. The first speaker was forced out of the company. I survived – just because I was doing something the company needed doing. But I was finished too, and I left a few months later.

'Don't ask for more money'

> I mean, don't do a good job then immediately use it to put in a pay claim. You lose out later, when you are not in that sort of position.

'Look at the toilets'

I had to go around looking at progress in thirty subsidiary companies. That doesn't give a lot of time for detailed financial studies. I worked out my own short cuts. For example, they may tell you they are big on people management. Check that out by looking at how the workers eat and take breaks. And look at the toilets. That tells you what's really going on.

Several of his 'leadership tips' indicated how sensitised Peter is to status symbols. He talks disparagingly of the widespread use of cars as status indicators. He is far from impressed by someone's title. Grand titles on business cards are the subject of his scorn: 'Why not just use your name? That's what you want to be remembered by isn't it? Look behind the boasts.'

I have become suspicious when someone tells me 'I don't want to be surrounded by yes-men'. Usually that's the sort of person who hates it if someone disagrees with them . . . Then there's the person who says 'I'm telling you this in confidence'. Do you trust that sort of person? I don't.

'Democracy and leadership'

Democracy. It's a lovely idea, in principle. But often you can't have it as a leader. Everything is slowed up. But also, you look weak. Sometimes you have to show what's needed. What must be done . . .

'Make a good first impression'

When I arrive at a reception area, I never sit down, however long I'm kept waiting. Why? Because you must make a good first impression. If you sit down, what happens when the person you are visiting arrives? He's standing over you. If you are sitting down, you are at a disadvantage.

'The fate of the leader'

The fate of the leader is to be vilified eventually. Particularly by your successor who's got to mobilise the company and show that things are changing for the better. So anything you have achieved has to be done down.

'Keep your expenses honest'

Never cheat the company you work for. It's stupid. It gets noticed. I was entertaining a client once. We stopped for me to buy petrol. I paid for the petrol on my company card, and bought some firewood, which I paid for in cash. The client told me much later that he saw then I was someone to be trusted. That was how we got the first contract with his firm.

'Share bad news'

Of course, clear communications are important for good leadership. Don't be afraid to share bad news. Sometimes there are legal reasons you have to withhold some things. But share what you know, and say what you can't announce yet. That way, your people will trust you.

Integration

The ideas in this chapter, although complex, offer a set of related maps. The earlier maps gave us stories of leadership as observable and objective behaviours of leaders which influence followers.

These new maps present leadership as a social reality, 'invented' by the perceptions of the group, including leader and followers. The processes of social invention also create organisational culture. Our maps indicate how acts take on cultural power, which is one way of thinking about symbolism. Hence culture is an important factor in understanding notions of leadership and the symbolic nature of leadership.

The more distinct or stronger the culture, the more cogent the symbolic field of the group/organisation, and the easier it is for leaders to manage the meaning. Employees find it easier to orientate themselves and to frame their experiences in line with the goals of the leader and the future state envisioned and proposed.

Popular work referring to culture tends to assume that each organisation has a culture. Although some works make it clear that culture may be unitary, there is often a clear emphasis on the notion of the multicultural nature of organisations.[14]

Culture consists of common values, norms and fundamental ideas about the organisation – an organisation's expressive and affective dimensions, forming part of a system of shared and meaningful symbols, manifested in myths, ideology and values and in multiple cultural artefacts (rites, rituals, metaphors, language etc.). We have seen in the second platform of understanding that as symbolism, leadership is an ideology designed to support the existing social order by providing a rationale for framing the experience of the led. Culture as a symbolic system emphasises organisations as cultural units containing more or less manifest symbols and symbol systems which are shared by members of the organisation. Over time, patterns of action and symbols mutually reinforce. There may be little objective evidence to back up the story, but a joke about a leader's drinking habits is reinforced every time the executive drinks cabinet is replenished.

Smircich and Morgan, as with many other organisational researchers, have tried to understand how constructions of reality (managing meaning) affect organisational or in this case leadership actions. They set out to develop a theoretical understanding which emphasises the sense or meaning which followers attach to actions and articulations of the leader. To understand these processes better is to understand how the leader frames the social reality and exercises influence through the followers' interpretations of their behaviour. From the work of Smircich and Morgan we see that the way in which organisational members define their situation and the need for leadership to frame their experience is of critical importance with respect to effective leadership. Shared meanings (between group members and between individuals and leaders) is seen as the basis for collective action.

McWhinney develops the notion of shared meanings through his idea of leadership and myths. Myths represent institutionalised meaning structures where thought and action are related in a purposeful way. In modern organisations meaning is derived mainly from its strategic orientation, strategy serves to develop a shared understanding of the environment through mission and vision statements and leadership is thus seen as the management of meaning.

In a conventional sense, leadership has been seen as a question of influencing others to act in a certain manner through a transference of ideas about some desired action from the leader to the group. For those adopting the 'management of meaning' as the basis for effective management, leadership is about establishing a common understanding of the situation and the desired future state. However, the problem for leaders is how to put such ideas into practice.

The new picture of reality of leadership offered by the symbolic approach, emphasises the subjective and emotional elements of followers' sense-making and in their framing of reality, which is in contrast to the objective and bounded rationality of more conventional leadership approaches. It can be argued that a symbolic treatment blurs the categories of subjective and objective, which become linked together through symbols, images and metaphors, so that both observable and symbolic realities have to be taken into account.

Leaders who consider the symbolic side of life may find it easier to deal with the dilemmas arising from different views (maps), rather than be surprised by them (as was the case of Mr Hall in the example on p. 107). Language and behaviour are more likely to avoid unintended confusions, if the leader is aware that 'my way is not the only way' of seeing things. The approach brings practical suggestions to otherwise abstract notions such as idealised influence and visionary leadership.

Getting personal

Of all the maps of leadership, this is the one where personal reactions seem most intense. Some experienced leaders are inclined to respond that they have been aware of the importance of the symbolic at work, even if they had not labelled it as such (rather like the character in Molière's *Le Bourgeois Gentilhomme*, who was pleasantly surprised to find he had been speaking in prose all his life). Other leaders and wannabe leaders find the maps unhelpful – either because they are considered statements of the obvious, or because they are considered too remote from practical steps for developing leadership skills.

The fundamental issue is your beliefs about the way in which you are assessed as a leader. Our earlier maps suggest that leaders have essential qualities observable through what the leader is, or what the leader does. The maps of this chapter offer another view. Leadership is what people *perceive* to be the most important aspects of the leader's behaviours and actions. The actions are those of symbolic significance.

You may also find yourself shifting understanding of leadership, away from a property of the leader, and more the property of a reality constructed by the words and actions of the leader, and the wider group involved in the situation. The most immediate implication is that leadership is more than being allocated the role or label of leader. Simply acting out the rules of being a leader makes sense to the workforce only if the map is that of the classical scientific management world, of leaders giving orders, and followers obeying them.

It may help you understand why a leader like Peter is sensitive to the status decisions in the car parking arrangements. Should the most senior director get the best car parking location? If so, the very recognisable vehicle reinforces its symbolic significance every time employees pass by, every day of the week. Should the directors get executive toilets, while permitting unhygienic conditions for other employees? We are not suggesting there is a 'right' answer to such questions, although we have our preferences. Our point is that you as a leader may benefit from understanding why such actions are not trivial, and are possibly highly significant, and how they set up recurrent patterns of behaviour, actions reinforcing beliefs.

The Bulner Gates challenge

Finally, we return to the challenge offered at the start of the chapter. You may recall that you have been recruited as new chief executive officer, having acted as a lead consultant developing a business plan for the Bulner Gates organisation, where your last assignment had been to restructure the finances in face of declining orders and profitability. The plan has been reluctantly accepted, and resulted in the resignation of the chief executive. Your nomination as replacement CEO was supported by a major institutional shareholder. What will be your first actions in your new job?

If you attempted this, review your earlier notes, and have another go, in the light of what you have gained from the materials in this chapter.

There is no right way to go about such a task, although there are ways more conditioned by your historical maps, and other ways which attempt to act according to a careful reading of the situation, linked to appropriate leadership maps. If you follow the maps of this chapter, you would pay attention to the symbolic consequences of your proposed actions. In carrying out the map-reading, you would also try to assess the maps of those you will be trying to communicate and influence. Perhaps you remembered the case of Mr Hall in the Smircich and Morgan example, where the leader initiated a plan to overcome a corporate problem, yet failed to anticipate other ways in which the staff might 'read' his plan. Should you emphasise the future success of the company, if your new plans are carried out? Should you acknowledge that some of your workforce will be worried about their jobs, and you will have to bring some workers bad news (adding that your policy is to do everything possible for those leaving, and those staying)? In thinking of the impact of your first announcements, did you consider whether you were likely to be compared with the departing leader? Or whether your previous role would have considerable significance in the sense made of what you say?

In discussing such cases with successful leaders, we often found considerable differences in the ways the leaders would deal with the case, and what they would do first. What they shared, however, was a view that was deeply influenced by their personal maps, and which showed a sensitivity to the maps of those with whom they were dealing.

Summary

This chapter provides us with an important difference in the nature of leadership mapping. The maps introduce the assumption of leadership as being socially constructed. This contrasts with earlier maps which assume the existence of a phenomenon with an essence that can be studied and identified. The shift has been described by the more formal terms described as a move from essentialist to constitutive mapping.

Essentialist maps are presumed to have a 'correct reading' of its (essential) features. For example, the essentialist trait maps assumed the existence of universal and essential traits. Constitutive maps, being socially constructed, offer the possibility of more than one reading or interpretation. The notion of a fundamental or essential *reality* shifts towards *perceived or assumed realities*. Alternatively, readers may prefer to avoid the idea of a reality at all (a position found in postmodern map-readings).

One of the most widely accepted essentialist maps assumes that organisational groups act rationally under the influence of rational thinking. Organisations thus make sense of their reality by exploring its rational elements. The maps we met before this chapter are from the family of rational essentialist maps. They are mostly modernist, which differentiates them from the older less rational and pre-modern maps.

Leadership in the pre-modern maps has been interpreted (read) as groups being influenced through activation of ancient symbolic systems. However, such older maps may still be essentialist. For example, Jungian archetypes have been assumed to be universalistic and transcending cultural contexts. These older maps are sometimes rediscovered in more modern treatments in which the leader is attributed with a sense of the mythical as a means of achieving change.

Although multiple or fragmented cultures were also possible within essentialist maps, they are more commonly found in constitutive ones. Here, the different perspectives within an organisation may be ascribed to subcultures who read the organisational map differently.

The popular treatment of new leadership concepts such as transformational leadership tends to assume a unitary culture with a unique and shared vision. These maps have helped us to become more familiar with concepts such as the management of meaning and sense-making. However, the maps still present dilemmas of compliance and cultural fragmentation which are not anticipated from the unitary concept of a shared vision.

The vocabulary of myths and of symbolic meaning tends to be associated with a constitutive reading. Dilemmas arise when they are examined within an essentialist reading which seeks the fundamental reality behind the myth or the symbol. This has been the case with popular treatments of vision-making which assume the process as producing the fundamental goal or mission for transformational change.

Concepts such as vision, culture, culture change and even leadership still tend to be treated within an essentialist reading. An alternative method of map-reading is to accept a more fully constitutive reading which acknowledged the possibility of multiple socially constructed perspectives. This helps as we consider the processes associated with charismatic leadership and of pseudo-charismatic leadership. In both cases, the leader provides meaning to group members. We no longer see the leader as *possessing* charisma, but the leadership process as one within which group members *make sense* of leadership in terms of charisma. The shift is one which gives salience to processes establishing personal, group and organisational identities.

Notes

1 Grint, K. (1997) *Leadership: Classic, Contemporary and Critical Approaches*, Oxford: Oxford University Press.
2 Smircich, L. and Morgan, G. (1982) 'Leadership: the management of meaning', *Journal of Applied Behavioral Science* 18(3): 257–273.
3 Pondy, L. R., Frost, P., Morgan, G. and Dandridge, T. (eds) (1982) *Organizational Symbolism*, Greenwich, CT: JAI Press.
4 Berger, P. and Luckmann, T. (1996) *The Social Construction of Reality*, New York: Anchor.
5 Turner, B. (1992) 'The symbolic understanding of organizations', in M. Reed and M. Hughes (eds) *Rethinking Organization: New Directions in Organizational Theory and Analysis*, London: Sage.
6 Hollinger, R. (1994) *Postmodernism and the Social Sciences: A Thematic Approach*, London: Sage.
7 Rosenau, P. M. (1992) *Post-modernism and the Social Sciences: Insights, Inroads and Intrusions*, Princeton, NJ: Princeton University Press.
8 McWhinney, W. (1992) *Paths of Change: Strategic Choices for Organizations and Society*, Newbury Park, CA: Sage.

9 Schein, E. H. (1992) *Organizational Culture and Leadership: A Dynamic View*, 2nd edn, San Francisco, CA: Jossey-Bass.
10 Ibid., pp. 373–374.
11 Martin, J. and Frost, P. (1996) 'The organizational culture war games: a struggle for intellectual dominance', in S. R. Clegg, C. Hardy and W. A. Nord (eds) *Handbook of Organization Studies*, London: Sage, p. 602.
12 Peters, T. and Waterman, R. (1982) *In Search of Excellence*, New York: Harper & Row.
13 Weick, K. E. (1995) *Sense Making in Organizations*, Thousand Oaks, CA: Sage.
14 Alversson, M. and Berg, P. O. (1992) *Corporate Culture and Organizational Symbolism*, Berlin and New York: de Gruyter.

Trust and the dilemmas of rationality and freedom

Orientation

A fistful of diamonds

Two diamond traders in London's Hatton Garden examine a handful of precious stones. They agree a sale. The buyer says she needs three days to obtain the finance for the cash transaction. The deal is agreed. There has been no discussion of the authenticity of the information provided about the origins and specification of the stones. By tradition, such deals have been conducted with no legal or written exchange. Their bedrock is the intangible bond of trust between the two traders.

Michael Howard, the leader of the British Conservative Party, told delegates to the 2004 party conference that voters had lost trust in politicians of all political persuasions. He concluded that it was no longer possible for politicians to make promises to the electorate.

Chief executive Gerald Ratner at a private function made a joke to the effect that his company's products were of very poor quality. The remark was reported, and the entire company collapsed within months, having lost the trust of its customers, other important stakeholders and financial analysts.

'One more weekend,' the project leader pleads with members of the team. 'I'll see it's worth your while.' There is a silence around the room, before a team member stands up and says that he's heard it too many times before, and would rather leave the company than ruin his family's weekend plans yet again.

We experience episodes such as these, directly or indirectly at work, and in our social lives. In each case, the outcomes of a relationship, often involving a leader and followers, seem to be intimately connected with the trust, or lack of it, in the relationship.

What is trust and why is it important for leaders?

These examples may have started you thinking about trust. We would like you to reflect on these and make a few notes on your personal map of trust in leadership processes. You may have taken the topic for granted, in which case it is worth spending a few minutes at this stage to reflect on your beliefs (Box 6.1). You may find that your ideas are influenced by the maps you have recently examined in earlier chapters.

As we have seen, the earliest theories of leadership took the 'something special' approach. Charisma was assumed to be a gift from the gods. It brought with it rights and capabilities which resulted in unthinking loyalty. There was little need to define trust any further – it 'went with the territory'.

Later researchers found it important to include trust in their leadership models. Robert House suggests that the behaviours of charismatic leaders demonstrate two fundamental components: competence and desirable characteristics as role models. These two features induce *trust* in the leader's ideology, as well as triggering a range of other emotional reactions. The most likely conditions for triggering such emotions are where followers are experiencing stress and distress.[1] Peter Northouse, in his summary of transformational leadership theory, includes building trust among a wide range of associated constructs.[2] Warren Bennis and Burt Nanus, in a much-cited study, collected the views of nearly a hundred leaders, and identified trust (along with developing a clear vision, being 'social architects' and having positive self-regard) as a differentiating attribute of transformational leaders.[3] David Goleman suggests that people will not automatically trust each other with sensitive information, and that the relationship has nothing to do with technical

Box 6.1 The trust challenge

How is your map-making coming along? If you have been practising the challenges in earlier chapters, you will have had several attempts. Perhaps you are feeling more confident at summarising your basic assumptions and beliefs about a topic as a first map, and then testing the map against other evidence.

Our focus for consideration in this challenge is the trust relationship between leader and followers.

- From what you have read and experienced, how important would you consider trust to be for successful leadership? Why do you reach the conclusion you have reached?
- Can you think of situations in which the level of trust in a leader is particularly important?
- Can you think of situations in which the level of trust in a leader is relatively less important?
- Have you noticed something surprising about the way trust is dealt with in the maps of leadership that you have come across?

competence (being an expert).[4] A leader has to be trusted in order that followers are prepared to open up regarding their fears and vulnerabilities. Career failures through lack of integrity have been noted in several empirical studies, and integrity has been highly valued in other studies both of leaders and their followers.[5]

Overview

Two platforms of understanding

The studies of trust are widely distributed, and rarely attempt to integrate their conclusions with the broader body of work in the field. For that, we have provided a thorough meta-analysis conducted by two American psychologists, Kurt Dirks and Donald Ferrin. This work constitutes our first platform of understanding. From it, we are able to see the manner in which the vulnerabilities of individuals play out in high or low trust relationships.

A second platform of understanding is drawn from the sociological perspective of Anthony Giddens. This work derives a theory of trust emerging as a consequence of the conditions of modernity which include the separation in time and space of individuals from the technologically embedded systems that have to be trusted. Giddens argues that trust in people (rather than in technological systems) is a means of protection against deep anxieties of identity and existence. It is constantly renewed through personal processes of reflection, yet remains always open to the dread of loss of trust, which leaves the process also open to challenge and disruption.

Contextual materials

The contextual materials introduce a range of ways in which trust and leadership have been examined. Dean Tjosvold has examined how cooperation has been downplayed in comparison with competition mostly in the context of team leadership. A second account connects creative leadership and trust-based leadership through the metaphor of trust-based methods of horse management. A macro-perspective of trust is provided by the work of Francis Fukuyama.

Platforms of understanding: trust and leadership

We will look at two platforms of understanding:

- Dirks and Ferrin's meta-analysis of trust in leadership
- Anthony Giddens on trust and identity.

Dirks and Ferrin's meta-analysis of trust in leadership

Dirks and Ferrin examined published research on trust in leadership conducted since the 1960s.[6] They compared the various studies in a meta-analysis. As indicated in Chapter 2, a meta-analysis examines data from different studies which are likely to have different approaches, intentions, measures and even definitions. The result simplifies and brings order to what previously was likely to be a complex and confusing body of work.

Concept definition

As might be expected, operational definitions of trust were found in abundance. Rousseau and colleagues offered a definition of trust which, in their view, captured much of the variety of the various studies: 'a psychological state comprising the intention to accept vulnerability based upon positive expectations of the intentions or behaviour of another'.[7]

This definition indicates the centrality of a psychological approach (we will consider a sociological treatment in our next platform of understanding). However, Dirks and Ferrin claim that the definition is consistent with approaches found in economic as well as psychological studies. More specifically, they locate their work within the realm of expectation theory.

The two referents: direct and distal leader influences

The literature was classified according to the focus of the trust process, described as its *referent*. Dirks and Ferrin describe two kinds of *referent*. The first is trust in a *direct leader*; the second concentrates on trust in *organisational leadership*. This distinction, they argue, has important practical and theoretical implications. For example, if research shows that trust is most strongly associated with direct reports, organisations should focus resources on establishing trust at each level of leader (supervisors, middle managers and executives). If the more significant referent is organisational leadership, the processes of trust development are likely to require theories of more indirect influence.

Studies often fail to clarify whether they are concerned with direct or indirect leader referents. This is made more confusing as they also introduce two perspectives, which appear to be connected with but cannot be totally identified with one rather than the other referent.

Direct leaders appear to be a particularly important referent of trust. This supports the need to view leadership as an important concept at all levels of organisation and the potential pitfalls of simply concentrating our efforts on understanding leadership through the actions of the top leadership team, or of the edicts of the chief executive officer.

The two perspectives

The *relationship-based perspective* focuses on the followers' perceptions of the relationship with the leader. Trust is studied as a social exchange process. Social exchange deals with individual willingness to *reciprocate* care and consideration expressed within a relationship. In its emphasis on consideration, the perspective has much in common with management style studies, in which consideration is a major dimension. Clearly, such a style takes account of the vulnerabilities of followers, and propensity to trust.

The *character-based perspective* focuses on the perception of the leader's character.[8] Followers attempt to draw inferences about the leader's characteristics such as integrity, competence and openness.

In everyday terms, we may consider the relationship-based approach to be one in which considerations of benevolence (and its converse, malevolence) are core. The character-based approach is more concerned with considerations of fairness.

Is a transformational leader a relationship-oriented leader?

According to the different perspectives on trust, individuals observe the leader's actions and draw inferences about the nature of the relationship with the leader and/or the character of the leader and these inferences, it is argued, will influence the trust in the leader. The transformational leadership actions and behaviours make sense of reality for the followers, and seem to be more likely than transactional actions to be associated with empathy and benevolence. Trust may indeed be stronger if the leader exerts an idealised influence, or shows individual consideration.

Transactional leaders put more emphasis on character-based issues of integrity and fairness. For example, a transactional leader is able to operate by virtue of followers' trust in the leader's capability for delivering a contractual arrangement. The diamond traders have no strong concerns about the benevolence of their relationship, as they exist within a social world in which transactional integrity is taken-for-granted. The transactional leader in an industrial context promises rewards and punishments in a range of sales and production exchanges. There is an emphasis on integrity, fairness and dependability ('That's not a threat, that's a promise').

These considerations suggest that although trust in a transformational leader is more likely to be relationship based than character based, the situation is not clear-cut. Idealised influence, for example, seems open to character-based trust relationships. The relationship perspective is uneasily close to management style theories.

Disentangling the perspectives

Dirks and Ferrin report on the findings of their meta-analysis of the primary relationships between trust in leadership and the concepts and constructs discussed.

Box 6.2 Locating trust in leadership maps

In the development of transformational leadership theory, Bernard Bass and co-workers derive four factors, the four Is:

- idealised influence
- inspirational motivation
- intellectual stimulation
- individualised consideration.

Can you see how the model suggests ways in which a transformational leader's behaviours induce trust, and therefore increases the prospects of achieving transformational goals?

Dirks and Ferrin differentiate between relationship-based and character-based referents of trust. Which referent (focus) seems more aligned with transformational leadership processes? How might an understanding of the implications of different referents help a newly appointed leader, installed after the departure of a popular leader, who perceives a lack of trust of her leadership role?

They conclude that research on trust in leadership has tended to treat the two perspectives (relationship-based and character-based trust theories) as functional equivalents, recognising the same determinants of trust and predicting the same consequences. The authors suggest this as a problem for understanding, proposing that the theoretical perspectives are conceptually distinct.

Significantly, they argue that their study indicates that trust in leadership is significantly related to attitudinal, behavioural and performance outcomes. This lends credence to the numerous references made by leadership gurus linking trust to organisational effectiveness.[9] Transformational leadership was found to have a substantial relationship with trust (Box 6.2). However, the meta-analysis fails to identify precise causal processes involved.

Conclusions

Past organisational research has demonstrated a lack of clarity in the trust construct.[10] Basically this study hypothesised that trust in direct leaders would have stronger relationships with job performance, satisfaction and altruistic organisational behaviours, than trust in organisational leadership. It also proposes that trust in organisational leadership will be strongly associated with organisational commitment.

Definitions of trust, it was argued, may seem to have a common conceptual core. However, researchers have attempted to measure trust along different and multiple dimensions, usually associated with cognitive, affective and overall forms of trust.

The researchers concluded that the operational definition would have a strong effect on the empirically established relationship between trust, its antecedents and consequences, thus supporting ideas that trust in leadership is a multidimensional construct. An important finding was that direct leaders appear to be a particularly important referent of trust. This supports the need to view leadership as an important concept at all levels of organisation and the potential pitfalls of simply concentrating our efforts on understanding leadership through the actions of the senior team.

Overall, this article offers a useful theoretical framework going some way towards clarifying different perspectives on the development and consequences of trust in leadership. It gives focus to the question why trust in leaders might be desirable, and addresses the issue (often skirted over) of how trust may be developed.

Anthony Giddens on trust and identity

Anthony Giddens has written extensively and profoundly about trust in the social world. He considers that trust is a social necessity under conditions of modernity. By modernity Giddens means a world dominated by the perspective of rational thought and of rationally informed behaviour.[11]

We may contrast pre-modern and modern environments of trust. Pre-modern societies had a localised and immediate environment of trust. In a modern environment, technological changes have contributed to a shift in the nature of trust, which has become 'distantiated' in time and space. In one sense of the word we trust our bank and our various investing institutions to protect our savings (even extending to our extremely virtual e-banking account). We trust our holiday flight to transport us safely to our destination. That is not to say that we remain in a permanent and unconcerned condition of trust. Concerns about flying persist, and each story of financial corruption or governmental malpractice disturbs us.

Modernity operates through a 'disembedding' process of symbolic tokens such as money, which have become increasingly abstract. (*What* is an e-bank? *Where* is its money located?) Also, there is the increasingly abstracted set of relationships implied in trusting expert systems such as an airline. Trust is inevitably, in part, an article of faith.

Giddens summarises his analysis as follows. Trust is related to absence in space and time, and to a lack of full information (distantiation). He considers trust to derive from faith (belief) in an individual such as a leader, or in a social system. When it comes to trust through faith in the abstract systems such as banks and airlines, we are concerned not with their moral but functional reliability. He then defines trust to make explicit the difference between the moral basis of trust in people, and the functional basis of trust in systems:

> Trust may be defined as confidence in the reliability of a person or system, regarding a given set of outcomes or events, where that confidence expresses a faith in the probity or love of another, or in the correctness of abstract principles (technical knowledge).[12]

In this definition we see that trust in a leader places responsibility on the individual who trusts. This is one of the consequences of modernity, in which our personal decisions are believed to be ultimately open to some degree of free will. Trust involves psychological risk, whereas in pre-modern societies, trust might be no more than the fatalistic acceptance of a cosmologically determined destiny.

Trust and reflexivity

All human action is routinely connected with a monitoring of the action, albeit mostly without conscious awareness of the process. The monitoring permits us to connect what we do with our explanations (theories) on which we claim to ground our actions. The consequence is a process where the personal actions and thoughts about actions are mutual influences. This is the process of *reflexivity*. It leads to considerable stability of social exchanges, yet is open to revision, for example, when we experience a jolt to our expectations through word or action.

Returning to the conditions in what Giddens refers to as late-modern society, personal reflexivity has departed from the more stable processes enacted in traditional societies. The consequences of modernity include a heightened interest in, and willingness to challenge, the legitimacy of the 'old' grounds for behaviour, and a far greater tendency to consider future possibilities. This appears to imply an enthusiasm for the new. Giddens argues that the case is rather for presuming the modern condition to be one of 'wholesale reflexivity' in which every facet is open to revision. The revision arises through the processes of actions and reflexive monitoring of actions. In these terms we have to see trust as a fragile and universal human condition, yet recurring in differing forms under changing circumstances.

The psychology of trust

Giddens draws on his sociological writings, as on a range of psychological theories, to explain his understanding of trust. One of his specific contributions is the importance of a person's sense of identity and security in the realities of existence. He has coined the term *ontological security*.

Why are people not overwhelmed with the uncertainties of life in general, and particularly with those differentiating modernist society? Giddens employs developmental psychologists, such as Erik Erikson, to consider trust as involved in developing self-identity.[13] A religious upbringing contributes a further powerful means of developing and sustaining a sense of faith and trust in the ultimately unknowable.

Learning to trust others is an important part of learning to trust ourselves. Trust, in this perspective, is a necessary protection against deepest doubts, not just in another person, but in one's basis for self-understanding and therefore identity. The betrayal of trust opens the psychological floodgates to anxieties of the deepest kind.

For a leader, then, the possibilities become clear. In relationships, the leader plays a part in the development of trust, the containment of uncertainties (Giddens prefers the term ambiguities) or the persistence of anxieties.

The transformation of intimacy

Present-day leaders can no longer expect the trust from their followers that would be granted to the clan leader of an earlier society. The fragility of trust to which we referred previously has been revealed by considerations of delocalised experiences (distantiation), and more complex and ambiguous social relationships. An appeal to 'trust me' can trigger those acts of reflexive kind, by the attention it draws to the possibility of reflection on the untrustworthiness of the speaker. If we are to believe opinion polls, most political leaders produce such consequences through their speeches. The reflexive process is particularly evident in the reactions of substantial numbers of listeners, to the appeals of political leaders, 'distantiated' through the mass communication media. When trust has to be 'worked at', an openness or self-disclosure by the leader becomes vital, as part of a developing process of mutual understanding. When Michael Howard claimed that politicians had lost the trust of the voters, he was showing the outcomes of an intuition, or a deeply reflective social process. For Giddens, trust remains a fundamental feature of contemporary social and organisational life, always open to scrutiny, and therefore always a source of psychological tension.

The permanence of the trust relationship

The analysis is of particular interest to anyone interested in leadership. It presents a treatment of a renewable dynamic process that differs from psychological treatments of trust. It points to a phenomenon that is constantly under reflective review by social actors. (Compare this with the sense-making in the maps of Chapter 5.)

This differs somewhat from the common-sense view that trust takes a lot of building, but is something that can be destroyed for ever in a single act perceived as untrustworthy ('After that, I was never able to trust him again . . .'). It offers a theory relevant for exploring the 'irrational' condition of unconditional trust associated with followers of the charismatic kind of leader. Giddens tells us that a key may be found through considerations of the reflexivity processes of followers to the specifics arising in the situation impacting on self-identity.

This leaves us with the particular and contrasting case of the charismatic leader. A charismatic style seems to weaken and even turn off the customary vigilance of personal reflective processes of followers engaged in the shaping and renewing of social actions and beliefs. The creative process and the dramatic performance both call for suspension of disbelief. After Giddens, we may see the suspension of reflexivity as an important way of understanding charismatic influence processes.

Contextual materials

We consider three contextual readings in this chapter:

- Dean Tjosvold's study of trust, conflict and collaboration
- Trust-based leadership: lessons from the horse pen
- Francis Fukuyama's treatment of trust.

Dean Tjosvold's study of trust, conflict and collaboration

The studies of trust tend to disregard the consequences of a lack of trust. To go more deeply we need to study work concerned with conflict, competition and cooperation. A model addressing tensions in work groups has been developed over a period of years by the researcher, Dean Tjosvold. The work presents a map of processes informing team leadership. The researcher suggests that trust operates in tension with competitive and individualistic action. Neither competitive behaviour nor trust supporting behaviour is an adequate basis for group effectiveness.

Tjosvold captures his experience and research findings in the book *Team Organization: An Enduring Competitive Advantage*.[14] In it he examines how teams balance their much reported process losses with productivity gains through synergy arising from collaborative (and trusting) relationships. His fundamental position is that the various forces for competition within team members contribute potential benefits as well as disadvantages to team progress. Competition hones personal attempts to 'shine', thus raising the bar for norms of performance. In this respect, he points to the oversimplistic view that harmony and cohesion are universally desirable group traits.

Tjosvold argues that since Taylorism and the rise of scientific management as a philosophy in practice, thinking about productivity has had an individualistic bias. This has contributed to the downplaying of what he considers to be an overwhelming body of evidence that *collaboration* has considerable merits within teams. He acknowledges the potential of teams to engage in self-limiting behaviours through being too preoccupied with collaboration.[15] He considers this to support the belief that group interaction is of itself a simple and direct source of productivity losses. Yet he insists that the practical evidence is different, citing overwhelming evidence that cooperative groups can be more productive than individuals working competitively or independently.

The cooperation maxim: constructive controversy

Tjosvold draws on the historical work of Morton Deutsch to arrive at the cooperation maxim.[16] Far from regarding conflict as bad, these views explain how conflict may even be necessary, so that minority opinions may be effectively integrated. Evidence for this has been found among a range of working teams including engineers, customers and technical sales teams. Indeed, it is the *avoidance of conflict*, rather than conflict itself, that is more likely to reduce a group's effectiveness. The ideas suggest approaches of team and personal development as the route to effective conflict resolution. They also indicate the significance of reflection and learning within effective teams.

Tjosvold draws on much of this work to develop a model which a team engages in visualisation of goals, developing a shared perspective, thus achieving more committed (empowered) members, working in innovative ways, reflecting and learning from their actions. These processes interact, although not necessarily in a simple stage-by-stage fashion. The leader directs a great deal of effort towards the manner in which the teams operate on each of the components.

The model has the appearance of a synthesis of elements from a range of sources. This gives it a considerable sense of familiarity. The terms are also in rather common currency in organisational practice. It is clearly consistent with the underpinning principles of constructive conflict and developmental team learning. It avoids a simple dichotomy of 'conflict is bad, cooperation is good'. It offers a sophisticated basis for introducing trust into team-based leadership.

Trust-based leadership: lessons from the horse pen

An unusual study of trust-based leadership has drawn on claims made for non-traditional methods of horsemanship.[17] The claims include the achievement of rapid and efficient interactions in which trust is gained between the human and unridden foals, or even between human and horses with fear of human contact. This story begins when the methods of a Californian cowboy came to the attention of academics in a European business school.

The Horse Whisperer was a Hollywood version of the story of Monty Roberts and his methods of dealing with horses. The film brought international attention for his approach, which has since become a recognised – and in many cases, preferred – alternative to earlier approaches to working with horses. In complete contrast to many traditional approaches of 'breaking' the horse into a condition of compliance, this approach is founded on non-violent training, and on the recognition of a horse's instinctive desire to be part of the herd. From a study of such behaviours over a period of many years, Monty Roberts developed a method that permits him to win the trust of a horse within half an hour, so that even a previously unridden animal accepts saddling, and then a rider. Demonstrations have convinced thousands of knowledgeable spectators that this new approach works. After one such demonstration, Queen Elizabeth the Queen Mother endorsed the method, and encouraged its wider use. Since then, Monty has communicated the methods in television appearances, books and hundreds of personal demonstrations.

The development of trust-based leadership in the United Kingdom began with a meeting between an enthusiastic horse rider, Sylvia Arnold, and Kelly Marks, one of Europe's leading advocates of trust-based methods of working with horses. Kelly had worked with the original horse whisperer, Monty Roberts, and incorporated his ideas alongside her own passion for what she calls intelligent horsemanship. Sylvia was captivated by the demonstrations, and had persuaded her husband, John Arnold, then head of Manchester Business School, to become involved as well. After one event, the Arnolds discussed the implications with colleagues who were already interested in leadership. On his next tour of Great Britain, Monty Roberts visited Manchester Business School.

In the autumn of 1999, a workshop was offered on non-traditional leadership approaches, at the British Academy Conference. The Manchester-based group, supported by Ian Lawson of the Industrial Society, presented emerging ideas about horsemanship and creative leadership. The dangers of drawing simple analogies between horse management and human leadership were made all too clear by the participants. The obvious differences can become a communication barrier. The reaction sensitised the group to inappropriateness of a great deal of animal behaviours as models for improved human action. Such methods are particularly dangerous and morally repugnant if translated to a handbook for human leadership.

Nevertheless, the logic being developed was as follows. Creative leadership has an easy-to-understand meaning as leadership concerned with bringing out the creativity inherent in others. It is a facilitative style of leadership perhaps found at its purest in the leader of a team engaged in a structured creativity technique such as brainstorming. The new methods of intelligent horsemanship seemed close to creative leadership, and on Ian Lawson's own research on trust-based leadership at the Industrial Society.

The case against using the 'intelligent horsemanship' metaphor is that it risks reinforcing inappropriate leadership metaphors of dominance and dehumanisation. A second line of attack is that the method is a version of the so-called theory Y, or be-nice-to-the-workers approach, which has its own problems in competitive business environments. The third objection is that the methods are not yet accepted by many in the horse-breeding and horse-managing worlds. Finally, it has to be noted that the theory is a leader-follower one, thus omitting the issues of leader-group relations.

Linking creative leadership and trust-based leadership

Manchester Business School group had previously been involved in teaching and studying creative leadership work for some years.[18] To compare trust-based and creative leadership, the researchers listed features of the approaches identified in discussions with horse experts, and with participants on leadership courses. These included a set of visiting leaders of African nations, including two members of parliaments in their own countries. This produced a list of over twenty attributes. A high degree of match was found. This result was essentially one of face-validity of the proposition that creative leadership and trust-based leadership approaches are similar concepts.

Creative leadership was defined as a process that shifts (team) behaviours to outstanding levels by introducing helpful (benign) structures for creative actions. The trust-based approach was defined as a process that shifts untrained equine behaviours to cooperative ones by introducing helpful structures leading to 'join-up' (condition of acceptance and trust) and 'follow-up' (condition of mutually beneficial leader–follower activities). Both processes emphasise cooperation not coercion. The creative leader establishes a warm, supportive climate; the trust-based leader establishes a non-threatening 'space' and invites the horse in. No pain, no adversarial actions, no illegitimate influence processes.

Into the round pen: the next steps

Since the early experiments, the approach as a metaphor for trust-based leadership has been tested in a range of executive and MBA courses, accompanied some times by exaggerated media reporting. An article appeared in *Time* in January 2001 indicating that Manchester Business School was training executives to be better leaders, by having them tame wild horses! The more mundane truth is that the metaphor has been included in training courses, as a means of challenging assumptions about the nature of leadership. Its relevance is exemplified in the following enlightening comment of Monty Roberts on the power of gentleness:

> If you want to pursue [trust-based leadership] as a concrete practice, you must give up what I call 'the myth of the gentle'. There is a prevailing, virtual worldwide belief that equates gentleness with weakness, slowness and lack of discipline. When [in a tough situation] I am calm because I have learned that any other state of mind is detrimental . . . It is also *knowledge* that keeps me calm and free of any desire to dominate through fear. I am a willing partner . . . Gentleness is the true strength of the world . . . Violence always comes back in the form of more violence.[19]

Francis Fukuyama's treatment of trust

Francis Fukuyama, former deputy director of the US State Department, wrote several influential books exploring the nature of capitalism. He describes his work as understanding the human historical process as an interplay between two forces.[20] The one force is that of rational desire, the other a striving for freedom as moral beings.

The dilemma of irrationality

Fukuyama suggests that such a position addresses one of the dilemmas of economics (and thus, a dilemma of leadership from an economic perspective), namely the apparent refusal of individuals to operate in strictly economic fashion in a variety of contexts. He suggests that a worker withdrawing from a working contract may be striking as much for economic justice as for economic gain. The entrepreneurial leader is motivated by recognition as well as the anticipation of disposable wealth.

The historical analysis suggests that primitive societies sought recognition through physical conflicts, more recently displaced into economic struggles. Fukuyama sees the process more as leading to the spiritualisation of economic life. Thus, in Japan, he sees the energies of the earlier *samurai* or warrior class as displaced into business. In other cultures a similar transformation has occurred, so that energies directed towards war became displaced towards entrepreneurial actions. This treatment addresses the dilemma of irrationality by offering a motivation for behaviour grounded in personal needs that transcend economic considerations, motivated by the personal need for recognition and self-respect.

Origins of workplace trust

Fukuyama traces trust in the workplace to its cultural origins. A culture's economic organisations develop out of an interplay of the culture's family and state arrangements. He suggests that there are three elements to consider in the emergence of organisations: the family, voluntary arrangements outside the family, and state-owned or -sponsored institutions. His principal thesis is that a strong family-based culture (such as China) tends to have weak voluntaristic arrangements and strong state influences, a view to be found in Weber's writings on China. Family values, then, are not necessarily connected with economic success for a society. Fukuyama suggests that the combination produces differentials in the trust relationships found in different cultures. He differentiates Japan from China in this respect, although his analyses here, and elsewhere, draw on contemporary economic conditions rather than on historical critique.

We can take from Fukuyama the notion that leaders will find cultural conditions strongly influencing their attempts to engender trust among their followers. He illustrates the cultural shaping with numerous examples such as leadership in the high technology multinational corporation, Wang Computers (Box 6.3). Pioneer An Wang automatically assumed that his successor would come from within the family. In contrast, American employees and financial analysts found this an unconvincing rationale.

Box 6.3 Trust and the Wang dynasty

An Wang represents the successful immigrant entrepreneur. Arriving in the United States from Shanghai, the computer business he founded became a great commercial success internationally. Founded in 1951 it had grown to a billion-dollar heavyweight by 1984. An Wang appointed his American-born son Fred Wang to take over the company. Ambitious and senior executives reacted by leaving the company, substantially depleting its management. Within a year Wang Computers had begun its serious decline. Within a few years, it had lost 90 per cent of its capitalisation, and eventually was to file for bankruptcy. Wang the elder decided he had made a big mistake, and removed his son from the leadership role.

Many dynasties survive the appointment of the chosen family scion (IBM was one), sometimes for several generations of leader. The Wang case needs to be examined as illustrative of an instinctive cultural trust that the son was the right leader, perhaps a trust that would blind a Chinese founder to other cultural realities in the United States. What An Wang saw as the rightful destiny for his son, his executives probably saw as ill-judged nepotism depriving them of recognition to be considered as leaders.

Whereas in China, the availability of the son of the founder would have been something to celebrate, and a leader to be trusted, in the United States the cultural context had produced quite different reactions among the workforce.

Integration

The psychology of trust

For Dirks and Ferrin, understanding of trust in leadership has been hindered by an absence of integration of the findings of the many and varied studies involving the construct. Their meta-study therefore may be seen as a map constructed after a careful study of the nature of many fragmentary earlier maps of the territory. Their work suggested that trust (the territory represented) could be defined as a psychological state comprising the intention to accept vulnerability based upon positive expectations of the intentions or behaviour of another.

The definition is as interesting for what it does not say, as for what it does say. It does not say anything about how trust develops or deteriorates. Rather, we are left with the assumption that such changes have something to do with changes in psychological state, which in turn draw on intention to accept vulnerability, and expectations of behaviour. Yet, it is the creation, maintenance and rupture of trust that are the aspects of the phenomenon of interest to leaders. This gives weight to the suggestion that trust is associated with transformational leadership (evidence of change processes associated with trust). It also gives weight to the converse possibility that any signal of lack of integrity in a leader risks revealing a kind of negative vulnerability, that is to say, a condition in which a breakdown of trust is possible. We have here the start of a theoretically based reason why leaders should at all costs avoid statements that might be taken as 'hostages to fortune' as indicating a lack of integrity. It is an argument that most leaders would already have accepted on pragmatic grounds, although fewer are able to resist the temptations in practice. The example of Gerald Ratner mentioned at the start of the chapter serves to illustrate the consequences of actions triggering off strong emotions around what is interpreted as a betrayal of trust.

The map also indicated that the strongest empirical relationships involving trust derived from those studies taking a direct (as opposed to a distant) leader perspective. This begins to suggest a dilemma for the organisational leader in needing to win the trust of employees who are more vulnerable (to use the vocabulary of the trust definition) to their direct leader. The dilemma is worse for the leader who believes there are dangers in becoming 'too close to the workers'.

The second distinction made in the meta-study was between two aspects of trust, the relationship-based and character-based perspectives. Clearly, the remote leader is forced towards being trusted through a character-based approach, associated with fairness; for a more relationship-based approach, the leader has to overcome the remoteness, perhaps through adapting a more direct style (popularised as 'leading by walking about').

The psychological perspective of itself is abstract, and apparently dilemma free. Only by connecting it to the more immediate concerns of leaders are we able to develop richer insights.

A sociological treatment of trust

Our second platform of understanding addresses the nature of trust, but makes no direct reference to leadership, so we have to work a little harder at its integration. Giddens represents trust as a fundamental characteristic of a person's identity. When he notes trust as arising from confidence in the probity or love of another, or in the correctness of abstract principles, we see overlap with the two referents of trust identified in Dirks and Ferrin's study.

The approach also indicates how trust in a leader has been fundamentally influenced through contexts of increasing complexity and ambiguities. This is a strong theoretical approach leading to the possibility of a leader being remote (distantiated) from others, and unable to interact directly, as was the case in early cultural forms, where leaders were local and directly accessible. Dirks and Ferrin arrived at a similar conclusion through their empirical finding from leadership studies that local leaders had stronger trust relationships than did distant ones.

The treatments appear similar. Trust emerges within a rationalistic culture, as having a non-rational grounding. It concerns vulnerabilities (Dirks and Ferrin) or else psychological dread (Giddens). However, there are differences relevant to leaders. The psychological approach has little to offer regarding the recovery of lost trust. The sociological approach suggests that trust is more fragile, always under scrutiny through personal processes of reflection, fragile, yet more of a state of a necessity for individual identity, so that trust is not so much lost as temporarily set aside. Dishonoured leaders are reinstated; deceivers are forgiven; reconciliation, while often a lengthy and painful process, remains a theoretical necessity, and a practical possibility. In contrast, charisma is sustained for as long as reflection is subjugated or set aside, a process whereby the followers achieve some sense of self through acceptance of the security offered by the charismatic experience.

Dilemmas of rationality and compulsion

Giddens offers a universalistic theory of trust from a sociological perspective. The meta-analysis of Dirks and Ferrin takes the complicated and fragmented studies of trust and represents them as an equally compelling map from a psychological perspective. Yet leaders may still feel there is further work needed to secure some insights of practical value

We return to the recommended process of developing a critique through the exposing of dilemmas. There are clues that offer a point of departure within the maps themselves. Dirks and Ferrins position their theorising within expectations theory, pointing to its significance in both psychological and economic theory. They develop their map of rational expectations around sets of rational benefits to the psychological or economic actors involved.

The dilemma emerges with recognition that behaviours cannot always be explained through rational expectations. Trust and loss of trust appear to be constructs for which fully rational behaviours do not seem adequate explanations. That is to say, the willingness of an individual, or social group, to trust a leader is not influenced by completely rational interventions. The 'instruments' of trust are documented in such terms as a 'compelling vision'. One highly charismatic leader regularly demonstrates the non-rational side of the process in a television programme where he acts as a corporate trouble-shooter. He appears to win considerable trust through an approach in which he declares his passionate and utter belief in the course of action he is urging on the directors of the firm undergoing the experience.

Giddens notes that our world is that of late-modernity, dominated with the perspective of rational thought and of rationally informed behaviour, but always unable to deal adequately with systems and personal dilemmas in a thoroughgoing rational manner.

Within the contextual materials, Fukuyama explains the dynamics of trust as arising through cultural and individual interplay between two forces, one of rational desire, and the other a striving for freedom as moral beings. Again we have the dilemma of trust, in terms of rationality and non-rational forces.

These universalistic treatments contrast with the micro-level of the studies of trust and its alternatives. For Monty Roberts, the strongest relationships are trust based, whether they are relationships among humans, or for people with other sentient creature such as horses. The core aspect of the relationship is voluntarism and cooperation rather than influence in its other formats. This was found to approximate to creative or invitational leadership approaches. Tjosvold developed a theory of cooperation in groups which is counter-intuitive, perhaps a dilemma, for many leaders who hold taken-for-granted beliefs that human behaviours are innately competitive, and, under modern conditions, inherently rational.

Getting personal

The chapter began with a few anecdotes involving trust indicating how important it could be for a range of leadership situations. Then the maps, and much of the contextual materials, took us a long way away from the real-life challenges which face business leaders. We can move towards these practical dilemmas following our advocated procedures of working out our own journeys and our own maps with assistance from the general maps provided.

Is trust exploitative?

We are aware of several dilemmas of widespread concern. They emerge as we 'get personal' in our leadership courses. One of the most important is whether the very concept of trust is to be trusted! For many leaders and wannabe leaders, the maps of trust are taking them into very alarming territory. Some express it forcefully: 'There's no chance that trust works in our company . . . trust is a way of exploiting the gullible . . . to survive, you have to say one thing and mean another.'

In effect, the leader who makes disparaging remarks about the company's products is implying that the customers are foolish and gullible, failing to understand the realities of commerce. This also assumes it to be a shared belief. Giddens follows developmental psychologists in suggesting that core beliefs are an important part of our self-identity, perhaps learned from our earliest family and cultural experiences. The dilemma is whether leaders can develop trust even in unpromising circumstances (Box 6.4). That is the personal dilemma we all face. We have to confront it, as the belief operates in a self-fulfilling way as our actions reinforce our beliefs. The trust-based leader is as convinced in its power, as the sceptical leader is in its lack of authenticity.

Box 6.4 A dilemma of loyalty and trust

As a leader, you are in possession of information that a business unit and associated manufacturing facilities will be closed down. The information has been decided at corporate headquarters, and an announcement will be made in ten days' time. Any premature announcements could have legal consequences. The director of human resources tells you she is considering leaving to take up a better-paid post in another company. She is partly influenced by the uncertainties, and could be persuaded to stay with appropriate reassurances. You know she would be very helpful in managing the close-down procedures. What do you do? Do you try to dissuade her from moving? You could tell her that you hope to have some interesting new changes to tell her about shortly. Or you may take her into your confidence. In which case, would you want her to guarantee her silence, either verbally, or more legalistically in writing?

These approaches have different implications and consequences. Taking her into your confidence shows how trust occurs in a two-way relationship. She needs to trust your assurances; you need to trust her with sensitive information. However, it may well be that in real life you have already undertaken a commitment to not passing on the information. These are the extra dimensions which produce hard-to-resolve dilemmas in real life. Furthermore, in real life you will always find pressures of time to reach a decision. 'Buying time' (although often necessary) is rarely enough to constitute a complete strategy.

Trust as a process to be developed

In thinking through this dilemma, we suggest you consider the lessons available from the maps of the territory. You may compare the situation with that of the diamond traders, operating in a condition of unconditional trust. This reminds us that a specific crisis or episode is not isolated from a context. The traders repeatedly reaffirmed their culture of trust through their actions. The lesson is that as leader, you may need to have worked at the culture in advance of the current crisis.

When trust is absent

Even when you find yourself in a condition where trust seems absent, there may be possibilities as a leader for a trust-based approach. Anything you say is open to the cynical response 'why should we trust you?' You may hope to learn from the inspirational speeches of charismatic leaders at times of crisis. Or you may return to the definition provided by Dirks and Ferrin. Trust refers to the condition of *vulnerability* which influences expectations. The leader may have to signal vulnerability – and by actions as well as words. This cuts across the model of trust in a leader's competence and strength. It is a relationship-based model not a character-based one. The leader 'goes at risk'. The leader may have to find a way of committing himself or herself – without being forced to. It is the tradition of the leader falling on the sword, or offering resignation as a demonstration of trust or honour. Ironically, it is a strategy that opposes the maxim offered earlier of avoiding offering a hostage to fortune.

Summary

The complexities of trust, a key feature of leadership maps, have been explored in this chapter. Detailed consideration has been given to the notion of a trust basis for leadership, and significantly the idea that trust is the essential ingredient for effective leadership. As noted in earlier chapters, notions of rationality are central to many leadership theories, and in this chapter we explore the emerging dilemma that behaviours within organisations assumed to be of a rational kind cannot always be understood as rational actions. Indeed, assumptions of thoroughgoing rationality may be undesirable manacles restricting freedom of thought.

The literature discussed has demonstrated how the growing interest in theorising about trust and leadership has led to some map-makers to be concerned about the poverty of practical guides on how trust might be developed by leaders and in providing insights which focus on more macro-analysis of trust at the organisational level. Dirks and Ferrin addressed the complexities and ambiguities involved and trust is examined as a psychological mechanism for understanding leadership effectiveness. Trust was mapped as having a widely accepted definitional focus, based on notions of vulnerability. Such a process remains a potential source of psychological tension for the leader as well as for followers.

Charismatic leaders may arguably be understood as individuals who are able to provide a focal point for followers to suspend individual freedom of thought, and thus deny their vulnerability to betrayal by charismatic leaders and their messages

Giddens offers an alternative approach to the analysis of trust from a sociological perspective. His mapping of the contemporary world is of a technologically complex globalising environment which requires new forms of trust into technologies which cannot be fully understood and therefore have to be trusted. He argues that trust in people (rather than in technological systems) is a means of protection against deep anxieties of identity and existence. It is constantly renewed through personal processes of reflection, although it remains fragile to disruption and betrayal. Giddens draws on developmental psychologists such as Erik Erikson to map trust as a component in the development of a sense of self.

Trust-based leadership offers a map that differs profoundly from many leadership maps which imply leadership as a control process. Trust-based approaches including leadership of creativity-seeking groups are based on cooperative behaviours and benign social structures, established through a warm and supportive work climate permitting creative and intrinsically satisfying personal conditions. These approaches address the dilemmas of rationality and control by introducing leadership maps which give preference to empowerment over control, accepting the leader's vulnerability to the values and needs of others within organisational groups.

Notes

1 House, R. J. (1976) 'A 1976 theory of charismatic leadership', in J. G. Hunt and L. L. Larson (eds) *Leadership: The Cutting Edge*, Carbondale, IL: Southern Illinois University Press.
2 Northouse, P. G. (2003) *Leadership: Theory and Practice*, 3rd edn, Thousand Oaks, CA: Sage.
3 Bennis, W. G. and Nanus, B. (1985) *Leaders*, New York: Harper & Row.
4 Goleman, D. (1995) *Emotional Intelligence*, New York: Free Press.
5 Yukl, G. A. (2002) *Leadership in Organizations*, 3rd edn, Englewood Cliffs, NJ: Prentice-Hall.
6 Dirks, K. T. and Ferrin, D. L. (2002) 'Trust in leadership: meta-analytic findings and implications for organizational research', *Journal of Applied Psychology* 87(4): 611–628.
7 Rousseau, D. M., Sitkin, S. B., Burt, R. S. and Camerer, C. (1998) 'Not so different after all: a cross-discipline view of trust', *Academy of Management Review* 23: 393–404, at p. 395.
8 Mayer, R. C., Davis, J. H. and Schoorman, F. D. (1995) 'An integrative model of organizational trust', *Academy of Management Review* 20: 709–734; Clark, M. C. and Payne, R. L. (1997) 'The nature and structure of workers' trust in management', *Journal of Organizational Behaviour* 18: 205–224.
9 Kouzes, J. M. and Posner, B. Z. (1995) *The Leadership Challenge: How to Keep Getting Extraordinary Things Done in Organizations*, San Francisco, CA: Jossey-Bass; Bennis and Nanus, *Leaders*.
10 Clark, M. C. and Payne, R. L., 'The nature and structure of workers' trust in management' [see note 8].
11 Giddens, A. (1990) *The Consequences of Modernity*, Cambridge: Polity Press.
12 Ibid., p. 34.
13 Erikson, E. H. (1965) *Childhood and Society*, Harmondsworth: Penguin; Winnicott, D. W. (1974) *Playing and Reality*, Harmondsworth: Penguin.
14 Tjosvold, D. (1991) *Team Organization: An Enduring Competitive Advantage*, Chichester, Sussex: Wiley.
15 Steiner, I. D. (1972) *Group Process and Productivity*, New York: Academic Press.
16 Deutsch, M. (1985) *Distributive Justice*, New Haven, CT: Yale University Press.
17 Rickards, T. (2000) 'Trust-based leadership: creative lessons from intelligent horsemanship', *Creativity and Innovation Management* 9(4): 259–266.
18 Rickards, T. and Moger, S. (1999) *Handbook for Creative Team Leaders*, Aldershot, Hants: Gower.
19 Roberts, M. (2000) *Horse Sense for People*, London: HarperCollins, p. 208.
20 Fukuyama, F. (1992) *The End of History and the Last Man*, New York: Free Press.

7 Do strategic leaders matter?

Have I got what it takes to be a strategic leader?

Do strategic leaders matter? 'Some do, some don't, and a lot more could.'[1]

Orientation

The significance of strategy in business school studies

One of the defining features of business schools is their widely shared treatment of corporate strategy within the MBA curriculum. A visitor to leading schools internationally is likely to find, at the appropriate time of year, students heading for their lectures, each carrying the definitive corporate strategy text for the course. In the 1970s it was a little book by Igor Ansoff, entitled *Corporate Strategy*.[2] Later this was replaced by a handful of rather larger books, including at least one by Michael Porter,[3] and a general textbook of readings and cases such as the multi-edition work by Gerry Johnson and Kevan Scholes.[4] Most recently, the curriculum would demand that they carry more books, to cover newer additions to the strategy curriculum from other 'thought leaders' such as Andrew Pettigrew (the behavioural context of change),[5] Ikujira Nonaka (knowledge creation),[6] and C. K. Prahalad and Gary Hamel (core competences strategy is widely recognised as 'what they teach you at business school').[7]

Have I got what it takes to become a strategic leader?

Strategic leaders are differentiated from other sorts of leaders by their contributions to shaping the strategic future of organisations. The terms may be widely applied – to military and political systems as well as economic ones. Even the leaders of religious institutions have to contribute strategic as well as religious guidance.

How might you set about establishing if you have what it takes to be a strategic leader? Contemporary selection processes of strategic leaders involve careful examination of the candidate's track record, together with psychological and social assessments through test batteries and interviews. The process remains one surrounded by conceptual uncertainties and situational factors. An organisation may place strong weight on factors such as selecting a leader perceived to be one able to bring a different strategic approach to that of the previous incumbent.

A high-level competence generally associated with strategic leaders is cognitive complexity. Such an approach tends to imply that strategic leaders have unusually rich cognitive maps permitting them to deal with more complex organisational and environmental challenges. Elliott Jaques proposed that cognitive complexity is revealed particularly by the timescale into the future that a strategic leader is able to operate.[8] The hierarchical nature of leaders in Jim Collins' scheme identifies strategic leaders with the highest (fifth) level of competence, one that combines cognitive complexity with moral sensitivities.[9]

As a would-be strategic leader you will probably acquire feedback from time to time about your strategic capabilities through experiences evaluating you in practice or psychometrically. A component within such assessments will be evidence of your own self-belief as a strategic leader. At a crude level you are more likely to be perceived as a strategic leader if you believe in your capabilities, and more likely to be rejected if you do not.

Do strategic leaders matter?

Our strategic challenge is suggested by the quote at the start of the chapter. In everyday terms, does strategy exist as something to be discovered by information collection and analysis? If so, do strategic leaders make a great deal of difference (beyond commissioning the best MBAs they can hire)? The issue is one which has generated considerable debate. One group of map-makers have argued that strategic choice mediated by leaders is what gives organisations a competitive edge. Other map-makers (the strategic determinists) believe that strategy is determined by objective factors in the competitive environment (Box 7.1).

Origins of the strategy movement

Igor Ansoff claims to have invented the discipline of corporate strategy, a claim sometimes contested by Peter Drucker.[10] At very least, Ansoff's *Corporate Strategy* taught a generation of business leaders in the 1970s the techniques of SWOT (strengths, weaknesses, opportunities, threats) analysis, weighing up the tensions between a company's internal strengths and weaknesses, and its environment's threats and opportunities, exposing the strategic dilemmas facing the company.

Michael Porter later developed a series of conceptual models which analysed the forces present in competitive environments as a way of revealing appropriate

---

Box 7.1 The strategic challenge: do strategic leaders matter?

The importance of strategy hides a dilemma for strategic managers. If strategy is a matter of identifying the best strategy, the importance of the leader's insights diminishes. Strategy is essentially a matter of information processing. If, on the other hand, there is some strategic choice open to the strategic leader, there is scope for imagination and creativity. The strategic leader makes a profound difference.

- Can you think of circumstances when strategic choice is likely to be very limited?
- Can you think of circumstances when strategic choice is likely to be less restricted?
- What have these considerations led you to conclude about the importance that a strategic leader may have in strategy formation?

---

strategies.[11] His vocabulary, associated with his five forces model, and proposed strategic options, gained wide currency. Executives now talk freely of niche strategies and strategic entry barriers, ideas and terms popularised in Porter's work (although traceable to earlier industrial economic theories).[12]

Pendulum swings: internal structures and industry structures

It has been suggested that research in strategy has swung like a pendulum.[13] In the 1960s the emphasis was on the firm, and its internal structure. The work provides rich case-based accounts of interest to industrial leaders and management teachers and researchers. In the 1970s and 1980s, the pendulum swung in recognition of the under-explored strategic implications of industry structures. The push on the pendulum came from efforts of researchers drawing on the economics literature. The swing took the emphasis away from concepts of direct relevance to strategic leaders such as the tools and techniques developed by the corporate-level writers. Unsurprisingly, the role of the business leader was less central (except as a player in the drama known as the strategic choice debate: could leaders and their actions make a significance difference to the strategic choices open to a company?).

In the 1990s, the pendulum was pushed back towards internal structural issues for gaining competitive advantage through deployment of the firm's resources. A range of themes relevant to strategy was emerging, under a generic title of resource-based theories of the firm. The role of the leader was back on the research agenda, as a means of knowledge capture and exploitation, although still as one possible influence, rather than as a major initiator of change (Boxes 7.2 and 7.3).

Box 7.2 Leadership strategy and performance

Strategy as a business subject has been grounded in several perspectives or maps. Some maps have acknowledged the significance of leaders and top management teams. In others, the role of the leader is missing. Furthermore, the field acknowledges the importance of practice-based evidence (cases), although it is a field in which leading academics move into international consulting firms, thus providing a rich set of concepts.

Early maps can be traced to classical writings, such as Alfred D. Chandler's exploring in depth the historical development of the new types of international firms such as General Motors.[14] Much emphasis was placed on the relationships between strategy and structure. The mood of scientific management inevitably supported maps which indicated ways of planning, and of working out the routes towards desired goals, means–ends analysis, SWOT analysis, which were the precursors of later analytical frameworks, such as Michael Porter's five forces model.[15]

Other maps helped reveal strategy as a dynamic process with behavioural aspects which cannot be totally pre-planned. More recent maps have turned our attention to the quest for unique advantages or competences, and to identifying how such competences may be converted to competitive advantages. These maps include those in which knowledge acquisition and conversion processes play a part in the firm's strategy. In a seminal article, Prahalad and Hamel argued that in fast-changing and uncertain (turbulent) environments, leaders will be judged by their skills at identifying and exploiting core competences in ways which even change our thinking about the nature of the firm.[16] A broader theoretical debate has developed around the firm as a means of managing such resources. This has become known as the *resource-based theory of the firm.*

One extended debate is whether there is such a thing as strategic choice – with possibilities of creativity encapsulated in a strategic vision. A counterview is that there are objective aspects of a firm's environment which make strategy ultimately deterministic, and the role of leader that of a vehicle for the establishment of 'correct' strategy, and as a means of authorising its execution or implementation.

A study of research themes in the major journal, *Strategic Management Journal*, showed six broad maps since the 1980s:[17]

- *Strategy and top management:* involving leadership, methods of planning and modelling strategic decision-making and change.
- *Strategy and its environment:* including and extending the early strategic-fit ideas.
- *Strategy and performance:* often including studies at the level of strategic groups, corporate strategy and financial measures.
- *Growth and market entry:* including entry processes and strategic advantage models.

continued

- *Industry and competition:* competitive and industry analysis, and the theory of strategic groups sharing strategic characteristics.
- *Resource-based theory of the firm:* a firm's distinctiveness is embedded in its unique resources or core competences.

The research agenda has swung *away* from the earlier interest in environment and fit (as the approach proved less tractable for dealing with complex and dynamic environments). Interest has swung *towards* assessment of performance with increasingly deep financial models and *towards* resource-based theory, and particularly aspects involving alliances and capabilities or competences. This swing has effectively meant that leadership issues have remained a part of strategic theorising, but somewhat overshadowed by the other approaches, and in particular, the resource-based theory which has been able to accommodate newer ideas of knowledge acquisition, technological innovation processes and multilevel strategies (global, international, national and corporate levels).

The maps are those indicating the emerging key theories of strategy (themselves examples of core competence development). The theories largely *conceal* the debates regarding the economic and behavioural theorists, dilemmas of the 'unplannability' of strategies within turbulent and fast-changing environments, and the influence (or lack of influence) of leaders and top echelon teams.

Overview

Two platforms of understanding

Our platforms of understanding examine two maps of the territory. The first is from Afsaneh Nahavandi and Ali R. Malekzadeh, at the Arizona State University. The chronological focus of their study was the period of new leadership emergence (1970s and 1980s), and their work helps us understand the dilemmas of strategy formation and implementation during this period. The second map is that of Kimberly B. Boal and Robert Hooijberg, who examine theorising of what is known as top echelon theory.

Both maps indicate that top-level leaders can make a difference. However, leaders' influence is only one factor involved in effective strategy formation and implementation. This provides some support for a strategic choice view of leadership (as opposed to the view that strategy is essentially deterministic). The studies also indicate the dangers of studies at different organisational levels. The impact of top leaders tend to be found in strategy formulation, and that of lower-level leaders/supervisors as moderating factors in strategy implementation.

Box 7.3 Strategy in complex environments

Elements from early models of business/environment fit are still relevant to business strategists. With the pendulum swing, simple gap analysis and SWOT techniques had been extended into wider environmental applications as PEST (political, economic, social and technological factors) analysis. However, such extensions only highlighted the complex and dynamic nature of the business environment, and the difficulties in planning as if the environment were predictable and stable.

This led to a high-tension debate in the 1980s between the strategy pioneer Igor Ansoff and the management theorist Henry Mintzberg.[18] Mintzberg was particularly concerned that strategic planning had ignored the unplannable components in strategy. The thrust of his argument is that strategy can never be fully pre-planned. The process would otherwise have a deterministic form which denies the actual uncertainties of business environments. Mintzberg proposed a way of thinking about strategy as a map which was being repeatedly refined and upgraded with increasing knowledge of the territory of the map. In other words, strategy (map) and journey (implementing strategy) are thoroughly interrelated. This is the notion that strategy emerges through practice. The term *emergent strategy* implies this mutual interactive process.

Strategic attention has turned to high-velocity environments, and the acceptance that strategy can no longer be restricted to simple models of stable environments, and the search for synergies of production or marketing kinds. Emergence is generally accepted as an important aspect of strategy mapping in high-velocity environments.

Contextual materials

The contextual materials provide a range of examples of strategic leadership. The first introduces a model of tipping point leadership as a means of achieving strategic change. The second is a case of an information-based strategic process. The third case presents the ancient strategic wisdom of Sun Tzu and its reapplication (remapping) by a modern IBM executive. The final extended case outlines a period of strategic turbulence involving a hostile take-over attempt of a global sporting corporation.

Platforms of understanding: strategic leadership

We will look at two platforms of understanding:

- Nahavandi and Malekzadeh's investigation into strategic leadership
- Boal and Hooijberg's review of themes in strategic leadership.

Nahavandi and Malekzadeh's investigation into strategic leadership

Do leaders play an essential role in an organisation's strategy and performance? Afsaneh Nahavandi and Ali R. Malekzadeh carried out a thorough investigation of empirical studies of the impact of leadership and strategy on performance.[19] They showed how the literature gave some comfort for two opposed viewpoints on the impact of leadership in addressing the critical question 'Do strategic leaders matter?'

This is the debate which examines strategic determinism and strategic choice. The determinists propose that strategy is a process of identifying factors determined by environmental, structural or cultural factors. The strategy is thus not *created* by insight on the part of a leader but *discovered* by analytical processes. Non-determinists' views propose that the leader has strategic choice, which eventually influences the corporation's success.

Formal studies are claimed by each camp to support their view. However, some of the ambiguities can be explained by looking at the studies in closer detail. The studies have tended to examine two different levels of influence: top leaders, and leaders throughout the organisation, thus including team leaders and first level supervisors.

Indeed much of the work has focused on individuals who would not have been considered leaders in the early trait-based era of leadership research.

Strategy formulation and strategy implementation

For leaders outside the top leadership cadre, there has been little scope traditionally for influencing strategy *formulation* in practice. Even strategic choice advocates would consider that the impact would be through a lower-level leader influencing the *implementation* of strategy. For top leaders, the strategic choice advocates would consider that the most significant influence a leader can bring to bear is in strategy formulation.

The majority of studies have focused on implementation. The widely accepted view is that leaders are unable to modify behaviours and beliefs so as to be more effective in implementing a strategy. Consequently, in line with the dominance of contingency theory for several decades, an impact arises if the leaders are *matched* to the strategies (compare contingency theory). If a new strategy is brought in, new leadership practices, and probably new leaders responsible for implementation, have to be introduced.

The general thrust of this analysis is that leaders influence implementation as one among a range of so-called intervening or contingent variables. However, different styles and functional backgrounds may be needed at different stages of implementation, and for different kinds of strategy. For example, entrepreneurial and pioneering strategies require leaders at all levels with greater capabilities for dealing with uncertainties, and with risk management; cost leadership may require process engineering orientation and skills.

The role of leader in strategy formulation

A relatively minor proportion of studies examined the role of leader in strategy formulation. Here, the leader is studied as a main factor impacting on strategy and performance (Box 7.4). Three broad classes of factor have been given particular attention: *leader's personal values* (which may extend to the personal values of the top management team), *demographic characteristics* and *personality constructs*. Some studies have found demographic, personality, personal values and interpersonal factors can have an impact on the choice of strategy, giving support to the strategic choice perspective.

Box 7.4 How leaders make a difference

Large numbers of variables have been tested for explanations of leader impact on strategy and organisational performance. No variable has been found as always being associated with improved performance. This conforms to the predications of contingency theory (that circumstances moderate the impact of variables on outputs such as a change in performance of an organisation).

However, demographic variables which have been associated with performance change include the following:

- *Functional background:* general or cross-functional experience may support more radical changes than experience within a professional function.
- *Age:* younger leaders may be more likely to be change oriented.
- *Prior experience:* leaders selected from outside may be more change oriented.
- *Cognitive style and orientation:* leaders with an internal locus of control (belief that events can be influenced by personal efforts) are believed to be more entrepreneurial, better during times of crisis, and to design and support more innovative strategies. Leaders with an external locus of control may be better at supporting and implementing cost differentiation strategies.

However, other studies have been less clear-cut, so that the strategic determinism position cannot be completely rejected. The authors suggest that an impact on performance by strategic leaders is the more generally confirmed position, perhaps weakened by methodological difficulties of studies (failure to distinguish formulation and implementation impact; the overlooking of moderating factors on performance).

An integrative framework

Nahavandi and Malekzadeh offer an easy-to-understand integrative framework of strategic leadership. The researchers suggest that the strategic leader may be considered to provide a 'main effect', or operate to provide moderator or intervening variables between strategy and outcomes. They suggest challenge-seeking orientation and the need for control are dimensions discriminating strategic orientation of leaders. High challenge-seeking leaders are innovative in their strategic choices. High control leaders wish to retain control over decisions and actions. This gives a typology of four strategic types:

- *High challenge/low control* leaders seek change within a process of delegating and sharing responsibilities.
- *High challenge/high control* leaders would seek challenges but expect more conformity to their prescribed strategy, retaining control. Innovation, for example, would be 'micro-controlled' for costs.
- *Low challenge/high control* leaders would advocate centralisation and seek stable environments.
- *Low challenge/low control* leaders would encourage participation under conditions in which major change is unlikely. Most often found in organisations not facing tough competitive challenges or fast changing environments. Some cooperatives, communes, and social clubs operated under such conditions (although these groups may also have high challenge leadership).

We should remember that such typologies simplify the realities of organisational practices. Leaders may have a preferred or dominant style, and yet behave differently (according to situational theories of leadership).

Boal and Hooijberg's review of themes in strategic leadership

Kimberly B. Boal and Robert Hooijberg reviewed the field of leadership and arrived at the widely accepted view that the 1980s and 1990s were decades of substantial changes in leadership research.[20] They suggested that the changes involve three streams of research. These are essentially

- strategic leadership research
- new leadership
- emergent leadership.

They traced a resurgence in top management research to earlier work under the rubric *upper echelon theory*.[21]

Upper echelon studies

As indicated by our earlier platform of understanding in this chapter, many of the leadership theories up to the 1980s had become increasingly interested in supervisory level leaders, and thus effectively concentrating on supervisory theories of leadership 'in' organisations (path-goal, contingency, leader member exchange focus). In contrast, strategic theories of leadership are concerned with leadership 'of' organisations.[22]

In an influential article in the mid-1980s, Donald Hambrick and Phyllis Mason proposed that strategy in organisations reflected characteristics of its top executives ('upper echelon'). The impact of the contribution was to help redirect attention towards strategic level issues. Hambrick and Mason highlighted aspects in the way the leader(s) thought, and the values they held. Essentially they were proposing that leaders within an upper echelon 'made a difference' through their cognitive styles and belief systems.

The discretion of the strategic leader

At the time when upper echelon leadership research was developed, one of the influential theories of strategy, widely taught in business schools, was that of Michael Porter.[23] Specifically, his method of identifying an organisation's optimal strategic 'position' indicated that with correct analysis, there was no need for leadership intervention in setting strategy. (Strategy could be carried out by well-trained MBAs.) A related debate was rumbling on between a rational school of strategic planning, identified with Igor Ansoff's pioneering work,[24] and a theory of emergent strategy, advocated by Henry Mintzberg.[25]

This again raises a dilemma of strategic choice: 'Can I, as a leader, create a unique strategy for my organisation, or is it a process best left to a team of strategic planners?'

Hambrick and co-workers found a way of dealing with this dilemma. They identified *leader discretion* as a critical component of effectiveness, describing the idea as a bridge between two kinds of theory, one claiming priority for leadership creativity, the other claiming priority for environmental forces.[26] This theory neatly sidesteps the 'either/or' debate of strategic choice. It indicates that creativity may be possible, as a form of leadership option.

Three issues for strategic leaders

Based on the perception of increasing turbulence of organisational work,[27] Boal and Hooijberg argue that the essential features of concern for strategic leadership are *absorptive capacity*, *adaptive capacity* and *managerial wisdom*.

- *Absorptive capacity* has become a central concept within knowledge management theory, and involves a capability for knowledge capture and utilisation (learning).
- *Adaptive capacity* is the potential for change, and has been linked to what some researchers call strategic flexibility.[28]

- *Managerial wisdom* manifests itself in a sensitivity to change in the environment, and to behavioural patterns of others. The former involves what is sometimes referred to as environmental scanning or discernment.[29] The latter has become the focus of attention for researchers into social intelligence and the related concepts of emotional intelligence. It is suggested that a strategic leader's skills at such knowledge management processes are significant through their influence on her/his actions throughout the organisation.

Contextual materials

We consider four contextual case studies in this chapter:

- Bill Bratton's experience of tipping point leadership
- Information-based strategies
- Sun Tzu and business strategy
- A battle of strategies: when leaders fall out.

Bill Bratton's experience of tipping point leadership

The tipping point concept had become popular enough to enter into 'management speak' by the early years of the new millennium. According to advocates Chan Kim and Renée Mauborgne, strategic transformations occur where there is a rapid shift (they talk of a hurdle crossed) in strategy orientation and strategy implementation.[30] There are four hurdles (or tipping points), two of reorientation and two of implementation. As implementation throws off unexpected outcomes, the process is more of a series of tipping points, rather than a single linear sequence of four stages.

The reorientation of strategy involves a shift in assumptions and beliefs – the *cognitive hurdle*, and a shift in resources – the *resource hurdle*. The implementation involves a shift in *motivational* and *political* factors. These are the four steps of the model, the 'what' of strategic change. The authors indicate the 'how' of strategic change illustrating with the rapid and transforming changes that have been achieved and credited to the strategic leadership of New York Police Chief Bill Bratton.

New York City is famous for the scale of its buildings, its pace of life, and for its rich cultural contribution in the shaping of modern America. It is also famous for its social problems and the challenges of policing. The city suffered its greatest single catastrophic event in the Twin Towers attacks of 11 September 2001. His leadership at the time of crisis contributed to the reputation of the Mayor, Rudolph Giuliani. Our story links Mayor Giuliani with his redoubtable police commissioner, Bill Bratton.

Bratton has a track record of achieving impressive and sustainable strategic change, initially in Boston at district level, then as chief of the Massachusetts Bay Transit Authority ('the terror train') and eventually as superintendent of the Boston

Metropolitan Police. In each of his assignments, Bill Bratton developed a strategic style exemplifying the four stages of the tipping point model.

Prior to Bratton's appointment at the New York Police Department (NYPD) in 1994, the city faced a crisis of confidence in the safety of its citizens in public places. There was increasing movement out to the suburbs, leaving whole areas derelict. Drug crime and vandalism were on the increase. Bratton had already been credited with the one bright spot, the highly visible improvements to the infamous New York Transit Authority (NYTA) within a few years after his arrival from Boston. In New York, his strategic plans were credited for clear progress made in addressing and dealing with the major sources of social discomfort and dangers. In the media, Bratton's achievements were simplified as the success of his controversial *zero tolerance* strategy.

Overcoming the cognitive hurdle

'Winning hearts and minds' has become a leadership cliché. Bratton developed several powerful approaches, which he modified to meet each new set of circumstances. One might be termed '*back to the shop floor*'. Managers 'see' their jobs differently after they (re)encounter the realities of the shop floor or the front line. Policing permits many opportunities for introducing this strategic shift plan. At the NYTA, Bratton initiated an edict. Starting with himself, his officials were to travel to and from work and to other official functions on the transit system. Subsequent discussions became more grounded in practical realities.

'Meet the public' events were introduced (a plan he had found successful in his time in Boston). Such meetings helped confirm the view that the police were preoccupied with dealing in serious crimes, ignoring 'petty' crimes of all kinds, whereas the public were far more concerned with day-to-day encounters with 'vandals and vagabonds'. It was from such confirmation that the policy of zero tolerance became internally accepted. Another approach involved communicating his messages internally. Aware of the low priority of circulated paperwork, he recruited a journalist to support internal communications, which became more immediate and involving, including video messaging at roll calls.

'Sidestepping' the resource hurdle

Effective, quick-moving leaders find ways to use existing resources in the short term, while lobbying for more for the future. Bratton tended to win more resources for his people; he also worked at targeting 'hot spots' in using what he had. For this sort of change he used hard facts to back his arguments. He was able to show, for example, that the policing of drug activities was inadequate and misdirected (it had been a Monday to Friday operation by custom and practice, and contrary to the evidence that drug-dealing was a seven-day-a-week business).

The motivational hurdle

Under conditions of crisis (the tipping point condition), motivation is enhanced through a process of focusing on key groups of middle-range leaders. Bratton's particularly effective plan involved the 67 district commanders, each with between 200 and 400 staff. The commanders were mandated to be present at twice-weekly strategy review meetings where they were quizzed by a panel including senior officers and significant outsiders.

Participants were notified at short notice that they were to present the work of their precinct. The format ensured that there was little possibility for excuses or blame-laying. The process encouraged acceptance of responsibilities for strategy formation and execution. Each presenter was expected to speak about the summary information culled from their computer databases, and explain the significance of the revealed crime statistics on operational decisions for dealing with the hotspots. In this way, the commanders were visibly accountable for their actions. This tended to be a motivational bonus for those showing leadership abilities, although a less pleasant experience for the weaker leaders. A further consequence of the plan was a trickle-down effect, as the precinct commanders began organising their own mini-strategic reviews at precinct level. Bratton worked at communicating a message that spoke to his officers at all levels, block by block, precinct by precinct, and borough by borough.

Knocking over the political hurdle

Bratton had learned the hard way that political intrigues could block strategies and people. He had been briefly sidelined, earlier in his career, paying the price for ignoring or crudely confronting political opponents. Over time he developed his plan for dealing with opponents of his strategies. Internally, he moved swiftly to isolate the 'unconvertable opponents', if necessary removing them from positions of (negative) influence.

Externally, he concentrated on building coalitions (his relationship with Mayor Giuliani has already been mentioned). The coalition was necessary to overcome resistance from the courts who feared that the zero-tolerance strategy would multiply their workloads, and make their justice system unworkable.

Information-based strategies

In the UK ambulance service, John sets strategies that have life or death consequences for everyone living and working in a large metropolitan region of England. He is charged with setting and implementing the strategy for the region's emergency health services. His approach is strongly influenced by his background as a London School of Economics graduate. Taken on as a National Health Service graduate with 'fast-track' leadership potential, he was conscious of the opportunities for better service that could be achieved though new technology.

This of itself is a widely held rationale for contemporary change programmes. Information technology (IT) has been lauded for its capacity to deliver great gains in efficiency. Increasingly, the leadership challenges have been seen as winning the support of employees who see the threats to their work far outweighing the gains to some corporate ideal of efficiency. A specific and not atypical example in a related service can be cited. In the United Kingdom, the three major emergency services are those of police, fire and ambulance forces. At the time when John was introducing his change programme for the ambulance service (2002–2003), regional police forces were resisting efforts to bring about greater integration. More spectacularly, the fire service had entered into a bitter industrial dispute which had led to prolonged actions including 'limited cover' withdrawal of labour and days of action ('strikes'). At the heart of the confused claims and counter-claims was the issue of 'modernisation', with substantial elements of acceptance of new technology.

It should be noted that the ambulance service is an integral part of the National Health Service. The fire service has a different governance system, with wage and conditions determined in a complex fashion through regional authorities whose budgets are subject to national governmental negotiations. Whereas John was able to offer leadership direction, the negotiators within the fire service dispute appeared to be relatively uncoordinated and leaderless. (The government minister, John Prescott, himself a former union official, for example, was unable to act as a leader; the spokesperson for the various regional authorities was similarly unempowered.) Operationally there are other differences. The fire service has a less frenetic pattern of calls. The scope for efficiency gains is greater. The opponents of the Fire Brigade Union claim there are too many 'custom and practice' procedures which are jealously preserved from management attempts to achieve efficiencies.

John's strategic approach was based on the recognition of the shared value of the unionised staff and the managers, namely that they were all in their jobs to help save lives through delivering the best possible medical support. In practice this goal was achieved through managing changes to practices of personnel attending emergency and non-emergency calls through the region's mobile medical units (ambulances). Advanced tracking systems and logistic programmes had demonstrably improved response times to emergency calls, and onward to hospital accident and emergency reception areas. The technology also provided comprehensive data that could be analysed for more strategic decisions. For example, it pinpointed the demand peaks and troughs. This demonstrated the need for changes in shift patterns involving more unsocial hours. Such changes still required negotiations, but the evidence was presented in formats that were clear and not disputed, as primarily directed towards necessary improvements in reaction time, and therefore aligned with shared values. Negotiations were broadly successful, and in considerable contrast with the bitter disputes as other public services at the time sought to achieve modernisation strategies.

Overcoming the 'big brother' syndrome

John was aware of the 'big brother' aspect of the implementation of such a strategy. The tracking devices could have been used to examine the location of specific ambulance crews at all times, as a means of monitoring and controlling working practices. This is a well-known example of a technological change seen as a managerial opportunity and as a threat to those affected. Some years earlier, the installation of tachometers, identifying speed profiles in commercial cabs, was widely attacked by drivers as 'the spy in the cab'. By John's consistent emphasis that the technology changes would be directed only towards implementing the agreed strategy of improving emergency response times, the anxieties of the union membership were managed without disruption. Improvements were also measured so as to permit open discussion of productivity rewards.

Over time, the technology was used to influence other stakeholders, as more and more sophisticated evidence emerged of hotspots calling for special attention; these included identification of localities and even time-peaks of specific kinds of medical emergency such as coronary emergency call-outs. Ambulance fleets were redeployed to take account of such data. Importantly, the data could be presented and discussed to evaluate the evidence of improvements in call-out times.

Sun Tzu and business strategy

Mark McNeilly was a successful business strategist for the IBM corporation. He became increasingly impressed by an unusual source of inspiration, namely, the wisdom of the great Chinese general Sun Tzu, whose ideas are still influential after more than two millennia.[31] Since McNeilly's book was published it has gained international attention, and been followed by other successful books, including one 'updating' the ancient military wisdom of Sun Tzu for modern military leaders.

McNeilly's interpretation of Sun Tzu's Art of War

Working from a scholarly English translation of Sun Tzu's work, and drawing on an interest in military history, McNeilly concluded that the principles were (with appropriate updating) still valid for military strategists. He further concluded that they offered rich insights for business strategists. He then offered six strategic principles:

- win all without (all-out) fighting
- avoid strength; attack weakness
- deception and foreknowledge
- speed and preparation
- shape your opponent
- character-based leadership.

The principles are not totally self-explanatory. *Winning all without (all-out) fighting* suggests that victory is better if the former enemy is not destroyed, but dealt with so as to become a future ally. *Deception and foreknowledge* argues for preparing for strategic initiatives, holding in mind the dangers of directly signalled attack on the competition's strong points. *Shape your opponent* involves all sorts of interactions with competitors, including negotiations and alliances, taking into account a psychological appraisal of leadership characteristics. Where possible, taking advantage of emotions of competitors is an advised approach. *Character-based leadership* is a form of trait-based leadership style, with ethical principles, through leading by example and with integrity. The style is presented as one that can be developed through study and practice.

From Sun Tzu to modern business strategy

McNeilly first argues that business strategy has evolved from military strategy. He argues that the six principles encourage a more creative approach to strategy that might have avoided some of the corporate downsizing caused by one-dimensional strategic thinking.

In illustration of ignoring the principle of win all without fighting, he gives chilling examples from industries which have entered price-wars, such as airlines and cigarette companies. His conclusion is that strategists seem to forget that a 'battle' for market share should be seen as a means to corporate survival and prosperity, not an end of itself. The Sun Tzu principle supports the increased interest in the past few decades in strategic alliances, even among firms in a competitive marketplace.

He illustrates the principles at work in high technology companies such as computers where great efforts are made to retain customers for new generations of product. Competitive firms attack each other's products, and the veracity of claims, in trade press releases, and any other media channels available.

He expands with a commercial example which has become a well-known classroom illustration: Sir Gordon White of Hanson plc achieved a hostile take-over of Smith Corona, during which there were various smokescreens involving bid offers. The deception reduced the vigilance within Smith Corona, and helped Hanson acquire additional shares at a reasonable price on the open market.

McNeilly also describes IBM as changing an earlier strategy of secrecy, aiming towards more openness in the 1980s and 1990s. This resulted in employees sending out mixed messages, often criticising products of other IBM divisions. The company decided that such displays of openness had gone too far. The new head of IBM, Louis Gerstner, set about discouraging such public displays of infighting, as a matter of corporate policy.

A battle of strategies: when leaders fall out

What happens when powerful leaders become locked in a strategic dispute? Our example from the world of sport suggests that a rational model is sometimes inadequate for exploring or explaining events. The case may be usefully studied in conjunction with Sun Tzu's *Art of War*.

The football club

Manchester United developed its worldwide fame in the 1960s under a charismatic manager Matt Busby, whose 'Busby Babes' included George Best, arguably, the second most famous and gifted footballer worldwide (after the Brazilian Pele). The Busby Babes won many trophies, and their fame was enhanced after a tragic air crash ripped the heart from the team. The club became overshadowed by another English team, Liverpool, for over a decade, and a series of managers failed to revive its success, until Ferguson's era in the 1990s.

Manchester United had for many years been owned primarily by a local family. Former chairman, Louis Edwards, was a successful meat trader. His son Martin had steered the club towards a more professional format as a public limited company. In a football world of extremely dubious financial arrangements, Manchester United Football Club had become regarded as a financially well-run business.

The financial model

Manchester United set a new financial model for British football clubs, developing three revenue streams: match attendance fees, merchandise, and media rights. The oldest stream, match attendance, remains the largest, and still growing through extending seat numbers (at 67,000 seats in 2004, substantially greater than its English rivals). Merchandising through a megastore is growing globally, although still with a slight majority of revenue from home sales. The newest and most exciting stream comes from media rights, which could build on its existing television station.

The manager

After the charismatic Busby, the club struggled to find stable leadership, and playing success. Alex Ferguson at first appeared to be yet another unsuccessful manager, but after going close to dismissal for poor results, he began what was to be the second golden era for the club, winning multiple trophies including the European Cup and in doing so matching one of Busby's greatest achievements.

Ferguson, like Busby, was a working-class Scot, an able but hardly outstanding player in his day, but whose managerial passion had secured unexpected success with an unfashionable Scottish club (Aberdeen). His combative nature helped him cope with the religious bigotry surrounding football in Glasgow. Over time he developed a reputation for nurturing talent with a fierce patriarchal style. This was combined with a temper that could explode into violence. He was noted for the 'hair-dryer' style of delivering a rebuke upon a hapless player who he considered had let him and the other players down.

Famously, in 2003, such an incident with his most famous player left the England team captain David Beckham with a facial injury from a boot, kicked in anger by Ferguson in a post-match locker-room outburst, after a dismal playing performance by the team. Shortly after the incident, Beckham left the club for Real Madrid, arguably the most glamorous team in the world, celebrated for its superstars, *Los Galacticos*. The drama was played out in the national and international press. Support was divided, although Ferguson appeared to retain much of the popular support of the club's fan base. An earlier indication that he was considering retirement preceded a dip in the club's playing performances. At 62 he indicated his intentions of staying on to take the club to even more success.

John Magnier and J. P. McManus

As the club began to prosper under Ferguson's managership, so had the manager. He negotiated a remuneration package that compared favourably with his superstar players. A favoured relaxation was horse racing, which had produced a friendship with two major shareholders in the club, John Magnier and J. P. McManus. The Irish entrepreneurs were highly successful racehorse breeders. Magnier had left school at 16, but since then had built up his multimillion pound international business around a stud in County Tipperary. Their business interests widened to include a substantial minority share in Manchester United through their investment vehicle Cubic Expression. According to one United investor, the Irishmen were focused and shrewd investors, unlikely to be investing in the club for sentimental reasons.

Rock of Gibraltar

Rock of Gibraltar was a racehorse initially owned by John Magnier, and whose early promise over the mile distance continued to be displayed. At its retirement to stud in 2001, the horse had become one of the all-time greats based on winnings and calibre of races won. Its fame, by then, however, had extended far beyond the racing world. 'The Rock' had become the centre of a high-profile legal wrangle between the one-time friends Ferguson and Magnier.

The dispute

Ferguson and Magnier met and became friends after the Cheltenham Festival race meeting in 1997. The origins of the dispute have been traced back to an alleged snub suffered by Magnier after one of his horses won a prestigious race (The Gimcrack Stakes) in York, England, in 1999. By then, the two had benefited from the friendship, with Ferguson's name linked with Magnier's business activities, and Magnier offering Ferguson access to horse-racing opportunities. Magnier suggested his friend Alex Ferguson make the acceptance speech. The request was denied by race course authorities in a manner that angered the Irishman.

In 2001, Rock of Gibraltar was a potential winner of the Gimcrack. Magnier offered joint ownership to Ferguson, and an arrangement was made between two friends, with little attention to legal documentation. He registered the horse jointly in the name of his wife and his friend Alex Ferguson. The horse won, and the new co-owner was able to make the acceptance speech. Magnier had the satisfaction for the perceived slight by the York racing establishment.

The horse and new co-owners continued to do well. When the horse went to stud, however, the fragility of the legal arrangements became painfully clear. Ferguson believed he was entitled to 50 per cent of any subsequent stud earnings. Magnier claims this was a misunderstanding. The success of the horse while racing had meant that first year stud earnings were an estimated £10 million. At stake was a half-share in future earnings estimated at between £50 million and £200 million, based on the continued virility of Rock of Gibraltar in servicing 150 mares a year at a fee of £65,000 each time. By November 2003, Sir Alex and Magnier and associates were embroiled in a bitter legal dispute.

The next moves, January 2004

The story began to attract media attention. Rumours of a potential take-over of the football club had persisted, with the two Irish shareholders among the possible candidates. A slight increase in their shareholding in January 2004 to 25.5 per cent fuelled the rumours.

At the same time, the media reported vigorous and visible interventions through the football club emanating from Magnier and associates. A formal document was lodged calling for explanations for claimed irregularities including the club's transfer dealings, criticisms of the directors and its treatment of Sir Alex's contract renewal. Documents were leaked to the press. The Football Association launched an inquiry.

Shareholders United (a shareholding group of supporters dedicated to protecting the club from commercial predators) claimed there to be a dirty tricks campaign being waged through an investigations company. Shareholders United were later to mobilise, claiming control over approximately 18 per cent by September 2004, and affirming their intentions to fight off any corporate take-over of the club. Demonstrations of shareholder support occurred at race meetings where horses owned by Magnier and McManus were running.

To calm matters, the United board issued a statement outlining their probity, distancing Sir Alex from the commercial dealings with players, and indicating their intention to initiate changes that would make transfer proceedings more transparent. They also confirmed that the manager's new contract would be signed as a rolling one-year agreement.

The new superstars

As these events developed, another team had established itself as the outstanding premiership team. After years in Manchester United's shadow, Arsenal FC became league winners, and were to achieve record numbers of games without a single loss in the period 2003–2004. Additionally, Roman Abramovich, a Russian billionaire, had bankrolled Chelsea FC with unheard-of financial resources. Chelsea even succeeded in enticing away Peter Kenyon, a major member of Manchester United's top echelon, as their own executive director. As Arsenal and Chelsea flourished, United's performance declined in the national league and international championship competitions, despite efforts at recruiting a new generation of top international stars.

Cubic Expression increases its holding in Manchester United

In the summer of 2004, Cubic Expression, the company conducting the financial affairs on behalf of Mangier and McManus, increased its holdings in Manchester United. Press speculation was that a take-over was now a distinct possibility.

Enter the buccaneer

The strategic situation became even more complicated, in the shape of a second potential take-over bid from the American Malcolm Glazer, who had already achieved a take-over of the Tampa Bay Buccaneers football team. His shareholding increased to roughly 20 per cent. His public statements indicated his interest in Manchester United as a long-term investment, and that a take-over could not be precluded. Glazer, an immigrant entrepreneur, had built his family business into a retailing empire, before becoming interested in football ownership. His investment in the Buccaneers had involved tough leveraging of assets, although at a level considerably lower than the value of Manchester United. Prior to his bid for the Buccaneers, he was not noted as a sporting enthusiast, although a son has shown interest in soccer. If he were to make a bid for United, it seemed likely he would need another well-leveraged deal, possibly involving the Buccaneers.

Cubic Expression indicated that they were not interested in a take-over in the foreseeable future, nor were they interested in selling their 30 per cent holding. Over a period of months of take-over speculation, shares climbed from £2.40 in the summer of 2004, to a high of £2.85 in September 2004. The nominal value of the club rose from roughly £650 million to over £800 million.

In the autumn of 2004, Glazer increased his shares in the club close to the 30 per cent mark that would trigger a formal take-over bid. Talks between his representatives and the current directors of United began, and stalled with a brief statement that the board had rejected the bid for its high gearing (the asset base of the bidder was considered inadequate). In November 2004 Glazer's representatives won one battle and lost another. Three directors were voted from the corporate board at its general meeting. However, the financial institute representing the Glazer interests warned against the launching of a hostile bid, and withdrew its services. On Thursday, 12 May 2005, Glazer launched a successful take-over bid. His victory was sealed by the acquisition of the shares of Magnier and McManus.

The strategic leadership issues

The story abounds with strategic leadership issues, and quite a few dilemmas. Successful entrepreneurs appeared to be making strategic decisions that cut across commercial interests. Why did a formidable entrepreneur appear to give away the rights to one of the world's most valuable stallions, Rock of Gibraltar? What strategic considerations leads the owner of a retailing firm to invest a sizeable proportion of his investments first in an ailing American football team, and then to express interest in a different kind of team in a different sport, in another country? How might the interests of the other shareholders (Cubic Expression, Shareholders United) influence a plan for take-over?

Integration

We began the chapter with a critical approach to the very heart of leadership studies, by asking whether strategic leaders actually made a difference. Our platforms of understanding indicated that the question cannot be taken lightly. Nahavandi and Malekzadeh report that the evidence is far from conclusive. Whereas studies frequently show that leaders make a difference, there is less clarity regarding which particular features are significant, and under what circumstances. The somewhat ambivalent evidence, however, may be attributed to unsatisfactory methodologies for investigating an issue that is more complex than it may appear. (Note, also, the difficulties that researchers experienced in identifying universal traits associated with exceptional leadership.)

They suggest two factors most likely to differentiate strategic preferences, namely a challenge-seeking orientation, and a need for control. The two challenge-seeking styles are more associated with innovation. High challenge/low control leads to participative and open cultures of change; high challenge/high control leads to a more autocratic or directive style of change. Of the two challenge-averse styles, low challenge/high control leaders are best considered for roles within cost-differentiating strategies, and low challenge/low control in benign climates where decisions and responsibilities are widely distributed.

Boal and Hooijberg also report that the literature shows leaders make a difference through their cognitive styles and belief systems (values). The leader influences an organisation's absorptive capacity, adaptive capacity and managerial wisdom. The issue of strategic choice was further refined through the concept of *leader discretion* as a bridge between two kinds of theory, one claiming priority for leadership creativity, the other claiming priority for environmental forces.

Our first two contextual case studies gave examples of leaders who made a difference. Each fell into the category of a senior executive, but neither had the simple and direct power of a chief executive officer of a private corporation. They were essentially *implementers of policy* and *formulators of strategy* . Their leadership discretion covered the manner in which they set out the strategy through which they would achieve their policy guidelines. In these specific examples, we see the contextual subtleties which transcend the simple question – are you mainly a strategy formulator or implementer?

Their leadership discretion can be understood by the implied contrasts with earlier leaders. Each introduced quite new approaches for their organisations. In some ways they had comparable styles. Each favoured a heightened attention to evidence authenticated on databases, as a means of strategy implementation. Each used such methods for more effective resource deployment and appropriation. In addition, each showed sensitivity to political considerations, both internal and external to their organisations.

The principles of Sun Tzu's *Art of War* were used to suggest strategic ways of making a difference often ignored by leaders who became engaged in 'tit-for-tat' strategic exchanges. We may become aware of limitations of following the six principles by once again seeking the dilemmas it suggests. For example, the first principle, of winning all without all-out fighting, has the future intention of seeking better and trusting relationships with former enemies. Yet following other principles, that of deception, or that of trying to take advantage of your competitor's emotions, suggests such a long-term outcome to be unlikely. Several of these principles seem to risk cutting across the principle of character-based leadership, described as demonstrating integrity and trustworthiness.

McNeilly distinguishes between deception that involves making false statements, and deception that arises from calculated withholding of information for corporate self-interest. These limits seem more about what is legally permissible, than what might be ethically dubious. As we have been suggesting throughout the book, leaders have to decide how to deal with such dilemmas, according to his or her beliefs and values.

Our final contextual case study illustrates a typically complex competitive strategic situation, with several leaders seeking to formulate and implement strategy. The nature of the competitive environment shifted as the story unfolded. We have suggested that the narrative is close enough to a battle for Sun Tzu's *Art of War* to be a useful map for studying the case. Insights into the behaviours of the protagonists may be suggested by the mapping of charismatic leaders in Chapter 4.

Getting personal

There is a fundamental challenge raised in this chapter for practising leaders. Do you or don't you 'make a difference' in your strategic efforts? Put another way, does your contribution matter, in organisational performance?

We have suggested that a strategic leader has to be accepted as such. Mostly this is a competitive process with other would-be strategic leaders. Do you relish such a competitive path to leadership success? You may well have some evidence of the impact you make on selection panels. Regardless of your untrained capabilities you are likely to benefit from professional advice in development sessions such as role playing the applicant. Mental rehearsal of appraisal encounters is another valuable possibility.

We have seen how the impact you have as a leader may be mapped as the management of meaning. Your current work provides a wealth of materials that you can use to reflect on and understand your impact on those around you. These are cues and clues to how others may see you as a strategic leader. Other maps you may wish to consult arc those of transformational leaders found in Chapter 4.

Box 7.5 Remaking your personal map

● What sort of strategic leader am I?

We posed this question slightly differently at the start of the chapter. Have you got what it takes to become a strategic leader? Experienced leaders will have had the opportunity to relate the strategic maps to personal experience. In this way, it may become possible to approach afresh the question 'What sort of leader am I?' Perhaps the integrative model of Nahavandi and Malekzadeh suggests clues. You should have a sense of your own concern for challenge, and therefore your likelihood of flourishing in an environment requiring innovation and entrepreneurial leadership. A sense of your need for control as contrasting to willingness to encourage (empower?) followers will indicate the style with which you would approach your leadership tasks.

Wannabe leaders have to take a view less based on direct leadership experiences. As an alternative self-reflection exercise, you may find it valuable to ask yourself about your ideal leadership role. What would you be doing? How would you be doing it? Do any of the leadership maps help you in this? The more convinced you are of the future you have pictured, the more likely that the exercise is tapping into your values and self-beliefs.

Whether experienced or wannabe leader, treat this reflective exercise as a starting point for further reflection and discussion with someone who knows you well, and whose opinion and feedback you will respect.

What can we learn from the super-hero leader?

Unease at the super-hero leader is growing, and there is even a dilemma of role-modelling. If he or she is such a great leader, how can they be good role models for less charismatic personalities? How can I hope to emulate them? Not every leader will have Bratton's personality. However, it is possible to extract some of the strategic ideas. For example, you may wish to study the four hurdles and ways in which tipping points may be encouraged. This particular model leaves open the possibility that you will accomplish this with a charismatic style, or through a more considered and reflective style (Box 7.5).

Summary

The fundamental dilemma of strategy mapping is whether strategic leaders make a difference. This has produced considerable debates between those who believe that strategy is essentially predetermined by objective circumstances, and those who believe there to be strategic choice. The latter maps consider that the characteristics of a strategic leader and other top echelon executives will make a difference.

Strategic leadership may be seen as more concerned with leadership *of* organisations, in contrast with other forms of leadership *in* organisations.

A widely accepted competence associated with strategic leadership is that of cognitive complexity. The assumption is that leaders who have unusually complex mental maps are best suited to deal with highly complex environments. A further assumption is that such individuals are in rare supply.

The cognitive complexity approach implies that leaders matter according to appropriateness of *person/environment fit*. Nahavandi and Melekzadeh's framework identifies the leader's orientation towards control and challenge as two important factors of strategic style which can be used as to consider person–environment fit.

Trends in mapping organisational strategy have swung towards interest in resource-based theories which emphasise knowledge management, intellectual property and innovative potential of knowledge workers. These approaches imply a more deterministic view of strategy formation. Careful empirical studies leave the issue unclear. Strategic leaders may be a 'main effect' or one among a range of factors contributing to strategic effectiveness.

Strategy maps also offer the distinction between the more deterministic approaches of identifying the appropriate strategy, and the less deterministic ones which assume strategy to be emergent as efforts are made to define and achieve organisational goals.

If strategies are largely deterministic, the significance of the strategic leader is minimal. Strategy can be safely left to a team of strategic planners. Hambrick and co-workers resolve this potential dilemma through the concept of leader discretion, which places leadership creativity as a component partly shaped by constraints identified through strategic planning.

The characteristics which differentiate effective strategic leaders from others also remain underdefined. Functional background and age and cognitive style are included among them, as is the cognitive complexity factor mentioned above.

Strategic transformations may be assisted through attending to critical and unstable elements for change. These tipping points may be cognitive, resource based, motivational or political.

At times the political personal driven components of strategic efforts may produce intense and ego-dominated dramas enacted by the strategic leaders. These episodes cannot be understood simply in terms of rational strategic behaviours.

Notes

1 Hambrick, D. C. (1989) 'Guest editor's introduction: putting top managers back in the strategy picture', *Strategic Management Journal* 10: 5–15.
2 Ansoff, I. (1965) *Corporate Strategy: An Analytic Approach to Business Policy for Growth and Expansion*, New York: McGraw-Hill.
3 For example, Porter, M. (1998) *Competitive Advantage*, London and New York: Free Press.
4 Johnson, G. and Scholes, K. (2002) *Exploring Corporate Strategy* [Text and cases] 6th edn, Harlow: Financial Times/Prentice-Hall.
5 For example, Pettigrew, A. and Whipp, R. (1991) *Managing Change for Competitive Success*, Oxford: Blackwell.
6 Nonaka, I. and Takeuchi, H. (1995) *The Knowledge Creating Company: How Japanese Companies Create the Dynamics of Innovation*, Oxford: Oxford University Press.
7 Hamel, G. and Prahalad, C. K. (1994) *Competing for the Future*, Boston, MA: Harvard Business School Press.
8 Hunt, J. G. (1991) *Leadership: A New Synthesis*, Newbury Park, CA: Sage.
9 Collins, J. C. and Porras, J. I. (1994) *Built to Last: Successful Habits of Visionary Companies*, New York: Random House.
10 For example, Drucker, P. F. (1954) *The Practice of Management*, New York: Harper & Row.
11 For example, Porter, M. (1980) *Competitive Strategy: Techniques for Analyzing Industries and Competitors*, New York: Free Press.
12 Thomas, H. (2004) 'Strategic management: its development and future directions', in A. Ghobadian, N. O'Regan, D. Gallear and H. Viney (eds) *Strategy and Performance: Achieving Competitive Advantage in the Global Marketplace*, London: Palgrave Macmillan.
13 Hoskisson, R. E., Hitt, M. A., Wan, W. P. and Yiu, D. (1999) 'Theory and research in strategic management: swings of a pendulum', *Journal of Management* 25: 417–456.
14 Chandler, A. D. (ed.) (1979) *Managerial Innovation at General Motors*, New York: Arno.
15 Porter, M., *Competitive Advantage* [see note 3].
16 Prahalad, C. K. and Hamel, G. (1990) 'The core competence of the corporation', *Harvard Business Review* 68(3): 79–93.

17 Thomas, H., 'Strategic management' [see note 12].

18 Mintzberg, H. (1990) 'The design school: reconsidering the basic premises of strategic management', *Strategic Management Journal* 11: 171–195; Ansoff, I. (1991) 'Critique of Henry Mintzberg's "The design school: reconsidering the basic premises of strategic management"', *Strategic Management Journal* 12: 449–461; Mintzberg, H. (1991) 'Learning 1, Planning 0: reply to Igor Ansoff's, *Strategic Management Journal* 12: 463–466.

19 Nahavandi, A. and Malekzadeh, A. R. (1993) 'Leadership style in strategy and organizational performance: an integrative framework', *Journal of Management Studies* 30(3): 405–425.

20 Boal, K. B. and Hooijberg, R. (2000) 'Strategic leadership research: moving on', *Leadership Quarterly* 11(4): 515–550.

21 Hambrick, D. C. and Mason, P. (1984) 'Upper echelons: the organization as a reflection of its top managers', *Academy of Management Review* 9: 193–206.

22 Hunt, J. G. (1991) *Leadership: A New Synthesis*, Newbury Park, CA: Sage.

23 Porter, M., *Competitive Advantage* [see note 3].

24 Ansoff, I., *Corporate Strategy* [see note 2].

25 Mintzberg, H. (1994) *The Rise and Fall of Strategic Planning*, New York: Free Press.

26 Hambrick, D. C. and Finkelstein, S. (1987) 'Managerial discretion: a bridge between polar views of organizations', in L. L. Cummings and B. M. Straw (eds) *Research in Organizational Behavior*, Greenwich, CT: JAI Press.

27 Eisenhardt, K. (1989) 'Making fast strategic decisions in high-velocity environments', *Academy of Management Journal* 32(3): 543–576.

28 Hitt, M. A., Keats, B. W. and DeMarie, S. M. (1998) 'Navigating in the new competitive landscape: building strategic flexibility and competitive advantage in the 21st century', *Academy of Management Executive* 12: 22–41.

29 For example, Osborn, R. N., Hunt, J. G. and Jauch, L. R. (1980) *Organization Theory: An Integrated Approach*, New York: Wiley.

30 Kim, W. C. and Mauborgne, R. (2003) 'Tipping point leadership', *Harvard Business Review* 81(4): 60–69.

31 McNeilly, M. (1966) *Sun Tzu and the Art of Business*, Oxford: Oxford University Press. McNeilly claims that the work influenced modern Chinese and Japanese military thinking and that its principles can be found in the strategies of successful western firms.

Dilemmas of gender and diversity

8

Sir, a woman's preaching is like a dog walking on his hinder legs. It is not done well: but you are surprised to find it done at all.[1]

Management gurus now know how to boost the odds of getting a great executive: Hire a female.[2]

Orientation

Most leaders regularly face dilemmas of diversity at work. The issues may involve a combination of features such as gender, ethnicity or nepotism (favouring a family member or friend). Discussion of such issues can be highly charged, with accusations of bias and prejudice. Here, more than in most chapters, each reader is likely to need a personal map. We pay particular attention to gender. This does not reduce the significance of other diversity issues such as ethnicity, social class, religious beliefs, age, physical or mental characteristics. Rather, we indicate how gender provides a map which happens to be worth comparing with maps of other territories of diversity.

What's different is dangerous

There is a socio-biological argument that suggests that any social or family group prefers a leader of its own kind. We have to consider whether such a view extends validly to a world of increasingly diverse social groupings, where it has been expressed in conjunction with views of supremacy and exclusion. It is sometimes summed up in the statement that 'what's different is dangerous'.

A diversity challenge

As an orienting challenge we invite you to examine your beliefs and assumptions about diversity and its consequences for leadership. Experienced leaders will be able to draw on their previous experiences. Less experienced leaders will still have some experiences of groups of various kinds to draw upon. These experiences might involve groups whose members were of similar educational background or gender or ethnicity.

Spend a few minutes considering the differences between highly diverse groups and more homogeneous groups (Box 8.1). You will find that several of the leadership maps you have studied will suggest ideas for this challenge.

Box 8.1 A diversity challenge for leaders

You have some experience of working with groups with very similar cultural and professional backgrounds. Now you have been invited to be a leader of a new working group comprising individuals with highly diverse cultural and professional backgrounds.

- What differences do you expect to find in the way the group members begin to work together?
- What might you as leader do differently in light of the changed situation you will be dealing with?
- Can you think of further possibilities suggested by any of the following maps you have studied?
  - team development theories (Chapter 3)
  - transformational leadership (Chapter 4)
  - management of meaning (Chapter 5).

The gender issue

Over several decades, women have moved into more powerful leadership positions (and more of them) around the world. However, the change is less noticeable in the most senior organisational positions with the greatest influence and power of decision-making.[3]

Whereas the earlier perceptions framed leadership in terms of attributes implicitly assumed to be more masculine, more recent perceptions have introduced attributes more likely to be associated with feminine styles. There has been a shift towards collaborative relationships: the rhetoric of empowerment advocates attention to supporting, encouraging and nurturing roles (Box 8.2). The changes are widely presumed to be associated with coping with increased uncertainties and complexities in the workplace.

Box 8.2 The vocabulary of gender studies

Analysis of the female leadership advantage takes us into the heart of the territory of diversity theory. One of the most powerful weapons for studying diversity, and specifically inequalities and prejudice, is that of interpretation and deconstruction of meaning. The studies have been aware of the significance of leadership as the management of meaning. For such reasons, vocabulary has become an important element in our understanding. Researchers differentiate between the terms sex and gender, preferring to use the former to refer only to biological categories, and the latter to refer to socially constructed differences. Sexuality is a matter of biological classification. Gender is defined by the manner in which sexuality is perceived in society.

Overview

Three platforms of understanding

The theory of female leadership advantage introduces some of the most urgent contemporary dilemmas of leadership. Arguments have ranged from ethical ones of human rights for equal opportunities, to pragmatic ones of more effective human resource management. In essence, there are two widespread sets of observations. The first is that women are found in far fewer key leadership roles than would be expected on simple statistical grounds. The second is that where women have occupied leadership positions, there is evidence of a more appropriate leadership style, particularly where the conditions call for transformational change. However, reviews offer conflicting conclusions.

We provide two maps through which we can explore the main positions in this unresolved debate.[4] According to Robert Vecchio, there has been a swing away from a dominant theory of male supremacy in leadership roles, which is being challenged by the mirror-image theory of female supremacy. Vecchio argues that each 'supremacist' view relies on simple categorisation into female and male behaviour categories, whereas each human possesses mixtures of the attributes (such as caringness or toughness). Alice Eagly and Linda Carli offer a critique of Vecchio's analysis, and claim there is solid evidence that female leadership styles in general offer performance advantages over those styles shown by male leaders.

Our third map by Stella Nkomo and Taylor Cox Jr outlines the main territories of diversity studies.[5] From it we see the narrow theoretical perspectives of discrimination, and the wider one of diversity as a neutral characteristic of heterogeneous social groups. The authors argue that a remapping of diversity could benefit from a perspective in which there is less polarising of issues into either/or and female/male categories, and more acknowledgement of both/and factors shared by males and females particularly (but not exclusively) in leadership roles.

Contextual materials

Our contextual case studies consider leaders, in contexts of gender and diversity. We begin with a political figure, Margaret Thatcher, chosen for the richness of its story, the depth of its documentation, its relevance to gender dilemmas of business leaders. We then look at Carly Fiorina, one of the few females to achieve highest office in corporate America, followed by a case study of the glass ceiling as seen through the eyes of an anonymous middle manager in a Chinese state organisation. Our next case is that of Roberto C. Goizueta, a Cuban refugee who shattered the glass ceiling at Coca-Cola to become the United States' first billionaire corporate manager. Finally, we review the global implications of diversity for leaders.

Platforms of understanding: gender issues and diversity

We will look at three platforms of understanding:

- Robert Vecchio's meta-analysis of leadership and gender differences
- Eagly and Carli's evaluation of the female leadership advantage theory
- Nkomo and Cox's review of diversity.

Robert Vecchio's meta-analysis of leadership and gender differences

Robert Vecchio conducted a meta-analysis of studies of gender and leadership styles in the 1980s and 1990s, to evaluate gender advantage theories.[6] He concluded that earlier assumptions of a male leadership advantage is being replaced by a symmetrical set of assumptions for a female advantage. For many years, the 'natural' superiority of male leaders was taken for granted, and he warns that a switch to a view of a feminine advantage repeats the error of a comparative gender advantage, again based on stereotypic reasoning.

According to Vecchio, early gender work was premised on an either/or dichotomy. Leaders (like other people) were *either* feminine *or* masculine, with distinct biologically determined characteristics. The styles were further simplified into either/or features, among which a concern for tasks or people was particularly significant. Later, gender became regarded as more socially determined. This offered the possibility that an individual might be high *or* low on *either* of two dimensions of task and relationships.

This led researchers to the view that a 'both/and' approach is superior (more effective) over the unidimensional either/or styles. Direct evidence in the workplace provides evidence that leadership behaviours cannot be predicted by a simple attribution of a feminine or masculine style dimension. Each leader displays a range of behaviours, some more associated with male leaders, some with female leaders.

Vecchio concludes that more careful empirical studies are required to establish where (if anywhere) relative superiority claims might be made based on gender differences.

Eagly and Carli's evaluation of the female leadership advantage theory

Alice Eagly and Linda Carli respond to Vecchio's analysis, and to his rejection of substantial evidence for a female leadership advantage.[7] They cast doubt on the reliability of earlier findings, including the retention of earlier work on gender which they described as belonging to the Goldberg paradigm.[8] Over thirty years earlier, Goldberg had raised the issue of biases in perceptions of males and females, using an experimental format designed to assess perceptions of *equivalent* behaviours of males and females. Yet Goldberg-type studies are included in Vecchio's meta-analysis seeking to assess *differences* in male/female leader behaviours.

The findings

The report concentrated on the full range of leadership styles well known from the work of Bass and co-workers, and measured by their Multifactor Leadership Questionnaire. Results were incorporated from leaders, peers, followers or more senior peers. Eagly and co-workers found forty-five studies of male/female leadership styles, each of which they considered had reached their criteria for inclusion.

The striking feature of the meta-analysis is evidence of consistent and significant differences between leadership scores for women and men for the transformational measures, from forty-four studies. All transformational subscales gave higher means for female than male samples, with the most significant being those of charisma (as idealised influence measures), inspirational motivation and intellectual stimulation.

In contrast, the male/female differences for the transactional factors were not statistically significant, with the exception of a weakly significant effect from the small number of studies (eleven) which examined management by exception. This means that transactional contingent reward, management by exception (passive) and laissez-faire styles were not found to provide significant gender-based differences.

Implications of the meta-analysis

As the researchers point out, the results are of considerable importance in evaluating the female advantage issue. Female leader styles were found in this study to be consistently and positively correlated with transformational leadership. They connect this finding with the major finding from an earlier meta-analysis, in which transformational leadership had been found to have a significant and consistent positive correlation with effectiveness.[9] Thus the two findings point to an association between performance and female leadership as stronger than the association between performance and male leadership.

A context of prejudice

The results were presented in the context of wide-ranging prejudice towards female leaders across cultures and working environments which contributes to what other workers refer to as glass ceiling effects, and which leads to continuing discrimination against appointment of women to top positions. They suggest that under such circumstances, women who do succeed are likely to be particularly effective.

The conclusions (including the aspirin effect)

Eagly and Carli conclude that the empirical evidence is clear. There is a potential advantage in looking at women for leaders with a transformational leadership style, which is particularly effective in supporting organisational change. However, this is offset by double standards and biases against women leaders, found especially in male-dominated environments.

They respond to a criticism of the empirical findings, that the statistical differences between male and female leaders only account for a rather small proportion of the total variance. They argue that addressing such differences may have considerable practical consequences. They back up their argument with the example of a medical trial in which aspirin was tested for effectiveness in managing heart conditions. As in the case of the female example, the aspirin effect accounted for a small proportion of total variance. Yet the medical experts considered the practical consequences to be so great that the trial was stopped so that the beneficial results could be shared as widely and quickly as possible (Box 8.3).

From this, we may choose to infer that the replacement of male with female leaders in organisational life will be justified. There are clearly revolutionary implications in such a claim. Readers may wish to reflect on the implications, taking a critical perspective, before referring to our critique in the integration section of this chapter.

Box 8.3 The aspirin effect: the significance of small effect sizes

Eagly and Carli produce statistical evidence widely used to back up the view that female leaders show more transformational qualities than male leaders. The evidence derives from a meta-analysis of contemporary studies that have applied Bass and Avolio's inventory of their full-scale leadership measure. The samples are mostly for middle-level organisational leaders, and the statistical evidence is clear. The female leaders sampled show significantly higher mean scores than male managers on the transformational scales. There were no significant differences on the transactional scales of contingent reward, management by exception (passive) and laissez-faire.

The results are accepted as an accurate finding from the available data. However, the relevance of the findings has been contested, on the grounds that the mean differences reported are relatively small. In statistical terms they can be said to account for only a small proportion of the overall variance.

The critique offered is that the result is statistically significant, but of little practical importance. Eagly and Carli argue, on the contrary, that the result is of considerable practical importance, drawing on what they call the *aspirin effect*.

The aspirin effect is a term associated with a very influential medical trial to test the effectiveness of aspirin on patients with heart problems. Even before the trial was completed, the data showed that there was a small but significant reduction in heart problems in the sample treated with aspirin, compared with the samples not receiving aspirin.

Approximately 3 per cent fewer people experienced heart attacks when taking the aspirin treatment. The result was considered important enough for the trial to end prematurely, so that all the patients could benefit from the discovery.

If we return to the leadership finding, an aspirin effect implies that organisations that identify the best female leaders they can find and appoint them to more influential positions would increase transformational practices with significant statistical and practical effects.

The argument has to be examined against the wider organisational map within which capable women are systematically overlooked for top jobs. The case on social equity grounds is clear-cut. Other factors may dampen the predicted effectiveness of such changes (just as other factors continue to contribute to the majority of heart conditions, with or without the aspirin effect).

Nkomo and Cox's review of diversity

Gender studies constitute one significant part of a wider body of work which has popularly been termed studies of inequality. A more recent terminology is that of diversity. We take as our map a careful review of diversity by Stella Nkomo and Taylor Cox Jr.[10] These authors suggest that diversity is a construct that poses considerable theoretical and practical dilemmas. Characterisations of diversity can be specific or very broad, and focused at the level of the individual, social group or society.

Definitions of narrow and wider scope

Diversity definitions of narrower scope tend to emphasise discrimination processes as consequences of diversity. Definitions of wider scope include the positive and negative consequences of individual and cultural differences, thus going beyond discriminatory effects. It should be noted that the terms narrow and wide are relative, with some of the narrow-scope definitions including a comprehensive range of discriminatory effects.

Nkomo and Cox offer a narrow-scope definition of diversity as focusing on issues of racism, sexism, heterosexism, classism, ableism and other forms of discrimination at the individual, identity group and system levels.[11] Race, ethnicity and gender are the 'big three' areas most widely mentioned in the narrower definitions of diversity.

For a broader definition, they point to the view regarding diversity as referring to situations in which the actors of interest are not alike with respect to some attribute.

Diversity and identity

For Nkomo and Cox, the diversity map helps us explore the nature of identity. That is to say, diversity is essentially concerned with diversity of *identity* as it is revealed for an individual or social group. They show how most theories of diversity directly attempt to explain the consequences of identity:

- *Social identity theory*, as its name implies, considers how an individual's identity relates to perceptions of self, and perceptions of others about one's self-identity.
- *Organisational demography* theorising has developed following a much-cited article by Jeffrey Pfeffer, which gave the field its descriptive label.[12] The field explores consequences of factors such as age, organisational tenure, education and functional background, and puts priority on those aspects of organisational life that can be accurately observed and codified. Organisational demographic studies also incorporate gender and racial factors.
- *Ethnology or ethnographic studies* offers explanations of identity in terms of cultural diversity. It includes the widely known studies of Geert Hofstede, with the

diversity discriminators of power–distance, uncertainty avoidance, individualism–collectivism and masculinity–femininity. (A fifth factor of Confucian values was later added.)

- *Race/gender studies* developed a broadly emancipative agenda, drawing on earlier theoretical perspectives of oppression, and of the processes of assimilation of under-privileged groups and values by the dominant social groups. Thanks to this work, the evidence of discrimination (most widely illustrated for women and non-white employees of either sex) is now overwhelming, and probably global as manifest in tokenism, exclusion and glass ceilings. Issues of identity tend to deal with psychological trauma, and with damage to self-identity of discriminatory practices.

Celebrating diversity

Race/gender studies are grounded in ethical or moral grounds for equality of opportunities. They consider the various ways in which diversity has failed to lead to equality in many walks of life, not least the workplace. This expresses respect for diversity, and the ethical imperative for granting equal opportunities for individuals of all kinds.

Of the other perspectives, the *organisational demographic* approach takes a more pragmatic approach, explaining why diversity may be a necessary feature for dealing with complex work problems. As we noted in Chapter 3, diversity is necessary for enhanced innovation, and for other effective organisational responses to complexity.

Remapping diversity

Nkomo and Cox suggest that much that is restricting and damaging in stereotyping arises from dichotomous ('either–or') thinking. For example, this thinking opposes 'women' as different from 'men' as simplistic polarities (tough–tender, rational–emotional, strong–weak). This is also known as having an *essentialist* model or map. If we map people in such a way, we may have difficulties coming to terms with behaviours contrary to our map – men who readily show their emotions in the workplace, or women who are assertive. They suggest the benefits in a different, *non-essentialist* or *interpretive* perspective. This helps us understand behaviours (and specifically gender relationships) as strongly constructed from our cultural and social roots, and reinforced by day-to-day experiences. Using this map helps us accept that beliefs about gender may be hindering leadership or followership (beliefs of our own or of our colleagues). Furthermore, it suggests that through reflecting on our beliefs, we may reach conclusions reshaping our practices in and beyond the workplace.

Contextual materials

We consider four case studies in this chapter:

- Margaret Thatcher
- Carly Fiorina
- The oriental glass ceiling
- Roberto C. Goizueta.

Margaret Thatcher

Margaret Thatcher is a leader whose political life justifies careful study. From humble origins, she became the United Kingdom's first woman prime minister.

> Eyes of Caligula, mouth of Marilyn Monroe (François Mitterrand).[13]

This strap line was to an article by Andy McSmith, the political editor of the *Independent* newspaper. The article, written in April 2003, had been prompted by the opening in London of an exhibition described as representing the iconography of Margaret Thatcher. The exhibition led to an incident in which a protestor, Paul Kelleher, had objected to a statue of Mrs Thatcher, which he considered to be revering a hated figure. He was arrested and charged after he attempted to decapitate her graven image with a cricket bat. McSmith recalled the impact that Mrs Thatcher had at the height of her powers, nearly twenty years earlier. In the United Kingdom, many people hated her vehemently as a heartless ideologue. Others admired her as a political and military leader.

The provenance of an icon

Margaret Hilda Roberts was born and brought up in the Lincolnshire market town of Grantham. A now-famous story tells how Margaret lived over the family grocery store, learning the political and economic lessons of hard work, independence and 'family values' from her father, a well-known local politician and former mayor of the town. From an early age she had the motivation to be in charge, and one of her first leadership appointments was as head girl at school.

The able scholarship girl went to Somerville College, Oxford, where she studied chemistry, and also became president of the University Conservative Association. It seems that she was already displaying some characteristics of her subsequent political career, so that we may assume that she was helped by an above-average intelligence, and a combination of her driving ambition to succeed, a willingness to work hard, a retentive memory and a strong physical constitution. She worked for a few years as an industrial chemist, also continuing her political education by standing for two 'unwinnable' seats to the Houses of Parliament. During that period, she studied and rapidly passed her law finals.

By her late thirties she had met and married her life-long companion Denis Thatcher, gave birth to their family (twins) and eventually succeeded in election to the House of Commons.[14] Her abilities were recognised when promoted by Prime Minister Edward Heath to education spokesperson and then secretary of state. As a government minister, she acquired a reputation for reading all the voluminous materials provided her by her civil servants. She would attend meetings with the information coded into a lawyer's brief, from which she would interrogate the officials in terrifying detail.

A capacity to attract controversy revealed itself. Many years later, her political enemies remembered her decision to halt free milk for school children. She had earned her first iconic label of 'Maggie Thatcher, Milk Snatcher', a chant that was to accompany her on her visits to schools throughout her time as minister. For supporters, it demonstrated a refusal to let sentiment overrule commercial necessities, and evidence of a capacity to take unpopular but sensible decisions.

The leader of the Conservative Party, Edward Heath, had lost the confidence of the electorate and of his own senior colleagues. Whoever wanted the leadership would have to challenge the incumbent, a risky business. Margaret Thatcher was bold enough to do that, encouraged by others with more credentials, who saw her role as one of damaging Heath, and opening the way for a more promising candidate to fight the Labour Party at the next election. Thatcher did more than damage Heath. She won the contest against her former mentor (who became one of her implacable opponents within her own party). With four years to go to a next election, the transformation from promising young politician to world figure had begun.

Mrs Thatcher's style

There is ample evidence that she paid a great deal of attention to her physical appearance. Within an awesome time-schedule she mostly found time for an early morning appointment with her hairdresser. She was in no doubt that this was a necessary contribution to the authority she expected to convey and be granted. In parliamentary debates, she cultivated a tougher-than-you style that delighted her supporters and infuriated her opponents. The style was anything but feminine, and it appeared to be a style that reflects the manner in which she ran her cabinet meetings. This style was yet another contribution to the polarising effect we have already encountered. To her allies, she was tough; to her opponents she was strident.
As she lost allies in the declining years of her career, the criticisms of her stridency became louder.

No one accused Mrs Thatcher of being soft on issues. She had a similarly brutal style in negotiations, famously over Britain's rights within the community of European nations. Her style was to offer no concessions in any respect, a form of no-negotiation negotiation approach. The veto was mostly used as a bargaining ploy. Thatcher used it to block any proposal that was contrary to her own position.
At first it worked among a shocked group of representatives unused to such methods.

Later it became counterproductive, and opponents remarked on the positive effect she had on uniting Europe (against her and British foreign policy).

Alan Clark, a cabinet colleague and notorious roué, was not alone in remarking in his memoirs on her sexuality. A Freudian view would suggest that Margaret Thatcher had been greatly influenced by her father, and was disposed to seek out similarly rewarding relationships in later life with older men, whom she was able to influence in a warmer and non-confrontational fashion. They would point to her marriage to Denis as an example, and her deep friendship with and admiration for President Ronald Reagan, as another.

Overall, Margaret Thatcher seemed to deal autocratically with the majority of men or women who worked for her; the style was to demonstrate her superiority (the demonstration of her mastering of the details of briefs would be one example of this). An even more ominous aspect of the style would be the public humiliation of victims, the most overt of which was with her minister Geoffrey Howe over a period of years. Howe was to play a significant part in her ultimate forced resignation.

Her first term (which began in 1979) was one in which an inexperienced prime minister might be expected to feel her way into the new job. Mrs Thatcher's style was based on conviction, rooted in the political values she had absorbed from childhood. Well before she became prime minister, she had arrived at the views of the evils of state intervention, and the merits of free enterprise. The philosophy of Friedrich von Hayek was one of the few ideas that united her with her Chancellor Nigel Lawson. Von Hayek's messages of liberation permitted her to spell out her intentions; her own lack of hesitation over right and wrong permitted her to act.

The new government was able to act swiftly, although initially the policies were crisis driven and less wholeheartedly shaped by the free market philosophy that was to become known as Thatcherism (sometimes defined as whatever Margaret Thatcher said or did). The architects of the medium-term policy installed were the two financial experts in the cabinet, Geoffrey Howe and Nigel Lawson, both of whom became increasingly unhappy with their relationship with a prime minister inclined to derive financial policy from philosophical rather than economic principles. In keeping with Margaret Thatcher's philosophy was the policy of privatisation, which began with soft targets such as the old Cable and Wireless company, then facing the prospect of rapid growth through technological advances.

Falklands and other conflicts

The economy was far from healthy, however, when a long-running dispute with Argentina over the territorial rights to the Falkland Islands flared up. The most bitterly disputed incident remains the sinking of the Argentine troop-ship, *General Belgrano*, with a great loss of life. 'Gotcha!' headlined the populist newspaper, the *Sun*. 'Rejoice!' proclaimed Mrs Thatcher. But others interpreted such displays of elation as vengeful triumphalism.

After the successful completion of the war, the re-election of Mrs Thatcher and her party the next year was a near certainty, with inevitable conspiracy theorists convinced that the Conservatives under the dominance of Mrs Thatcher had engineered an election-winning war. Although unemployment had risen to 3 million (an alarming figure economically) the 'Falklands factor' and the disarray of the Labour opposition ensured that Mrs Thatcher was elected for a second term.

The miners' strike, now famed in British social history, remains in public consciousness as a simplistic battle between two ideologies, led by two ideologues, Margaret Thatcher and Arthur Scargill. According to this view, Scargill and the miners lost, and Margaret Thatcher won. The Labour left had suffered its Waterloo. Privatisation became easier to implement, and legislation was introduced further weakening the power of unions to disrupt organisations and industries not directly involved in industrial dispute.

In 1987 Margaret Thatcher became the first prime minister to win a third successive term of office. Yet this triumph had been achieved at some political costs. There was continued hostility throughout Europe to the British (i.e. Margaret Thatcher's) tactics in dealing with the movement to achieve a single European currency.

Additionally, there was the symbolic significance of what became known as the poll tax. In principle, the idea was to achieve more control over local council spending, by removing local rates and replacing them with a centrally collected tax, calculated district by district. In practice, the tax proved a popular disaster. Now political style and events collided. The tax led to violent public demonstrations. It was clear to many Conservatives that Mrs Thatcher had to abandon the tax, or the Conservatives would have to abandon Mrs Thatcher. For someone of Margaret Thatcher's style, a U-turn was a political sin.

Downfall

Mrs Thatcher was about to be abandoned by the party that had shared her successes and helped her to the status of an international superstar. Arguably the manner in which she controlled her cabinet over a period of time reduced their capacity to seek more consensual solutions. In particular, her treatment of the much-respected Geoffrey Howe was eventually to prove a tipping point (see Chapter 7) as he made a dignified and damaging resignation speech to the House of Commons.

Her removal was rapid, and dramatically charged. In her final Commons speech she displayed many of the attributes of courage and self-belief for which she had been famed. Her reputation remains as a leader of charismatic style most often likened to that of Winston Churchill. Interestingly, after each of its two most charismatic leaders, the country voted for leaders widely regarded as lacking in charisma: Churchill was followed by the quietly spoken intellectual Clement Attlee. Margaret Thatcher was succeeded by someone she had considered as her preference, the modest and introverted John Major.

Carly Fiorina

Carlton S. (Carly) Fiorina has attracted attention as a business winner. Her success leading a major corporate spin-off (of Lucent Technologies in the 1990s) was to trigger international publicity. Her subsequent appointment as CEO of the Hewlett Packard organisation, and her leading role in a controversial merger with Compaq, propelled her into iconic status as business leader. American business heroes of the recent past have tended to be lauded as exceptional figures. The business press tends to offer portrayals of them as the ultimate leaders and role models. Yet, for someone whose potential as a role model is particularly potent, Carly has also been described as one of the most vilified women in corporate America.

The Hewlett Packard story and the Hewlett Packard way

The Hewlett Packard story has been a business school favourite for many years. Its high-tech origins and growth to a mega-star growth company in Silicon Valley at first captured the imagination of Tom Peters (although he subsequently felt that the company lacked the revolutionary zeal necessary to compete into the future). Collins and Porras cited Hewlett Packard as one of sixteen visionary companies 'built to last' through their founding principles.[15]

The company was founded in 1939 by two engineers, who (it is alleged) 'stood in a garage in 1939 and flipped a coin to see whose name would go first in the company logo'.[16] Their goal was to create a great innovative company driven by engineering excellence.

At the heart of the Hewlett Packard success was the HP way, an articulated statement of values and respect for employees and customers. Since the 1940s, care for employees meant an unusual policy of protection of employees from lay-offs. The culture had been inspired by the informal style of founders Bill Hewlett and Dave Packard in the 1940s. Their social and organisational innovations have been as acclaimed as their company's technical products. For example, they pioneered succession planning and management development schemes in the 1950s while the firm still only had some 500 employees. Their original scientific electronic calculator, the HP-35 in the 1970s, was hailed as an invention which changed the world, selling 300,000 within three years, against market estimates of 5000.[17] Its success helped charge up the Silicon Valley phenomenon, feeding the market need for more, faster, smaller, cheaper electronic products and their electronic components. Users of calculators saw prices fall to increasingly accessible values. Hewlett Packard continued on its highly innovative way with a steady flow of imaginative electronic products.

In the 1980s, the approach had been hailed as a proven commercial and human success. By the late 1980s, however, the great growth days seemed to be at an end. Moss Kanter mentions the firm twice, each negatively, in her book on how giant corporations were attempting to become more flexible. She cites a failed attempt to buy into a new market sector, and the firm's rejection of approaches from Apple's founders, Steve Jobs and Steve Wosniak.[18] Its stock price in 1990 had dropped below book value. By the time Carly Fiorina was appointed CEO, the company was increasingly seen to be losing out to competitive threats.

The truth, the whole truth . . .

The original vision of Hewlett and Packard was the creation of a company which would generate high value, highly innovative products. The story goes that Bill Hewlett championed the hand-held calculator product because he had a dream of an electronic slide rule. The growth in its core printer market in the 1990s, fuelled by the internet boom, was for low-price, value-for-money personal and office products. The company had struggled to accept the need for change. Even its own successful product in that market was initially introduced against considerable opposition within the organisation.

Fiorina accepted the need for change and directed her efforts to achieve what was needed. Inevitably, her efforts met with resistance. During the merger that would be the centre of her strategy, opposition became intense. Resistance was led by Walter Hewlett, the son of one of the founders, who had come to believe (rightly) that the merger would threaten the very core of the corporate philosophy.

The story of the Compaq merger had all the ingredients of a Hollywood movie. A high-profile (and female) chief executive faces a culture deeply rooted in its founders' vision and the HP way. Two extensive accounts were written, one with access to Fiorina, the other without. George Anders chronicles the rise of an outstanding communicator and business leader.[19] In some contrast, *Business Week*'s Peter Burrows argues that Carly Fiorina has been engaged in attacking the essence of the company's success.[20] Business commentators suggested that the personality-dominated decision-making process at HP had overcome its traditional beliefs and rational strategic considerations. On 7 February 2005, Fiorina resigned, an event that brought the change initiative to an abrupt close. Her strategic vision had failed to deliver.

Typical biographies of business leaders offer an unambiguous account of the great leader. A colourful private life or unusual personal characteristics tend to be downplayed or omitted completely. In some contrast, the business press seems rather interested in Fiorina's private life. Why might that be the case? Might it help in any way to comment on personality flaws? In which case, should a similar treatment be applied more widely in biographies? Or might the judgement on Carly have something to do with widely held assumptions and beliefs about the suitability of women for top executive positions?

The oriental glass ceiling

Cultural factors continue to exclude women from leadership positions around the world. Some cultures exclude women on religious grounds. These beliefs are defended by so-called traditionalist groupings and challenged by so-called reform or modernising tendencies. Religious traditionalists believe in the universal and timeless truth of evidence revealed through documents and other accepted sources.

Modernisers contend that perceptions of truth change over time and circumstances. Within most of the dominant religious traditions, traditionalists, in accord with their timeless belief systems, continue to define the roles that women are able to play in the religious offices and in society. Modernisers threaten the established order around the world, often risking splits or schisms with the accepted (orthodox) groupings.

We present the dilemmas of gender through the eyes of Ming Hsu (not her real name), a young Chinese woman working as a manager in a state organisation. She believes that executive opportunities for women in China are beginning to improve. However, she sees that there are particular aspects of Chinese culture that reinforce the western notion of a glass ceiling. She talks of the attitudes towards women in the workplace, which are themselves reinforced by cultural beliefs. There is still prejudice, she argues, against career women who are seen as neglecting family duties. 'Women caring for the family win more respect than women caring more about their career,' she explains. 'If she earns more than her husband, society looks down on him.'

She sees the need for sweeping legislative changes and anti-discrimination laws to change the situation and to change male attitudes. At work, what she sees as prejudice means that

> male staff tend to challenge women more than their male counterparts. There is a kind of double bind. If you are more successful at your job, you will be looked down on as masculine and lacking feminine charm. You contribute more to your family, and they will regard you as weak and unqualified for the job. Men can benefit their family by becoming a leader. It is easier to marry a caring and meek wife. A woman suffers and might lose her husband or her lover when she focuses on striving to become a leader.

Two of her special heroines as leaders are Lan Yang, chief executive officer of Sun TV, and Shihong Wu, the former general manager of Microsoft China. Her admiration is the greater because they both overcame the adverse reputation bestowed on women who are divorced (still likely to discredit the woman and her subsequent career).

> Yang's path to being a leader can be summarised as taking advantage of every opportunity, having a long-term mindset, and being diligent and having a strong will to succeed. [Wu's strengths are] a strong will to succeed, extreme hard work, and taking a career as her main life objective.

Roberto C. Goizueta

The case of Roberto C. Goizueta deserves close study as a clear example of a leader from a different cultural and ethnic background reaching the highest office in corporate America, and helping in the establishment of a powerful global brand. Goizueta was a Cuban immigrant who worked his way through the ranks of the Coca-Cola organisation, becoming president and chairman.

He was born into a prominent Cuban family, which in pre-Castro times owned a Cuban sugar refinery. Goizueta was born in Havana on 18 November 1931 to a prominent family in Cuba's sugar industry. He was educated in a Jesuit school in Havana, and later sent to a private academy in Connecticut. There he polished his limited English by watching the same movies over and over. He subsequently earned a degree in chemical engineering at Yale University, before returning to Cuba in 1953 to join the family enterprise.

A year after returning to Cuba he joined the Coca-Cola bottling operation in Cuba, rapidly earning promotion as a bilingual technical manager. However, the political conditions triggered his emigration to the United States where, like so many political refugees, he arrived with no more than a suitcase of possessions and minimal financial resources. He would later reflect that such an experience prepares you to take risks in order to achieve your goals.

His initial work was for the company's Latin American interests, but his energy and competence drew him to the attention of the company's senior executives. He was promoted to corporate headquarters in Atlanta: he became a vice-president at 35, and subsequently chairman. He was widely regarded as a detail and facts executive, although he was credited with leadership of Coca-Cola's global expansion activities of the 1980s. The corporate stock rose by over 7000 per cent during his tenure, and through retaining his stock options, he was eventually to hold 16 million shares, making him the United States' first billionaire corporate manager.

Diversity leadership

Dilemmas of a global kind

Diversity is an increasingly studied subject, with its specialist journals, databases, conventions, books and thousands of articles. The establishment of global organisations has added impetus to the subject. Each global organisation faces the dilemmas of diversity, starting with the diversity at the level of the top echelon team, almost always headed by a leader from the territory of the firm's national and legal origins. Where local headquarters are established, the issues of local and 'expatriated' leaders remain important.[21]

Nowadays, a greater acceptance of diversity on ethical and economic grounds can be found in many institutions and sectors internationally. Women have taken their place as presidents of state and held other high offices. Ethnic minorities have advanced within more dominant regimes in governments, universities, legal institutions and in a range of public service roles around the world. In Malyasia, Chinese leaders are accepted alongside the legally constituted majorities of ethnic Malays (Bumiputras). The courageous experiment in South Africa of a 'rainbow nation' initiated by the charismatic Nelson Mandela is an inspiration of diversity leadership, after its earlier regimes of colonisation and then separation (apartheid).

Organisational diversity and its difficulties

Organisations have accepted the principle of diversity management and, increasingly, the 'entry barriers' for previously restricted groupings are being relaxed. Progress has been claimed, as evidenced by data collection on targets or quotas. Yet the evidence is of slow rather than spectacular progress. In the United States where diversity affirmation programmes have been prominent, surveys suggest that the progress becomes increasingly restricted for non-whites, and for females in particular, at higher levels of leadership.

The meandering path: build your own corporation

Various studies suggest that successful women leaders have chosen to make a lateral leap to overcome the glass ceiling of corporate life. This may involve a meandering path away from corporates to founding a business of their own, then later moving in to head a larger and more traditional corporation.[22] A recurrent resolution of the diversity dilemma seems to be that of building your own corporation.

The profile of successful black leaders suggests a similar meandering path. A database of great American black business leaders of the twentieth century illustrates the pathways.[23] Thirty-one black leaders were identified (four of these were female) who arose in the context of a segregated society within which corporations developed serving the needs of the segregated black minority groups. Several were former slaves, or children of slaves.

The most numerous business leaders by industry sector were financial entrepreneurs (eleven) who set up savings and loan schemes, and insurance services where previously no poverty safety net existed. Typically, the leaders overcame severe discriminatory barriers to success, and the corporations were founded where white leaders were unable to compete.

The other main groupings were newspaper and magazine publishing (six) and personal care products (four). Smaller numbers of the leaders founded food and drink retailing firms, technical and construction organisations, and an advertising agency. See Box 8.4.

Box 8.4 Diversity: cognitive and non-cognitive factors

A general theory of dynamics of diversity is known as homosocial reproduction. Evidence from a wide range of sources supports the view, drawing on self-identity and organisational demographic principles. In general, the evidence also suggests that the tendency to homosocial reproduction reduces the capability of the group to display innovative and creative behaviours.[24]

The cognitive psychologist Michael Kirton provides a theory of diversity leadership which focuses on cognitive style.[25] According to Kirton, any social group will establish a shared culture based on understanding of individual cognitive styles, which discriminates primarily on a preference for incremental or radical change. The theory proposes that preferred style is a stable personality trait, although an individual may temporarily adapt a different style under environmental pressures. People seek environments and leaders consistent with their preferred styles. Conflicts arise as people of differing styles interact and seek to solve problems at work. Individuals will leave those environments that are too distant from their preferred style. A stable environment attracts and retains people of incremental style (adaptors); a turbulent environment attracts and retains people favouring radical change (innovators). Adaptive groups seek adaptive-style leaders; innovative groups seek innovative leaders. However, the most preferred leaders by their followers' in-group are those who are moderate adaptors in the adaptive groups, and moderate innovators in innovative groups.

Other researchers, such as McGill's Nancy Adler, have arrived at similar conclusions (homosocial preferences within multicultural groups, at the expense of improved creativity through diversity). Dr Adler puts her emphasis on non-cognitive influences, resulting in subconsciously framed assumptions and beliefs, including *stereotyping*. According to Adler, we are all prone to stereotyping, but we may be able to minimise self-fulfilling expectations, and treat our stereotypic beliefs as working propositions open to revision through direct experience.[26] Understanding cultural differences involves emotional intelligence: empathy, awareness of effects that individuals have on one another, and non-verbal components of communications.

Integration

The feminine advantage

From our platforms of understanding we begin to see the core issues of gender and diversity. The first dilemma engages with the issue of women as leaders, expressed as the feminine advantage. This view is contested by Vecchio, who sees it as having the same weakness as earlier models of male leadership supremacy, namely that it establishes a superior and an inferior group of leaders, according to gender. Furthermore, he considers that both models draw on a simplistic reduction of human behaviours into two categories of either male or female kinds. The feminine advantage view is strongly supported by evidence that women tend to have more transformational leadership styles, and that transformational leadership is well suited to contemporary turbulent business situations.

The aspirin effect

Eagly and Carli anticipate the criticism that the differences in means are modest, referring to the *aspirin effect*. This metaphor suggests that a modest difference between two populations induced by a causal variable (aspirin on heart conditions, in the original experiment) may be extrapolated to a worthwhile outcome in practice (reduced deaths from heart attacks). From this, we may choose to infer that the replacement of male with female leaders in organisational life will be justified through worthwhile anticipated gains in transformational leadership and through effectiveness of planned change programmes.

Some of the heat is taken from the debate if we consider that the statistical evidence of itself directly only supports the proposition that there is a larger proportion of women than men are reported as having transformational leadership styles. We are still unable to estimate what the proportion is. Nor are we able to say what other factors are likely to mediate between leadership and corporate success (as predicted in contingency or situational theories of leadership). Nor are we even able to say whether training can enhance transformational leadership styles for leaders deficient in such a style, perhaps minimising the statistical difference reported. These considerations show the dangers of confusing logical and deductive reasoning with exploratory and creative induction through metaphoric thinking.

What does seem to be *disconfirmed* is the existence of any evidence that men are more transformational than females in leading change processes. Even discounting ethical considerations (e.g. equality of opportunity), the preponderance of male leaders cannot be justified through any evidence of male leadership's superior effectiveness.

Gender and diversity

This chapter has a preponderance of studies on gender, as one specific aspect of diversity in the workplace. How justified are we in looking for generalisations relevant to the various other kinds of diversity that impact on business leadership? We have just suggested that inductive thinking is exploratory in nature, and we should treat generalisations as possibilities. For more certainty we need to find integration through theories which cover the various kinds of diversity, including gender. In the review by Stella Nkomo and Taylor Cox Jr we see the various theories which do that. The overarching concept according to the authors is that of *social identity*. This is a construct that we have not come across in the earlier maps of leadership. Such a broad concept serves as a starting point for understanding diversity in all its forms. It proposes a common social root to all discriminatory behaviours, as individuals find ways of dealing with 'selfness' and 'otherness'. We thus have the idea that glass ceilings, written about originally in the context of gender concerns, can be applied to discriminatory practices in general. More positively, to understand and reflect on gender dilemmas is to begin to develop further skills at dealing with those wider range of dilemmas. This approach permits us to compare more thoroughly the various contextual examples of the chapter.

Using a social identity map, we may be better equipped to understand the challenges that helped some leaders to shatter glass ceilings; we may understand how discrimination may have multiplicative effects, so that ethnic women leaders have tougher challenges ascending corporate pyramids than ethnic males, or white women. It helps us appreciate how 'the meandering path' to success is so attractive, as able leaders create their own organisations.

Getting personal

Each leader and would-be leader faces his or her highly context-dependent journeys. In this chapter we introduced the complexities that are largely hidden in the maps studied in earlier chapters.

The leader who has identified a rare talent among his or her subordinates will be all too aware of the dilemma of promoting, if that talent is from outside the dominant culture, gender, or (in Pfeffer's terms) outside organisational demographic norms of its traditional leaders. Are the lessons to be learned from a social identity perspective? What actions may help in dealing with assumptions and stereotypes of 'what's different is dangerous'? What are the predictable consequences of 'affirmative action' on expectations of those in the dominant corporate grouping?

The female wannabe leader, such as Ming Hsu in our case example, believes she faced a double-bind in her organisational life Success is hindered by prejudice, and rewarding by criticism of the woman as a 'bad' wife in order to succeed. We may note that the social identity processes involve multiple groups. Criticism of Ming Hsu as a bad wife is most likely to come from her peers. This is an experience shared by ethnic leaders, condemned for 'selling out' their racial kind for corporate advancement, or working-class leaders accused of being class traitors.

Making difference count

One strategy for successful leaders is to find ways of making difference count. The very rare example of corporate success achieved by Roberto C. Goizueta was in part through the acknowledgement of his skills at technology leadership. However, it was the valued difference in working with the company's Hispanic interests that also worked to his advantage. The effort to make difference count can also be found in the case example of successful black leaders founding businesses for black society where white leaders failed.

MBAs seeking corporate jobs are encouraged by their placement tutors to compile a compelling CV. The preference is to present a person with a considerable number of points of similarity to the majority of senior people within the organisation. These points include educational path, professional training, and job experience. Those candidates with unusual CVs are advised to find unusual jobs (there will be fewer applicants with appropriate credentials).

Candidates with military credentials should have more chances in jobs where the company already has a leader with a military background. Candidates who have worked for a not-for-profit charity may find more encouragement in for-profit sectors in the 'creativity' and service industries, and in work requiring creativity and innovation.

Summary

This chapter exposes some of the dilemmas of diversity facing leaders. It selects gender as a specific and critical issue of diversity where there may be a minority or even a majority of a group who may form a subgrouping requiring appropriate leadership treatments for reasons of equity or effectiveness of performance.

The fundamental dilemma of diversity is expressed in the tendency of social groupings to regard 'what's different as dangerous'. In gender studies this has led to what became regarded as the masculine advantage in many work groups, a view based on historical beliefs rather than empirical evidence.

While many of the issues and arguments associated with gender and leadership have a strong empirical basis, there are still conflicting conclusions which are seen to focus on notions of gender superiority. This has caused considerable debates about masculine and feminine values and behaviours and the implications for leadership styles.

Vecchio argued that assumptions of male leadership advantage are being replaced by a mirror-image notion of female advantage. He suggests that the empirical evidence is slight, and may give rise in the future to the same kind of gender-based stereotyping associated with the earlier male leadership advantage.

Eagly and Carli strongly oppose this idea. They suggest that there is ample evidence that there is an advantage in looking for women as transformational leaders based on the database analyses of such leaders, which suggests a stronger association between female leadership and a transformational style (itself believed to be connected with more transformational change potential).

Regardless of the resolution of the feminine advantage debate, the evidence does not justify the 'glass ceiling' barriers to female entry to senior corporate leadership roles.

Eagly and Carli ground the context of prejudice through a treatment of social role perspective that sees social beliefs articulated and reinforced by interactional cues in social groups. Specifically, we see that social role theory may be applied to develop an understanding of prejudice and the exclusion of individuals who are perceived to be undesirably different.

Some of the gender issues lead into understanding other kinds of diversity that impact on the development of leadership maps. Nkomo and Cox also take social construct theory as a broad concept to be found in various maps of diversity in work and social groups.

When people hold stereotypes about a social group, they may have difficulty in coming to terms with behaviours contrary to their map, due in part to the restrictive nature of such 'either–or thinking'. Using a map constructed on the basis of an understanding of social and cultural helps the leader to accept that beliefs about diversity may act to frustrate the practice of leadership. The contextual cases discussed in the chapter highlight the dilemmas of role incongruity, exposed through issues of gender and ethnicity.

One strategy for successful leadership of diversity is through permitting an open culture in which differences lead to improved knowledge sharing and problem-solving. Nevertheless, where the incongruity of the traditional female role with perception of traditional leader roles persists, women may be rejected as a leader because they are either too masculine or not masculine enough. In such circumstances women (and members of other socially excluded groupings) will continue to seek 'an alternative path'.

Notes

1 Boswell, J. (1953[1799]) *Life of Johnson*, 3rd edn, Oxford: Oxford University Press, p. 327.
2 Eagly, A. H. and Carli, L. L. (2003) 'The female leadership advantage: an evaluation of the evidence', *Leadership Quarterly* 14: 807–834, at p. 808, citing Sharp, R. (2000) 'As leaders, women rule', *Business Week* 20 November: 74.
3 Smith, R. A. (2002) 'Race, gender and authority in the workplace: theory and research', *Annual Review of Sociology* 28: 509–542.
4 Eagly, A. H. and Carli, L. L. 'The female leadership advantage' [see note 2]; Vecchio, R. P. (2002) 'Leadership and gender advantage', *Leadership Quarterly* 13(6): 643–671.
5 Nkomo, S. M. and Cox, T., Jr (1996) 'Diverse identities in organizations', in S. R. Clegg, C. Hardy and W. A. Nord (eds) *Handbook of Organization Studies*, London: Sage.
6 Vecchio, R. P., 'Leadership and gender advantage' [see note 4].

7 Eagly, A. H. and Carli, L. L., 'The female leadership advantage' [see note 2].

8 Goldberg, P. A. (1968) 'Are women prejudiced against women?', *Transaction* 5: 316–322.

9 Lowe, K. B., Kroeck, K. G. and Sivasubramaniam, N. (1996) 'Effectiveness correlates of transformational and transactional leadership: a meta-analytic review of the MLQ literature', *Leadership Quarterly* 7: 385–425.

10 Nkomo, S. M. and Cox, T. Jr, 'Diverse identities in organizations' [see note 5].

11 Cross, W. E. (1991) *Shades of Black: Diversity in Afro-American Identity*, Philadelphia, PA: Temple University Press.

12 Pfeffer, J. (1983) 'Organizational demography', in L. L. Cummings and B. M. Staw (eds) *Research in Organizational Behavior*, vol. 5, Greenwich, CT: JAI Press.

13 Quoted in McSmith, A. (2003) 'Me and Mrs T', *Independent on Sunday*, Life section, p. 1.

14 Uglow, J. S. (ed.) (1999) *The Macmillan Dictionary of Women's Biography*, London: Macmillan.

15 Collins, J. C. and Porras, J. I. (1994) *Built to Last: Successful Habits of Visionary Companies*, New York: Random House.

16 Leonard, D. (1995) *Wellsprings of Knowledge: Building and Sustaining the Sources of Innovation*, Cambridge, MA: Harvard Business School Press, p. 52.

17 Vogel, C. (1992) 'Thirty products that changed our lives', *R&D* 34(11): 42, quoted in Leonard, *Wellsprings of Knowledge*, p. 117.

18 Kanter, R. M. (1989) *When Giants Learn to Dance: Mastering the Challenges of Strategy, Management and Careers in the 1990s*, Englewood Cliffs, NJ: Simon & Schuster.

19 Anders, G. (2003) *Perfect Enough: Carly Fiorina and the Reinvention of Hewlett-Packard*, New York: Portfolio.

20 Burrows, P. (2003) *Backfire: Carly Fiorina's High-Stakes Battle for the Soul of Hewlett-Packard*, Hoboken, NJ: Wiley.

21 Adler, N. J. (1991) *International Dimensions of Organizational Behavior*, 2nd edn, Boston, MA: PWS-Kent; Adler (2000) *International Dimensions of Organizational Behavior*, 4th edn, Cincinnati, OH: South-Western.

22 Moore, D. P. and Butter, E. H. (1997) *Women Entrepreneurs: Moving Beyond the Glass Ceiling*, London: Sage.

23 Twentieth Century American Leaders Database, 2004, Harvard Business School, http://www.hbs.edu/leadership/ethnicity

24 Boone, C., Van Olffen, W., Van Witteloostuijn, A. and De Brabander, B. (2004) 'The genesis of top management team diversity: selective turnover among top management teams in Dutch newspaper publishing, 1970–1994', *Academy of Management Journal* 5: 633–656.

25 Kirton, M. J. (2003) *Adaption-Innovation in the Context of Diversity and Change*, London: Routledge.

26 Adler, N. J. (2000) *International Dimensions of Organizational Behavior*, p. 99 [see note 21].

9

Nice guys lose, don't they?
Ethical dilemmas

Orientation

Can't we leave ethics to theologians and philosophers?

Businesses exist as agencies of economic exchange. From this perspective, leaders are primarily concerned with achieving the economic goals of those businesses they are part of. Business leaders are judged on commercial grounds, and ethics come into the picture only if the business is economically damaged through charges of unethical practices. Ethics are relevant only as they introduce economic costs for compliance or non-compliance. In other words, ethical standards are established as rules and regulations, providing guidelines through which businesses are able to pursue their economic goals.

This time-honoured view is widely found in the world of business, noted tolerantly by Adam Smith, writing with the authority of a moral philosopher. It implies that the practice of business is of itself morally neutral, although Smith was wise enough to indicate that such freedom required legislation to prevent the freedom turning into collusion and monopolistic distortions to a free market. On these grounds we may well consider that business and ethics should be kept apart (Box 9.1).

Why leaders can't ignore ethics

This view turns out to be untenable in practice. Few dilemmas of business leadership are more evident than those concerned with ethical behaviour. For some leaders, matters of ethics arise as unwelcome intrusion in the pursuit of economic success. Nevertheless, such leaders have to find ways of assessing the risks facing companies that fall foul of regulatory guidelines (or, worse, of transgressing against legal restrictions). Crudely speaking, the dilemmas are whether the costs of being ethical will damage profitability. Leaders who wish to set high ethics standards in the practices of their organisations face different kinds of dilemma. For as they consider their business on a day-to-day basis, they become aware that ethical values do not come with a simple formula. Often there are conflicting values to weigh up.

Box 9.1 An ethical challenge

● Where does ethics appear on your personal leadership map?
● Which of the following arguments appears more compelling to you?

Argument one: as a business leader my direct responsibility is to my organisation. That means I am legally answerable to those who own the organisation. In a public corporation this duty is made clear by the framework of corporate law. My job is to maximise the worth of the company and the wealth of its stakeholders.

Argument two: my legal responsibilities in general are aligned with the well-being of the various constituencies making up the organisation and its network of employees, suppliers, customers, contractors and consultants. Well-run businesses create long-term prosperity. As far as possible businesses should establish codes of practice with minimal interference from government through legislation or regulation.

Argument three: there are no ethical dilemmas for me as business leader as long as I comply with the regulations laid down for the business. This is similar to the view that science is about *establishing* the truth and is morally neutral. The *application* of scientific knowledge is a different matter, which is best left to the democratic process.

'Whistle-blowing' is but one example where there are different actions possible, suggested by differing ethical considerations (conflicting loyalties for example). Internationalisation increasingly confronts leaders with practices that are considered acceptable and socially obligatory in one culture, and unethical in another. Loyalty may be opposed to truthfulness; giving someone special help may be opposed to treating everyone equally. A gift may be seen as a token of respect or as a bribe. Advancement of a family member may be seen as a necessary step to ensure continuity in a family-owned firm, or an example of nepotism to other candidates for promotion. On one hand, concealing information may be regarded as unacceptably damaging to individuals. On the other hand, revealing the information may lead to legal proceedings for breach of contract, or for colluding in insider trading.

However much we may wish it to be otherwise, business leaders are unable to ignore ethics in the workplace, any more than outside it.

Nice guys lose, don't they?

There is a revealing piece of business folklore, repeated with little challenge in many walks of life: 'Niceness is for losers'. The assumption is often presented in reversed terms in the epithet that winning is everything (the slogan of several sporting coaches). Winning nasty is better than losing gracefully, and you have to bend the rules to win. This perspective serves as a counter to exhortations about moral virtues. In this chapter we investigate how much truth there is the assertion that niceness is for losers. (Not a lot, as it turns out, although the claim is too loosely phrased to bear a great deal of analysis.)

Overview

Two platforms of understanding

Our first platform of understanding of ethical matters was prepared for a special edition on leadership ethics of the *Business Ethics Quarterly*. Joanne Ciulla argues that ethical behaviour is not an optional extra, but a vital dimension for understanding leadership processes. However, the evidence is that the leadership literature ignores ethical dilemmas, or pays lip service to high ethical conduct of good leaders. She invites us to consider what we mean when we refer to good leadership. Does 'good' refer only to effective in achieving economic goals? She argues that we then have trouble if such leadership is 'not good' for the moral well-being of followers.

In the second platform of understanding, the work of James MacGregor Burns on transformational leadership and of Robert Greenleaf on servant leadership is used to explore the rationale for the leader as guardian and guide to the ethical development of followers.

Contextual materials

Our contextual materials explore a range of ethical dilemmas. The case study of Jean-Pierre Garnier shows the clash of values of stakeholders in assessing the value added by a leader, as reflected by his remuneration package. Next we look at the dilemma of a leader faced with imposing a drastic change of conditions on suppliers. We finally study a leader who believed in what might be called ethical manipulation, comparing his beliefs with those who would see him engaged in a form of seduction.

Platforms of understanding: ethical leadership

We will look at two platforms of understanding:

- Joanne Ciulla's exploration of ethical leadership
- MacGregor Burns and Greenleaf's voices of ethical leadership.

Joanne Ciulla's exploration of ethical leadership

Joanne Ciulla conducted a deep exploration of leadership studies to understand the status of ethics. We can be in no doubt of her intention of providing a map: her review is entitled 'Leadership ethics: mapping the territory'.[1]

She suggests that the pressing issue for practising leaders as well as researchers is to understand how to confront the moral or ethical dilemmas associated with leadership. In everyday terms, the fundamental dilemma is between beliefs about morality (conduct) and beliefs about achievement (effectiveness or performance). Debates about whether Hitler was a good leader demonstrate how slippery a concept is the term good.

Tokenism of ethics in leadership studies

Ciulla's study suggests that ethical leadership is treated in a token fashion in most overview studies of leadership (Box 9.2). Tokenism is a term more commonly applied to the process of discrimination, in which an individual is accepted into a group as a token representative of a marginalised subgroup (e.g. by ethnicity or gender). The pressure for accepting the token individual is through a morally strong case. Through tokenism, the group avoids criticism of unethical behaviour, while not having to embrace it thoroughly. Leadership ethics is treated in a text in a tokenistic fashion if little effort is made to integrate it with the main concerns of the text.

Readers who have not encountered the term tokenism in a formal way may wish to consider whether their reading of leadership texts suggests evidence of tokenism in treatments of leadership ethics. They may also wish to consider what other area or areas of leadership studies may have been treated in a token fashion.

In a study of 1800 article abstracts, she found very few offering in-depth discussion and critique. Yet, many researchers and practising leaders directly or indirectly find a need to mention ethics as a 'good thing' for leaders to display. So much so that the textbooks tend to make an unequivocally positive reference to ethical behaviour, while at the same limiting the references to a few paragraphs, or possibly to a self-contained chapter, mostly without serious critique of the concept. Revealing evidence of marginalisation of the subject of ethics comes from the treatment found in Bass and Stogdill's encyclopedic *Handbook*.[2] Its thirty-seven chapters fail to reveal even a token chapter on leadership ethics. There is a brief treatment in the final chapter (which is on leadership in the twenty-first century) and an even briefer reference to James MacGregor Burns's argument that transformational leaders support the development of moral virtues.

Box 9.2 Tokenism in leadership studies

Joanne Ciulla suggests that leadership studies mostly treat ethics in a tokenistic way. Tokenism results from appearing to accept a morally strong case for inclusion of an individual in a group even if the dominant in-group would prefer not to. Tokenism implies lip service to the moral case, and the individual remains marginalised, although apparently accepted into the group.

The notion of tokenism is most commonly applied to discrimination of individuals within groups, as a consequence of their gender, ethnicity or other subgroup characteristics. A wider ethical argument of equality of opportunity has been decided upon, thus providing a moral or ethical benchmark. Wholehearted acceptance of the ethical principle threatens the prevailing (but comfortable) conditions of inequality. The group appoints a limited number of 'token' women, or members of a different ethnic background, and superficially treats them as equal to others in the group as a matter of principle. In practice, salary, preferment and social integration are unlikely to conform to the implied ethical values.

In preparing this book, we were conscious of the importance of dilemmas of unethical behaviours facing leaders. We were also aware of the dilemmas posed through diversity. Ciulla draws attention to the possibility that both issues are treated in a token way in many textbooks. Our treatment here is also open to the claim of tokenism, as we present each issue as a chapter. The reader has to decide on a case-by-case basis, for each topic in each book studied. Is the treatment one that is disconnected from the dominant issues found throughout the book, or is an attempt made to integrate the topics to reveal their importance and relevance?

The treatment of ethics in leadership studies

Ciulla concludes that leaders and researchers consider that ethics are largely a matter of practical knowledge, not requiring theoretical exploration. Unfortunately, a general lack of awareness of the accumulated body of knowledge often leads authors to simplistic rehashes of sophisticated ethical ideas.

The treatment is further hindered by what might be described as a reductionist approach. The treatment, originally applied in the natural sciences, relies on splitting down the complex and analysing the simpler elements. This approach is less powerful in investigating the broader nature of systems. Reductionism fails to help us understand broader issues such as personal ethics (any more than it helps us understand creativity, or soul, those 'ghosts in the machine'). The difficulty of dealing with leadership ethics is a consequence of the dominant approach to leadership.

The significance of 'good' leadership

The literature of leadership is widely concerned with differentiating superior leaders from others. This can be seen in the emphasis placed on leader characteristics. Trait theories searched for the 'right stuff' of leaders and leadership. They could be said to be seeking an explanation of what is good leadership. The dilemmas arise because the dominant methods are weaker at addressing the issue of what leadership should be doing in an ethical sense. Ciulla illustrates this through the evidence that, under some circumstances, effective results are achieved without placing a priority on treating people well. This approach to leadership is too concerned with describing what leaders do, rather than understanding the moral consequences of what is being done.

This was at the heart of so-called *theory X* management, which assumed that workers had to be coerced to perform according to corporate requirements. This makes theory X leadership good leadership. For contingency theorists, theory X leadership is good leadership under conditions where better productivity ensues from such a style, than from other leadership styles. If we define theory X style as good on the grounds that it produces better results (in terms of corporate goals) we are subscribing to a simple notion of good leadership based on situational effectiveness of results. It ignores considerations of whether the process is ethically sound in addressing the moral well-being and development of the followers.

MacGregor Burns and Greenleaf's voices of ethical leadership

Ciulla identifies two influential contributions to a deeper understanding of the performance/ethics dilemma. These are the ideas of James MacGregor Burns and of Robert Greenleaf.

We have come across Burns as a founding figure in the field of transformational leadership in Chapter 4. His approach has been diluted and appropriated into simpler, more widespread approaches concerned with transformation of corporate systems. His treatment was originally one that emphasised the transformation and moral development of followers.[3] Burns drew on the developmental theories of Maslow and others to propose that a leader is able to progress followers to 'higher' levels of ethical development. For example, preoccupations of survival of self may be transcended with commitment to broader ethical considerations in their ways of relating to others. Immediate gratification of needs (likely to be through transactional processes) is less pervasive, as consciousness grows of longer-term and wider considerations.

Burns has a model of leadership in which the leader is differentiated from followers as having a higher or more developed sense of ethical values. This view is uncomfortable for those who prefer a more egalitarian perspective. Burns is suspicious of efforts of consensus, as possibly reducing the possibility of moral progress. His process of transforming people requires in a leader a willingness to engage with the different values, and permit constructive conflict between them (on the grounds that the moral values will eventually outdistance more selfish and transactional perspectives). In the process, the followers are increasingly prepared for leadership roles themselves. The process thus addresses the weakness of more coercive leadership styles, which essentially reinforce transactional follower behaviours.

Robert Greenleaf is associated with the concept of servant leadership, outlined in his book *Servant Leadership: A Journey into the Nature of Legitimate Power and Greatness*.[4] Greenleaf was initially influenced by the mystical tale *The Journey to the East* by Hermann Hesse.[5] The main character (implicitly Hesse) and other travellers were accompanied by a servant, Leo, who attended to their chores and who sustained and uplifted them when they were struggling. When Leo mysteriously disappeared, the group loses its way. Later, it emerges that Leo was the leader of the group.

The powerful central idea in Greenleaf's book is that leadership is essentially about attending to the moral needs of followers; 'good' leadership results in followers who have themselves taken on the ethical values of the servant leader. The consequence, as with Burns's transforming leader, is the development of followers into morally responsible and autonomous leaders. Here autonomy implies the freedom and willingness to undertake the duties of servant leadership. The idea of servant leadership appeals to those with humanist as well as to those with religious value systems.

Ethics at the heart of leadership

Ciulla considers that Burns and Greenleaf help us understand how the moral dilemmas facing business leaders arise. Unlike the more dominant theories, they place the deeper moral issues at the heart of leadership, and deny the possibility of treating ethics as a desirable but optional extra.

They also reject the pragmatic argument that ethical leadership makes sound commercial sense. Maybe it does, maybe it doesn't. Although important, that is another question. For Burns and Greenleaf, good leadership is characterised as a categorical imperative, a means of enacting beliefs rejecting a narrower self-interest where it conflicts with wider general principles of moral philosophy. Or, in everyday terms, of treating people according to notions of morally acceptable behaviour, including that of reciprocity (treating others as you would wish to be treated). This does not eliminate the moral dilemmas facing leaders, but rather offers a starting map of the territory, which was Ciulla's original intention.

Contextual materials

We consider three contextual studies in this chapter:

- Jean-Pierre Garnier: the price of leadership
- Global leadership hits local difficulties
- The manipulative leader.

Jean-Pierre Garnier: the price of leadership

A surprising AGM

London, England, Monday 19 May 2003. The customary calm of GlaxoSmithKline's annual general meeting (AGM) was shattered by a vote against the remuneration package proposed for its CEO, Dr Jean-Pierre Garnier. The package was reported as providing a 'golden parachute' for the CEO of the second largest pharmaceutical company in the world, in the event of his dismissal before the 2007 termination date of his prevailing contract. The details were widely reported as amounting to $28 million.[6] The figures quoted were estimated by the Pensions Investment and Research Consultancy at $35.7 million (£22 million), disputed by GlaxoSmithKline, since it included some $12 million of already vested share options.

The story can be traced to the restructuring and merger activities of the world's pharmaceutical companies in the 1990s. Beechams merged with Smith Kline which then merged with Glaxo to give GlaxoSmithKline (GSK). The incumbent CEO, Dr Garnier, was hailed at the time as one of Europe's rising business stars.

The vote (marginally over 50 per cent against) was itself symbolic. It had no legally binding power over the board's decision, and was brought about by opposition from small shareholders (predictably opposed to perceived generosity in such awards) and institutional investors, particularly the representatives of the pensions funds through the Association of British Insurers. Institutional shareholders in the United Kingdom are traditionally hands-off, preferring to work discreetly towards protecting their interests (primarily, the contribution of the company to the value of their portfolios). It was believed to be the first time such a vote had carried the day. Standard Life, a major shareholder (holding 110 million shares), had already publicly stated its intentions of opposing the proposals.

The post-merger performance

Since the $195 billion merger between the British drug companies Glaxo Wellcome and SmithKline Beecham was completed in December 2000, the company had maintained its market leadership in the $300 billion global drug business. First-quarter results reported pharmaceutical profits had grown 11 per cent, to $2 billion, on sales of around $7 billion from 'megabrands' such as diabetes treatment Avandia and a recently launched asthma medication.

Shortly before the vote, Sir Christopher Hogg, chairman of GSK, had announced that the company had commissioned an independent inquiry into the remuneration packages of its executives. He also indicated that the opposition to the proposals would be taken very seriously by the company, regardless of the outcome of the vote. The vote followed new investor protection legislation passed in the United Kingdom earlier in the year. This represented one aspect among several that contributed to the incident, which was regarded at the time as a possible significant one for future pay deals for business leaders.

> Garnier, who is known as JP, has already wrung $580 million in cost savings from overlapping businesses. And the stock? Up 12% since New Year. Garnier is determined to make the new GSK 'king of science'. So he has reshaped the company's massive research and development effort into competing teams to boost productivity. The payoff could be big: the company should launch 15 new drugs by 2005. For JP, it's just the start.[7]

The merged company retained European (British) legal status, with many operations located in the United States as well as plants and research dotted around the world. As such, there are sometimes cultural ambiguities to manage. For example, the company appeared on one hand to hold the more robust American corporate view on CEO remuneration. Its public statement on the proposed package had originally been based on the argument that top people had to receive top rewards, in order for a world-class company to recruit the best leaders, and retain their services in a competitive world. Yet the company also retained its European cultural heritage, together with its notions of inequality, and collective contributions to achievement or failure, which contributed to beliefs about distribution of rewards. In Europe, debate regarding corporate 'fat cats' had been around for several years, fuelled by the payments received by senior executives of newly privatised organisations, who had in general failed to demonstrate their contributions to added shareholder value. The 'top people should receive top pay' argument had been considerably weakened as a consequence. The previous week, at the annual meeting of investors at the Royal & Sun Alliance, 28 per cent of votes were cast against the company's remuneration proposals.

That is not to indicate that the culture was particularly swayed by non-economic arguments. Opposition to the basic principle that top people deserved 'top' salaries came only from the distant voices of the outlying groups opposed to the more general structures of capitalism, and those seeking more social and environmentally sensitive institutions. These voices were less directly significant in this specific corporate incident (although they should not be discounted as contributing to the wider debate on corporate governance). The weight of opposition came from the institutional stakeholders who had already supported the even more important symbolic vote to reinstate the executive board of the company. They had no ethical quarrel with the principle of top pay for top people. Rather, they pointed out that the substantive vote was over what a failed executive should expect on termination of contract.[8] If Dr Garnier (as leader) was to receive a commission for the financial success of the merger, that was one thing. But the corporate performance since the merger was not as strong as had been predicted. They believed that the leader should also take the hit under these circumstances.

Nor were the prospects for the short term seen as bright. Key profit streams from its best-selling drugs were under challenge from cheaper generic drugs, as patents expired (and as had happened to the antibiotic, Augmentin, the previous year). The company had played down the prospects of replacements for its declining drug lines.

The corporate reputation of the drug giants had also been under threat from alleged lack of social responsibility in its policy to suffering in developing countries. This made them a target for criticisms.[9] Only a few months earlier, the State of New York sued GSK, together with the US major drug company Pharmacia, alleging that it inflated its drug prices.[10] The advantages of Glaxo's increased presence in North America and Europe were not gained without incurring associated disadvantages.

In an article for the *Guardian* newspaper, a few months before the GSK shareholders' meeting, journalist Sarah Boseley wrote the following on GSK's leader.

> It takes a big man to run the second largest pharmaceutical company in the world . . . Jean Pierre Garnier, who years ago lost some of his French identity, if not his accent, to the ubiquitous American initialising and became universally known in the pharmaceutical world as JP, doesn't wear a tie. Why would he? . . . Within his own parameters . . . JP is not only a big man but a good man. Some call him a humanitarian. He has been awarded the Legion d'Honneur by the French government. He has indisputably taken GSK several rungs higher on the ladder of altruism than any other drug company. But at the end of the day, he says, he runs a for-profit company. And if people are still dying of AIDS in Africa, it is because their governments are ineffective or do not care. It is not to do with the greed or indifference of the pharmaceutical companies . . . JP's vision is clear. He is willing to supply not just antiretrovirals but other medicines poor countries need for epidemics, such as malaria, at cost, he says. Combivir [a dual combination Aids drug] sells at $1.70 a day. For a Malawian woman . . . it might as well be the price of a flight on Concorde. His answer is twofold: order from GSK in bulk, perhaps for the whole of sub-Saharan Africa, and the price will drop and, secondly, persuade the rich countries to support the Global Fund so that poor countries will have the money to buy GSK's drugs. It's win-win for Glaxo. It need do nothing that is incompatible with the capitalist ideology of the marketplace or would upset the shareholders, even if it may seem ironic – to those who were baying for JP's blood over the recent offer from the GSK board to boost his pay to £20m – that he should be asking effectively for government subsidies.[11]

Opposition was further sharpened by pressures on the institutional investors. Pension funds, those sleeping giants, had been awakened by the 'pensions gap' facing ageing contributors and recipients. Corporate pension schemes were becoming difficult to manage, and therefore coming under closer scrutiny. The corporate investors found themselves searching for economies, and ways of cutting out any fat. The somewhat collusive relationship with corporations was changing. Glaxo had already indicated a scheme along similar lines, and somewhat more modest in scale, in 1992. At that time, there were more muted objections. When the new scheme came along, the timing, lack of corporate progress, the difficulties facing the institutional stakeholders, and the new legislation, were all factors that may have contributed to the dramatic vote.

The vote was hailed at the time as having historical significance. It made sense in different ways to different groups of people. The institutional investors believed they had sent out a warning against reward packages that were not linked to 'value added' promised by the leaders involved. The social-responsibility lobby took heart at future opportunities for drawing attention to other forms of corporate abuse of power. Small shareholders felt they had at last had some influence over decisions that affected their savings. Glaxo accepted the need to revisit their remunerations policies and procedures with greater inputs from disinterested outside experts. Other global corporations watched with interest.

Global leadership hits local difficulties

The year 2002 saw the widespread acknowledgement in the United Kingdom that macro-economic and socio-economic factors were signalling that the days of the corporate pension scheme were numbered. One multinational energy organisation faced a range of unwelcome issues. For some years, environmental groups have targeted its policies as exemplifying the iniquities of global capitalism. Initiatives by the firm to demonstrate its social consciousness have been largely ineffective in neutralising the negative message. Reports of suspected irregularities in contract arrangements in an African subsidiary received worldwide publicity, and were seized upon by environmental opponents of the corporation to justify their opposition. Further financial problems developed in the company, as it was forced to announce overestimates of energy reserves, which led directly to boardroom resignations. The company faced short-term and longer-term financial problems.

To deal with short-term financial pressures, various sources of revenue restructuring were examined. One attractive possibility involved a shift in the arrangements for supplying the company's distributors. These were locked in to a considerable extent, as each of the major energy suppliers had its own local distribution network. Current arrangements involved payment on delivery. The company considered that the distributors were making healthy margins, and that the company could make a significant and rapid financial hit by introducing a worldwide policy requiring the distributors to accept a more disadvantageous payment schedule.

The company carried out a financial risk analysis and concluded that strategy was one of the most promising in scale and speed of implementation. Speedy action was called for, and the change was announced as a global policy, leaving local managers around the world with no financial discretion in implementing the policy.

We learned of the implications facing one leader. An internal company source we interviewed reported that his leader

> is preoccupied with how he is going to get the acceptance of the distributors in his region. He's presenting the case strictly as a must financially for the company. He doesn't see there's going to be a lot of criticism, adverse publicity at a time where they've had to be really careful not to attract more bad press. He's living in a world where financial muscle is going to win over any other considerations.

Our contact told us that he was arranging meetings with his distributors where he would listen to their protests. Then he would try to find what non-financial arrangements might be possible, to make their situation more bearable in the short term.

This story comes from the energy industry, although similar examples of 'must do' implementation of decisions taken unilaterally through financial muscle can be found, for example, in retailing. The incident gives a vivid insight into a corporate culture within which strategy appears to be largely the exercise of financial power. The regional leader was well acquainted with applying the pressure required to force through unpleasant policy. He was himself under pressure to deliver on a series of financial measures. He had no discretion to fail, any more than he had discretion to waive the policy for any special cases. The distributors would eventually and unwillingly accept the change. A few weaker and less efficient ones might be forced out of business. The others would have been encouraged to find efficiencies of their own, thus becoming more competitive.

The manipulative leader

Manipulation: a clarifying definition

Broadly, we consider manipulation to be a form of influence process. It is a term generally used with implications of concealment of intentions or information so as to influence the willingness of the manipulated person or persons to comply with the wishes of the manipulator. In general, its use implies patterns of behaviour which lead to relationships within which there is little concern for the ethical or moral issues involved. The desired ends are more significant than such potential dilemmas. The term also implies that the process is in some way less acceptable than processes which conceal less of the leader's intentions. As Yukl pointed out, most leadership definitions imply the exercise of intentional influence.[12] We are therefore well advised to consider this particular perspective, which starts to set limits to 'acceptable' leadership practices on ethical or moral grounds.

A justification for manipulation

In our case study, we shall see a leader ('Roland') arguing that manipulation may be 'in the best interests' of his subordinates, or even more broadly as a necessary and effective way of achieving goals compared with more open (less manipulative) approaches. This turns the moral argument on its head. We are familiar with it, in dramas of family life. It is one resort for parents who have decided that the application of more direct approaches fail. ('She's too young to understand why we really do not want her to go on holiday with her boyfriend'.)

Was Roland a seductive leader?

One of us worked closely with an extremely able and successful executive whose career had been mainly within a large corporate organisation. Let us call him Roland. He was thoughtful and self-aware, responsible for others often of lesser self-awareness and social skills. Roland considered it important for him to achieve results. His view was that 'the company' (i.e. its decision-makers) arrived at high-order goals and objectives. The company, while demanding, was also ultimately aware of what were reasonable targets. The professionals for whom Roland was responsible were mostly cooperative, with some more difficult than others ('bloody-minded' according to Roland).

In work and outside, Roland had an easy charm about him. He rarely lost his temper, was adept in deflecting anger, and generally liked to find 'win-win' outcomes to potential conflicts at work. He tried to treat everyone with respect and courtesy (secretarial and support staff warmed to his approach). As his career advanced, he set himself a personal development programme and was able to bring many ideas into his work practices from his training in interpersonal skills, and even creativity management. He later became a successful independent consultant with briefs in reconciliation and change management. One of his favourite approaches was that of reverse negotiation: 'Let me work out what I think is best for you and how we might be able to achieve it together. You work out what you think I want and how we can both achieve it. I find we get better results than the old ways of doing this.' He often did.

One of Roland's principles was that he would try at all times to be as open and honest as he could. This would always have limits. He would relate the dangers of being told something 'in confidence' about a third party. For Roland, openness and honesty were not so much moral absolutes as potentially conflicting moral guidelines that had to be 'managed' repeatedly.

Roland had also realised that at times his wants did not coincide with those of others in the organisation. 'If I have to, I go in for manipulation,' he was known to remark.

> But I have some ground rules. I will never do anything I believe will be against someone's interests. So I might have to withhold some information, for example. Sometimes it all works out the better because of what someone did not know in the short term. But if I get asked, 'Is there something you are keeping back from me?', then I will admit I have been holding back, and I can't say any more until whenever I think I can be more open.

Roland had worked out an approach he believed could be called manipulative ('scheming, calculating, controlling') within his self-determined ethical framework. 'You may think it's manipulative, but I don't see there's anything wrong with the way I do it.'

He became a role model for many in his organisation. His leadership skills were highly effective and he was widely regarded as someone of great integrity. His style would win approval from leadership expert, John P. Kotter, who in his book *The Leadership Factor* indicates that the role of the leader is to influence 'through (mostly) non-coercive means'.[13] Roland preferred to use '(mostly) open non-coercive means' and had defined his own boundaries of what he considered to be acceptable influencing methods. He would probably not use the word coercion. It is not clear whether Kotter has some softer implied meaning here, as opposed to dictionary senses of coercion as compulsion, force, intimidation, bullying, oppression, cruelty and duress.

What then can we learn from Roland? Something about the practical pressures of leadership and the moral dilemmas of seeking to gain trust while being less than fully open with others? Something about the slippery nature of words like manipulative and honest? Something about the essence of trust-based leadership?

The seductive leader

Roland turns out to have a complex leadership style. In his own eyes he is sometimes 'forced to' be manipulative. In such times he attempts to be 'benignly' manipulative. We will benefit from taking more than one perspective on his case. Feminist writers Marta B. Calás and Linda Smircich have drawn attention to the unrecognised but widespread use of strategies of seduction in organisational and social life as a manipulative strategy.[14]

Does this make the seductive leader in some way the weaker party, resorting to 'wiles' of seduction to achieve goals? Where does this leave differences between male and female leaders? Is leadership more than a metaphor? Hardly any old metaphor: the mythology of seduction runs through our cultural heritage since the story of Genesis and Adam's 'Fall'.

Integration

At the start of the chapter we asked whether leaders can ignore ethics at work. For Ciulla, the answer is a clear negative. She argues that studies of leadership have tended to ignore ethics, concentrating on a search for the secrets of leadership through what leaders are observed to do, while implicitly being concerned with what good leaders do. Unfortunately, studies have failed to appreciate that good leadership means more than productive leadership. Ciulla calls for a recognition that good leadership refers to productive behaviour that is also grounded in moral or ethical principles.

This map helps us work out the difficulties with the taken-for-granted routes for exploring leadership which ignore ethics as a core component of good leadership, or treat such considerations as a convenient add-on. She offers a challenge to research on existing empirical evidence: suppose research confirms that treating people well somehow detracts from 'good' leadership measured only through short-term productive results? Are we to move towards 'teaching how to be nasty enough to be winners'? We can reshape the question in a more formal way to permit a critical examination of it. Suppose empirical evidence suggests that leaders who are successful in meeting economic goals are likely to have ignored ethical considerations of treatment of others? Does this evidence justify us in encouraging more leaders to be successful even if their actions ignore the well-being of followers? In such terms, Ciulla has revisited the old question of whether ends justify the means, this time in the context of leadership effectiveness and morality. For Ciulla, the answer is an unequivocal no.

We suggest that she has demonstrated why 'good' leadership cannot be decoupled from ethical considerations, and why leadership research requires to pay more attention to ethical issues. However, we would also consider that arriving at 'good' decisions remains problematic, and that ethical dilemmas remain to be confronted.

For example, there may be several conflicting views of ethical behaviour. Drug companies argue that medical advances have saved countless lives, and that sustained profitability within the industry creates jobs. To provide drugs at lower cost appears to be ethical, but in the long run damages the health of people by reducing investment in research, and the wealth of economies through destroying profits. As part of the same argument, the corporations require the best leaders, who can be attracted and motivated through being offered a share in the additional surpluses generated through their leadership. Similar reasoning permits diffusion of lesser 'incentives' throughout such organisations. Critics consider this unethical, arguing that the connection between the leader's rewards, and his or her contributions to profitability, is hard to evaluate. They also point to cases where the rewards are high, even when profitability is not.

Displacement of ethical responsibilities

The drug companies may be accused of failing to help the health of the poorest people in the world. They offer a compelling argument that it is the responsibility of governments, not corporations, to arrange for subsidies to permit low-cost drugs. It is not that the leaders are inconsiderate of the needs of others; rather their ethical responsibilities are for the long-term well-being of their shareholders, and that indirectly is in the long-term interests of a far wider set of beneficiaries. This is an example of *displacement of ethical responsibility*. By displacing ethical responsibility, a dilemma disappears: 'I am in favour of nuclear waste disposal, relocation of homeless people, and erection of wind-farms, but *not in my backyard.*'

Should business leaders attend only to their legal and corporate obligations, leaving ethical considerations to others? Or should they operate so that ethical concerns impact on their actions and decisions? This is a version of a well-known dilemma within the scientific community. Science was considered as the driving force of human progress, and many scientists argued that science should be distanced from considerations of the ethicality of its utilisation. However, there have always been scientists who concerned themselves with such matters, and who had common cause with those fearing the consequences of scientific discovery. The debate reached a wider public with the emergence of nuclear weapons: the first generation of weapons of mass destruction. There followed further debate around environmental impact and then genetic manipulation.

The ethics of 'doing my job'

In our case examples we saw how leaders dealt with dilemmas of implementing policies that were likely to be opposed by people. In each of these examples, the leaders took for granted that the task they had undertaken was to be discharged. One (unnamed) leader accepted the inevitability of a coercive policy, but sought to find ways of providing any (limited) help he could. Another leader (Roland) felt he was often obliged to influence people 'in their own interests' as well as in the interests of his company. He applied a litmus test to his behaviours. He would not behave in a way that he would object to, if someone else was applying it to him (ethical reciprocity). See Box 9.3.

Box 9.3 Notes on ethics and leadership

An area of ethical dilemmas for corporations arises in matters of environmental concern. The ethical imperative is broadly that of preserving the environments for future generations. Organisations, as consumers and converters of natural resources, are increasingly confronted with such ethical issues.

One widely accepted principle is respect for the survival of species facing extinction through change of habitat. The rights of humans to fish for food supplies are protected by organised culls of seals, a competitive predator for fish stocks. One corporate response has been the doctrine of sustainability. This accepts ethical obligations of avoiding damage to the environment, while holding to the beliefs in the social virtues accruing from technological innovation and progress through economic freedom to trade.

Corporations legally have an obligation to act in the best (economic) interests of their shareholders. As long as a majority of these shareholders support actions driven primarily by short-term economic considerations, there is only secondary interest in ethical issues. A pragmatic response has to argue for the economic virtue of ethical behaviours. There seems to be some supportive evidence for this.

Consideration for others, as an ethical construct, is close to what has become known (after Immanuel Kant) as a categorical imperative or moral absolute. It becomes a dilemma for leaders who concern themselves with operating in an ethical

continued

fashion under conditions where they have also committed themselves to corporate well-being through their leadership actions. This implies exerting leadership influence with the primary consideration of achieving corporate goals.

In the United Kingdom, the Co-operative Bank, founded as part of a communitarian movement, has preserved its ethical business values for over a century. Recently it has turned this ethical position into an economic benefit, proclaiming its decision to invest only in other companies of high ethical standards. It has avoided suspicions of pragmatism and opportunism because the strategy is well aligned with its long-held values. Other companies attempting to present a more ethical image tend to struggle to overcome the accusation of making dishonest and unethical claims of ethicality. Any evidence of actions contrary to the ethical claims is quickly brought to public attention by external pressure groups, often supported by internal 'whistle-blowers'.

Corporate development of environmental practices has often been described as a kind of moral development process, from unconscious and damaging strategies, towards conscious and socially responsible ones. For example, a company may be located on the path from non-compliance with prevailing regulations, compliance, compliance plus, commercial and environmental excellence, and leading edge.[15] A range of theories of this kind seem to share a sense of increasing salience of environmental issues for a corporation's strategic plans, culminating in deeply embedded acceptance of the competitive (rather than ethical) benefits accruing from social responsibility. The initiating motivation for change seems to be compliance with governmental or stakeholder demands.

One of the more cited bodies of work on moral development is that of Lawrence Kohlberg.[16] This work proposed the development sequence from pre-conventional morality, to conventional morality (socialised by family and legal conditioning) and post-conventional morality (social contract and orientation towards universalistic ethical principles). Kohlberg developed a methodology that remains popular, of presenting ethical dilemmas to sampled individuals. His work extended across large numbers of cultural groups, but ignored women. Carol Gilligan extended the work, and revealed a complex picture of responses. Applying Kohlberg's methodology, women appeared to be of a lower level of moral development than males in a range of samples. This research was to lead to recognition of the possibility that women and men held different moral orientations. The women tended to perceive moral issues in terms of care, empathy and compassion; the men more in terms of right, justice and fairness.[17]

In earlier times (perhaps through to the mid-1970s) most business executives believed (or at least stated publicly that they believed) they were responsible only to their shareholders. More recently, recognition of wider corporate responsibilities has grown. The Enron debacle may become viewed, in years to come, as the nuclear meltdown event, the Chernobyl of corporate responsibility.

Getting personal

A pragmatic word to the sceptical

When you came across this chapter you may have felt a sense of unease at its subject, ethics. If so, you are far from being alone. This is understandable, in that we tend to meet a proportion of people who are interested in business and whose interests are rooted more in the practical than the theoretical, and the economic rather than the philosophical. You may well have approached business and business leadership expecting to learn about influencing, and been surprised to find ethics as a subject of concern.

We have already indicated why you may find the subject of value. You may be unable to achieve your leadership goals, or resolve leadership dilemmas without an understanding of how ethics interplay with economics. Incidentally, this is itself an example of a *pragmatic* ethical approach: you are concerned with ethics as a means to achieving your ends.

Leaders are increasingly under pressure to conform to socially acceptable norms of various kinds. You have to show concern for the environment; your recruitment policy has demonstrably to avoid discrimination; you may be compared with other firms for how you treat your employees; you are expected to monitor ethical practices of suppliers, and avoid contracts with those not meeting required standards. The pragmatic argument is that *compliance is good for business.*

The evidence is that compliance can indeed be good for business. This pragmatic approach has its advantages: there may be opportunities for a 'balanced scorecard' of attention to economic and ethical objectives, so that you are not punished economically for your 'investment' in ethics.

Beyond compliance

The pragmatic approach has its advocates. Our own interpretation of the leadership literature is that the approach 'works' (it achieves its ends) where the simpler transactional leadership style works. Its success may bring advancement to the leader under such circumstances. There is ultimately, however, a weakness at the heart of the approach. Then ethical principles claimed are actually based on dubious claims, and may be revealed in behaviours when the ethical course of actions is compromised for (pragmatic) considerations.

These considerations (according to Ciulla) are second nature to a leader for whom ethics lies at the heart of leadership not at the periphery. The organisation is then more attuned to ethical possibilities in their work, rather than having to react to ethical pressure from outside. Another argument is that transformational approaches are more likely than transactional ones to lead to trusting relationships, as well as to a leader lifting the ethical horizons of others. The pragmatic approach is a wholeheartedly transactional one, which offers encouragement to pursue approaches placing ethics at the heart of leadership.

Can ethics be learned from a book?

Before you started reading this book, you will have developed personal ethical beliefs. Some of the beliefs will have come as 'moral instruction' from earliest years at home, at school and perhaps from religious instructors. Later there may have been intense discussions late into the night with friends. Freudian theory suggests that we develop our impulses from the most primitive kinds, to be influenced by social conditioning of what we 'ought' to do. This develops through our social experiences, and through indirectly acquired principles. If that was the entire story, there would be little room for considerations of 'the real me'. This develops as we each develop our personal maps. Studying leadership maps is just part of the processes of studying maps for wider personal journeys.

In other words, you have already learned far more about ethics in your map than you are likely to acquire from another textbook. What may be possible is for a book to suggest other journeys, and other experiences against which you can check your ethical ideas. See Boxes 9.4 and 9.5.

Box 9.4 Machiavellianism: beating up the nice guys

One of history's most famous (or infamous) leadership consultants was Niccolò Machiavelli, adviser to the powerful in sixteenth-century Italy. His advice was intended primarily to support and preserve the power of his 'clients'. There is an ethical basis to Machiavellian behaviour. It is that of pragmatism, whereby the ends (preservation of power) justify any means available. Such an orientation is understandable if the possible consequences of losing power include imprisonment, exile or death.

Nowadays, there is interest in the Machiavellian orientation in public life. It has been studied in connection with business leadership, although as a topic it tends to be omitted from many leadership texts. Nevertheless, it permits us to address one of the dilemmas of business leaders. In practical terms, it supports the popular belief that nice guys come last; that winning (the goal) is all that matters (i.e. the way you win is irrelevant, as long as you are not disqualified from the game for a breach of rules).

A famous business game (the red-blue game) permits individuals (representing groups) to negotiate and break the rules in order to win the game. One outcome is clear, intentions to deal ethically are fragile, and the game typically deteriorates into breaches of agreements and widespread Machiavellian behaviours. One of the learning points is that the process often results in 'lose-lose' outcomes in comparison with the potential gains if each side had behaved more ethically. Yet game theory (developed in experiments such as this one) remains an accepted discipline for understanding human decision-making behaviour.

In an Indian study of managerial ethics, the authors tell of an ancient text, the Arthashâstra or the science of material gain.[18] The Arthashâstra is written in the same mode as Machiavelli's much quoted *The Prince*. The focus is on the rights of the leader to impose their right to rule. The rulers have no moral sanctions restricting their treatment of their subjects, who have to accept the rules placed on them, or accept equally unrestricted and severe penalties. Ends (preservation of the leaders' rights to rule) justify the means to achieve that end, including an early proposal for spies and the science of deception to gain useful intelligence. Unlike Machiavelli, the Brahmin author, Kautilya, considered the ends to be an ordered regime with protection to the benefit to all under the law. At present, the concept of Machiavellianism has been more thoroughly studied than the related eastern concept, so the authors applied the western methodology to investigate ethics within Indian businesses. Machiavellianism was tested in experimental trials, requiring responses to various ethically challenging situations involving bribery, padding of expense claims, nepotism and insider trading. Machiavellianism was shown to be *situational*. This accords with a view that ethical behaviour in organisations is situationally mediated.[19]

Other studies have explored the Machiavellian orientation in samples of business leaders and others. The orientation appears to be correlated with manipulation, skills at persuading, resistance to being persuaded by others, and less concern with ethical considerations of their actions. One well-cited study compared managers, MBA students and MBA faculty. Managers showed significantly lower Machiavellian orientation than did the students and faculty.[20] Interestingly, there seems to be some evidence that Machiavellians have a lower sense of control over their environments.

Box 9.5 A myth of servant leadership

Best-selling author Terry Pratchett has created an alternative universe, beloved by millions of his readers. Although the universe is inhabited by many fabulous creations, their dilemmas are all too human. In *Thief of Time*, Pratchett created a servant leader character, Lu-Tze, who can be found in the garden of the five secrets, in the grounds of the monastery of Oi Dong, where reside the fighting monks of the order of Wen. His account captures the moral significance of servant leadership:

> And who is this Lu-Tze? Sooner or later every novice had to ask this rather complex question. Sometimes it would be years before they found out that the little man who swept their floors and uncomplainingly carried away the contents of the dormitory cesspit . . . was the legendary hero they'd been told they would meet one day. And then, when they'd confronted him, the brightest of them confronted themselves.[21]

Business leaders can no longer ignore servant leadership, nor related wider issues of corporate responsibility and governance. These subjects may even offer lessons for any ambitious executive, although we would personally be uncomfortable if servant leadership, and the transcendence of self-interest, are approached only in a narrowly self-interested Dilbert-like fashion. The boss sits smugly behind his high-status desk. He has enrolled for a crash course on servant leadership. Why? Because he has been tipped off that the meek will inherit the earth, and he intends to be there when the inheritance is handed out.

Corporate executives are often driven to succeed, in some cases by the spur of escaping from subservience to a leader or to an oppressive regime. MBAs generally do not invest large sums of money in their education to learn how to be a servant of any kind, even a servant leader. For many people, servant equals low and powerless, leader equals high and powerful. We invite readers to examine this perspective and place it in the context of our experience of the commercial world. In the process, new and enriching possibilities for leaders may be revealed.

Leadership and spirituality: the ethical dilemma
A servant leader is essentially a transcendent concept, one in which the servant leader transcends the narrow notion of self-interest at the core of all human behaviour. There are great moral and philosophical arguments regarding the ethical virtues of accepting servant relationship. These will cut no ice with many people.

Summary

In this chapter the fundamental dilemma between beliefs about morality and beliefs about effectiveness of performance have been explored.

We suggest that a widespread dilemma for business leaders lies in the tension between commercial well-being and ethical probity. The contextual issue comes from the structure or form of organisations as legally constituted primarily for economic considerations of the stakeholders. Statements about the importance of good leadership or strong leadership conceal dilemmas including ethical dilemmas. These dilemmas become critical when leaders considered to be good and/or strong are judged as unethical and criminally responsible for their leadership behaviours.

The fate of ethically flawed leaders at the turn of the twentieth century highlighted the need for leaders and other organisational stakeholders to develop more awareness about the taken-for-granted issues of good leadership or strong leadership. We follow the map of ethics in leadership developed by Ciulla. She points to the absence of interest in ethics by the map-makers we have encountered in our earlier chapters.

Tokenism

In her mapping of the territory Ciulla suggests that even when the subject of ethical leadership is mentioned, it is treated in a tokenistic fashion in most leadership texts. Tokenism involves the apparent acceptance of a set of values or beliefs by a group who would prefer to exclude the individual. The actions of acceptance are a means of protecting the group from objections of exclusion and perhaps from accusations of prejudice against the individual. Ciulla implies that the treatment of ethics in leadership maps is confined to a limited territory – a kind of conceptual *apartheid*.

The tokenism of ethical issues in leadership maps may reflect the way ethics is approached in practice. Espousing ethical policies for the business and then displaying contradictory moral conduct might be open to accusations of 'tokenism' just as in the case of diversity management.

The fundamental dilemma

Ciulla suggests that for most leaders, ethics is a matter of common-sense and not requiring any formal education into ethical theories. Within such common-sense mapping, she argues that the fundamental dilemmas for business leaders arise through attempts to deal with the tensions between conduct (morality) and performance.

One approach is for leaders to find a pragmatic justification of actions – morality in the service of corporate economic responsibilities. The organisational obligations require that leaders are effective (if they are not then their ethics is not usually an issue as their position as leader will be challenged on their lack of achievement). A different approach is to argue that morality is good for business. This is the pragmatic view that attention to ethics is aligned with business success.

The ethical imperative

Ciulla points to the dilemmas for those holding such pragmatic views: what to do when ethics appears to be damaging your business? She points to the ethical imperative of leadership developed by Burns in his theory of transformational leadership and Greenleaf in his model of servant leadership. Burns and Greenleaf place deeper moral issues at the heart of leadership dilemmas. These maps offer some moral certainty for leaders in terms of ethical values.

Burns introduced the concept of transformational leadership as one in which the leader lifts the moral horizons of followers. Any denial of this denies that which was essentially different about new leadership maps. Similarly, Greenleaf holds that good leadership results when employees find meaning in and take on the morality of the leaders.

This chapter raises the question of whether leadership is ultimately a moral process. If so, the ethical dilemmas of business leadership are not resolved. Rather, the challenge is that leaders work with organisations' stakeholders and the general public to accept higher levels of ethical behaviour. If so, leaders as role models have an *obligation* to align the values of organisational members with the leadership direction, and to accept that the morality of leaders and those being led can have a strong influence on mapping the leadership process.

Notes

1 Ciulla, J. B. (1995) 'Leadership ethics: mapping the territory', *Business Ethics Quarterly* 5(1): 6–28.
2 Bass, B. M. (1990) *Bass and Stogdill's Handbook of Leadership: Theory, Research and Managerial Applications*, 3rd edn, New York: Free Press.
3 Burns, J. M. (1978) *Leadership*, New York: Harper & Row.
4 Greenleaf, R. K. (1977) *Servant Leadership: A Journey into the Nature of Legitimate Power and Greatness*, New York: Paulist Press.
5 Hesse, H. (1989[1945]) *The Journey to the East*, trans. H. Rosner, London: Paladin.
6 For example, *Herald Tribune* and BBC websites, 20 May 2003.
7 *Business Week Online*, 11 May 2001.
8 Garnier would get two years' salary, bonus and benefits valued at about $6.5 million according to the reports: ibid.
9 The Glaxo official website at the time indicated social responsibility initiatives ('investments') which could be presented as not too different in scale to the remuneration package proposed for the CEO.

10 BBC website, 14 February 2003, citing press release from New York Attorney General Eliott Spitzer.

11 Boseley, S. (2003) 'Jean Pierre Garnier, head of Glaxo', *Guardian* 18 February.

12 See Chapter 1. See also Yukl, G. A. (2002) *Leadership in Organizations*, 3rd edn, Englewood Cliffs, NJ: Prentice-Hall, p. 2.

13 Kotter, J. P. (1988) *The Leadership Factor*, New York: Free Press and London: Collier Macmillan, p. 16.

14 Calás, M. B. and Smircich, L. (1991) 'Voicing seduction to silence leadership', *Organization Studies* 12(4): 567–602.

15 Roome, N. (1992) 'Developing environmental management strategies', *Business Strategy and the Environment* 1(1): 11–24; Roome, N. (1994) 'Business strategy, R&D management and environmental imperatives', *R&D Management* 24(1): 65–82.

16 Kohlberg, L. (1969) 'Stage and sequence: the cognitive development approach to socialization', in D. A. Goslin (ed.) *Handbook of Socialization Theory and Research*, Chicago: Rand McNally; Kohlberg, L. (1981) *The Philosophy of Moral Development*, San Francisco, CA: Harper & Row.

17 Gilligan, C. (1982) *In a Different Voice: Psychological Theory and Women's Development*, Cambridge, MA: Harvard University Press; Sharma, P. and Bhal, K. T. (2004) *Managerial Ethics: Dilemmas and Decision Making*, New Delhi: Sage.

18 Sharma, P. and Bhal, K. T., *Managerial Ethics* [see note 17].

19 Trevino, L. K. (1986) 'Ethical decision-making in organizations: a person-situation interactionist model', *Academy of Management Review* 11: 601–617.

20 Siegel, J. P. (1973) 'Machiavellianism, MBAs and managers: leadership correlates and socialization effects', *Academy of Management Journal* 16(3): 404–412.

21 Pratchett, T. (2001) *Thief of Time*, London: Doubleday.

Emerging issues and dilemmas

Orientation

Leaders with development dilemmas

These are the primary dilemmas for two participants in one of our recent leadership workshops. You will have your own dilemmas. If this book is to help, it has to offer you ways of dealing with those important and hard questions. We have argued that there may not be simple answers, but you still have to make decisions. We also argue that maps are useful for journeys, although you are far better advised to take maps found valuable by others, and rework them to help in your own leadership journeys.

> I'm just confused about being a leader. It's been two years since I left N—— [a multinational financial services organisation]. I had been a technical analyst and then a trainer. When they asked for volunteers during downsizing, I took advantage of the package they offered. So I took time out. The plan was to start a family, study for an MBA, find out what sort of leader I really am. As you can see, I'm well on the way to starting the family, and I'm finishing the MBA. But leadership! The more I've studied it and thought about it, the more confused I am. In my old job I had got to the state of believing I was working to a set of rules that were not right any more. I was talking to people, learning about new ways of changing things, more networking, sharing commitments and responsibilities to make work life fairer and better for more people. But it wasn't happening. Now I'm finding out about all these leadership theories but they still don't give me what I'm looking for. As it is, I'm going off the whole idea of leaders and followers.

> I know I have been a good leader in my present firm. Our results show that. But I wonder what would happen if I moved into another leadership position in a different type of business. Would I have to change? Could I change?

Overview

Throughout this book you will have become familiar with the metaphor of a personal leadership journey. Metaphors can be powerful means of discovering new possibilities and learning. Each chapter introduced maps of the leadership journey, often from the most respected map-makers. We also consistently encouraged readers to treat the general maps as starting points for their own leadership journeys.

The materials provided may still be regarded as platforms of understanding accompanied by more limited contextual materials. Now we have a somewhat different kind of situation. The personalised maps were always focused on the future, on journeys we expected or hoped to experience. But in previous chapters, the general maps attempted to describe territory as it has been experienced by map-makers and travellers. As we reach the end of this book, there are no general maps of such well-travelled territories from which to create our personal maps. We have to recognise that any general map of the future is less directly based on reliable evidence than maps of the past. Bearing that caution in mind, we can still learn from well-considered maps of that strange territory, the future.

Two platforms of understanding

Our first platform of understanding comes from Gary Yukl, a map-maker whose work has already been found in earlier chapters. He attempts an integrating conceptual framework which helps us understand the partial nature of earlier maps. The essential feature of his integrative model is that of reciprocal influence of its various components: leaders influence and are influenced by the specific situations they are placed in. We can no longer think in terms of simple cause and effects, but of systems within which the traits and behaviours of leaders may be among several factors initiating changes at a point in time, changes which are then mediated, so that outcomes are not easy to predict, and differ from situation to situation. Yukl includes leader power as a particularly significant kind of intervening variable.

Yukl's model helps us see how the early trait and behaviour theories ignored additional intervening and situational variables. The search for the complete set of traits can be seen to have assumed that leaders had a direct impact on their circumstances. That is to say, the map assumed a simple link between the special gifts of the leader, and his or her impact on the world. As long as we believed this possible, we went on assuming that the leadership effect could be transferred from one circumstance to another, simply by transferring the leader. The introduction of intervening and situational variables helps us to understand how the same behaviours could produce different results.

Our second platform of understanding is an interesting and thorough investigation of the leader of the past, and a proposal for the leader of the future. The map was drawn up by Joseph Rost as a guide for leadership in the twenty-first century. If Yukl has attempted to rescue leadership from its twentieth-century state of fragmentation, Rost has attempted to demolish the old ideas and replace them with a new model. Interestingly, the new model has a familiar feel to it. Rost seeks to deal with the definitional and ethical dilemmas at the heart of leadership studies, and to provide a coherent and consistent map. Like Yukl, he proposes that leadership be studied as a reciprocal relationship. He proposes, more originally, that the process occurs where there is *intention to achieve mutually desired purposes*. This is his universalistic definition. Rost further claims that the twentieth-century leadership paradigm (for that is the term he seems to be closely reformulating) has been forced into ethical dilemmas through ignoring the principle of striving to attain collective purposes. For one of the last times we offer readers an invitation to practise their skills of critique. If someone proposes a universalistic definition of leadership, what dilemmas might a leader face in studying this map? If adherence to the mutually desired purposes is accepted, what consequences arise from that part of the definition? We offer some suggestions later in the text.

Contextual materials

For our contextual materials we have introduced (and at times reintroduced) materials which we find provide food for thought. They hint at new maps, and the rewriting of the old ones.

Our first contextual map seems quite different from the maps of earlier chapters, while offering an alternative way of reaching similar territories. It deals with the social psychological approach to social identity, which has been recently examined for its relevance in reshaping our understanding of leadership and power relationships.

The approach has become associated with the concept of *prototypicality*, which offers an explanation into otherwise puzzling aspects of leader–member relationships. These include how followers identify strongly with their leaders, and yet regard their leaders as different and special.

We take a look at the high-profile concept of emotional intelligence (EI), and work through its maps, comparing them with well-established ones. The most controversial claim is that high EI leaders are far more effective than low EI leaders.

The next contextual map examines the much-discussed conditions of high turbulence in contemporary work contexts. The map-maker argues for a positive approach to turbulence to avoid ill-advised efforts to preserve the status quo.

Platforms of understanding: the future of leadership

We will look at two platforms of understanding:

- Gary Yukl's map of the future of leadership
- Joseph Rost's map of twenty-first-century leadership.

Gary Yukl's map of the future of leadership

In Chapter 1 we looked at the influential maps of leadership by Gary Yukl, concentrating on his ideas at the start of the period of new leadership studies in the

1980s. More recently he reviewed the state of the field at the start of the twenty-first century.[1] He confirms the important changes occurring since the late 1980s, including theories of transformational and charismatic leadership. His later leadership maps differed from the earlier thoroughly rationalistic ones, through attention to processes emphasising values and emotions, influencing followers to 'higher'-level aspirations. Yukl is concerned to address concerns regarding the conceptualisation and measurement of leadership processes. In our terms, he acknowledges the dilemmas remaining within contemporary conceptualisations of leadership.

Yukl enumerates a range of major issues:

- simplistic either/or thinking (or models) of leadership
- omission of relevant behaviours
- a focus on 'one-to-one' leader/follower processes
- dubious methodologies for measuring leadership.

Yukl notes the dangers of ignoring earlier theories as wrong, a point which recognises the dangers of an important antecedent of dilemmas, namely either/or thinking. He encourages us to see how older theories become a bedrock on which new theories arise, and to which new theories sometimes return in a more contemporary form

Simplistic either/or thinking (or models) of leadership

We are now familiar with the either/or nature of many leadership concepts. These led to much work on oversimplified two-factor models of leadership.

- Before the 1980s, there was the split into *task-oriented leaders* or *people-oriented leaders*.
- In the 1980s, *leaders* were differentiated from *managers*. It was suggested that managers did things right; leaders did the right things.
- New leadership studies offered *transformational* leadership as opposed to *transactional* leadership.
- *Charismatic* leaders (in modern contexts) were contrasted with *non-charismatic* leaders.

These dichotomies simplify the leadership concept, and encourage a stereotyping or categorising attitude. In our seminars, we noted not only the willingness of some leaders to accept the 'tick boxes', but also the restlessness and desire to explore more deeply of others. These were the leaders who were more naturally disposed to go more deeply into what we have referred to as leadership dilemmas. For example, a dilemma arises as we wonder whether we can divide up people into leaders or managers. We may also wonder at the kind of context in which a transformational leader never engages transactional processes. There are various ways of dealing with the dilemmas, some ways requiring a deeper critical examination than others. We believe that readers who have worked through the earlier chapters will be able to work towards their own views on any of these dilemmas.

Omission of relevant behaviours

The simplistic two-factor models are the most obvious ones in ignoring other factors of relevance to leadership. Charismatic leadership has tended to be studied in a way that inevitably puts great emphasis on the heroic leader. Transactional leadership is relatively weak on creating climates and communities for self-help and learning.

A focus on 'one-to-one' leader/follower processes

Dyadic theories (such as leader/follower exchange) simplify leadership into the impact of one person on another, and minimise the significance of contextual factors and distributed leadership. More generally, the absence of multilevel theorising (the leader, the core group, the organisation in its environment) has inevitably led to omissions of relevant factors. (Many factors have been identified in the vast numbers of studies of leadership, but the field is notoriously fragmented.)

Dubious methodologies for measuring leadership

The favoured approach to collecting data has been through structured surveys in ways that tend to be biased favourably towards the importance of individual leaders. Yet the information is more likely to report on frequency of a specified behaviour, than skilfulness in its enactment. The difficulties in gaining access to leaders 'in the field' has meant that few studies have been able to conduct follow-up studies, so that the stability of the data over time has to be assumed. The call for 'mixed' quantitative/qualitative designs has tended to fall on deaf ears.

Overall conclusions

The new leadership campaign has been waged with antiquated methodological methods. Enthusiasm for new leadership may have contributed to premature abandonment of earlier concepts (such as traits and 'classical' concepts of charisma). Yet, the newer theories have then reintroduced the old ideas 'through the back-door' (as in the case of charisma, 'tamed' to fit the proposed measures of transformational leaders, the 4Is).

The new charismatic and heroic leader all but overwhelms interest in distributed leadership concepts. However, the more thoughtful accounts of charisma direct us towards the dark side of ego-driven charismatic leaders, and sometimes to severe adverse consequences of the charismatic style.

Another emerging theme is awareness of ethical dilemmas. For Yukl, these arise once we consider the multiple obligations on leaders rather than obligations utterly directed to the needs of a dominant stakeholder (owners). The issue becomes one of resolving the dilemmas of conflicting obligations – to workers, owners and customers. To this list we could add obligations to family (the dilemma of work/life balance).

Joseph Rost's map of twenty-first-century leadership

In the 1990s, a scholarly and comprehensive study, *Leadership for the 21st Century* by Joseph Rost, attracted considerable attention among leadership researchers. The book was acknowledged by James MacGregor Burns as the successor to his own seminal contribution, written three decades earlier. Critics extensively reviewed the book.[2] Ciulla examined it, along with the contributions of James MacGregor Burns and Robert Greenleaf, as exemplars of major influences in the field.[3] The book received praise for its scholarly approach, and its thorough critique of the entire period of twentieth-century leadership. Its central message is that leadership in the twenty-first century should escape from an unhealthy dominance by thinking that was too close to the beliefs of a bygone era. This contention sat comfortably with emerging ideas about distributed leadership, ethical integrity of leadership, and the processes of mutual sense and meaning-making within change programmes.

Rost's ideas have been relatively ignored by the mainstream leadership paradigm, as if his roadmap for the twenty-first century is too contentious.

Rost is critical of much of late-twentieth-century leadership as grounded in faulty foundations. He further considers that there has been a lack of help for leaders (whatever the definition) to deal with ethical dilemmas. He is therefore also critical of the formal ethical canon whether based on religious or other moral philosophical grounds. The knowledge, he suggests, has little relevance for a leader facing conflicting duties and obligations. He considers that legislation aimed at promoting ethically desired results tends to reinforce leaders in a leadership mind-set of 'staying legal' rather than 'staying ethical'. He considers that this has become increasingly germane to situations of moral ambiguity, where people hold sincere views on opposing sides of dilemmas such as AIDS, affirmative action, environmental sustainability, freedom of information and intrusion on other rights, and differing cultural views of gifts versus bribery.

Rost has two main targets for his critique of twentieth-century leadership, and two prescriptions for the future. The targets are the lack of definitional clarity of the subject, and what he calls the fallacy of the industrial paradigm. The prescriptions for the future are a new definition securing a new theory of leadership, and a plea for a multidisciplinary treatment.

Lack of definitional clarity

Readers will be all-too-aware of the definitional confusions. Rost shows a striking grasp of the historical nature of this. He notes the confusions extended back to the

1940s, how Chester Barnard criticised the domain for its dogmatism and drivel. He then traces other major figures and their concerns, such as the more urbane recognition of the ambiguities expressed by Burns in the 1970s. Rost's careful examination of over 200 definitions he found in the literature led him to conclude that the numerous definitions mostly failed to untangle leadership from other related human activities involved in social intercourse.

He arrives at a surprising and interesting conclusion, namely that there is a universal definition implicit in the apparent diversity. The core definition had never been revealed because it has been confused by a failure (by everyone) to grasp the possibility that leadership is a term used to indicate a special kind of management. As an epigram, Rost suggests that leadership may be equated with good management. He also expands what good management is about, offering the following (twentieth-century) definitions:

> Leadership is great men and women with certain preferred traits influencing followers to do what the leaders wish in order to achieve group/organizational goals that reflect excellence defined as some kind of higher-level excellence.

> Management is an authority relationship (contractual power) between at least one manager and one subordinate who coordinate their activities to produce and sell particular goods and/or services.[4]

Rost retains the old term 'traits', which makes it unclear whether he excludes new leadership and transformational leadership from his definition of leadership in the industrial era.

Fallacy of the industrial paradigm ('leadership as good management')

Rost concluded that the multiplicity of definitions captured the various aspects of leadership within the industrial era (and specifically, within the twentieth century). Far from indicating large numbers of overlapping theories, they constituted a collective theory of the enactment and theorising about the core of industrialism. This core is explained in a study of the definitions, and societal beliefs, of the industrial society:

- a mechanistic view of organisations (the structural/functional view)
- management as the pre-eminent profession
- a focus on the person of the leader
- the primacy of organisational goals and goal achievement
- a self-interested and individualist outlook
- a utilitarian ethical perspective
- a technological and rational belief system or paradigm.

The assumptions were seen as:

- hierarchical control of followers by leaders
- unilateral top-down goal setting and communication flows
- leaders know best.

The thrust of the critique is that leadership as good management perpetrates the norms of the industrial era.

The universal definition

Rost offers the following as a definition for the future of leadership:

> Leadership is an influence relationship among leaders and followers who intend real changes that reflect their mutual purposes.[5]

The definition seeks to remove the ethical dilemma of the more general definitions of leadership that cover the behaviours of a Hitler as well as a Mandela. Its most imaginative aspect is its emphasis on *intentions* of leaders to act so as to reflect mutual changes. From our maps of ethics we can see that Rost's arguments are essentially grounded in ethical considerations and beliefs. His recognition of the mutual involvement of others with leaders is why his theory has been described as a *communitarian* one.

Communitarianism theories of a more democratic leadership form can be, for example, found and described vividly in work by Manz and Sims. They coined the term *superleadership* to imply that a collective leadership approach can go beyond what can be achieved by a traditional leader, however gifted that individual may be.[6]

Rost was later to recognise that the term *follower* was too close to the vocabulary and thinking that he wanted to consign to a former era (the industrial era), and was replaced in his work with the term *collaborators*.[7]

A multidisciplinary approach to leadership

Rost argues that leadership studies have been swamped by the dominant influence of the business leadership work (the industrial paradigm). However, he notes other disciplines, notably education, public sector and political leadership, each struggling to establish their unique silos of leadership know-how and theory. His proposal is that leadership studies should free itself from the dangers of being a single disciplinary approach, and reinvent itself in multidisciplinary form.

A critique of Rost's view of leadership

Rost's work was received in the 1990s as a significant contribution to leadership thought. For Rost, moral principles in the industrial era are those of an even earlier classical liberal philosophy which have paid more attention to the rights of individuals, and particularly material rights, at the expense of what might be called higher-level non-materialistic and altruistic considerations. He admits that he is no formal scholar of ethics, and calls for those who are to help provide models appropriate to the needs of the present time.

The general thrust of his argument might be taken in support of transformational leadership as pioneered by his mentor Burns. Yet leadership scholars have greeted his work warily. Critical evaluation has come principally from the field of ethics, where he has been particularly attacked for a misunderstanding of the ethical principles he considers to be inappropriate for leaders in their work practices.

His critics acknowledge that the principles of a more distributed and collaborative leadership concept have considerable appeal. His ideas are also seen as rich sources of debate. In essence they help us move away from the idea of a leader identified totally with an assigned role, towards the idea of a more flexible function, occupied by multiple players in a more complex set of relationships.

Despite his rejection of the philosophic tradition, it is pointed out that his most novel element in his leadership definition is that of ethical intentions, one of the concepts deeply studied by Kant. An ethical issue is how decisions are freely entered into, without coercion, manipulation or edict, within contemporary organisational structures. More seriously, his analysis is considered to be an inadequate treatment of the dilemmas raised in considering what is ethical leadership. His advocacy of a collectivist approach leaves unanswered the issue of absolute standards, or directive principles. He avoids the deep issues of the nature of 'real' leaders and 'good management'. His espousal of the Kantian principle of ethical intent requires further consideration of Kantian principles of ethical imperatives, which he sidesteps. These objections are hardly surprising: ethics as a branch of philosophy are generally considered to offer starting points, rather than complete maps for negotiating leadership journeys.

Contextual materials

We consider three contextual materials in this chapter:

- The social basis of influence
- Emotional intelligence and leadership
- Positive turbulence

The social basis of influence

Social cognition and social identity

Several crucial aspects of influence have been implied rather than thoroughly examined in earlier chapters. Leaders exercising influence have plenty of common-sense advice from common-sense books. The advice stops short of answering the question 'Why should I follow that person?' Or again, if the leader has to be able to support the sense that followers make of their world, or to be the manager of meaning, there is a need to understand how such meanings occur.

The processes through which individuals develop and retain shared beliefs and values are known as *social cognition processes*. An emerging theory places importance on how individuals in groups develop a sense of social identity. They suggest this helps us understand leadership, and the development of power relationships.

Although these processes are open to various social psychological treatments, the social identity theorists have tended to theorise around the notion of *self-categorisation*. Shared social views emerge through interactions and dialogue, which help in the production and maintenance of mental categories. Psychologists have used various terms to the mental categories, of which conceptual frames and schema are particularly popular.[8] These are relatively permanent mental constructions, drawing for their reinforcement not only on reflective personal use in thinking, but also on social acceptance through linguistic social exchanges and shaping.

Schema which categorise people help us make sense of our world, and might include concepts such as leader, somebody important, trouble-maker or potential husband/wife. According to this theory, the schema has a prototypical core which is connected at a neurological level with other members of the category which are conceptually more remote from the core. From experience, and through our social interactions, we build up rich schema (we could also call them mental maps). 'Real' leaders are leaders conforming most closely to the prototypic leader identifiable through our mental constructions. Non-leaders provide us with contrasts which help us locate the various aspects of our schema on leadership.

Prototypicality and the 'extra-ordinariness dilemma'

Social identity theorists have suggested that group members have greater chances of acceptance as leaders if they are particularly well able to represent the social identity of group members, and tend to be perceived as more effective leaders. Politicians (and many organisational leaders) try to show that despite other differences, they are really 'people like us'. This strategy implies that prototypical leaders are very ordinary, and is a kind of dilemma. Surely, politicians and leaders are well aware that they are in some ways unusual and perhaps extraordinary – by respect of their position power, for example? However, prototypicality does not have to infer *equivalence* of status, or of leadership capabilities. Group members are looking for leaders who are prototypical of their map of their idealised selves, 'someone like me' in many ways, 'someone I would like to become' in others.

In-groups and out-groups revisited

The categorising process turns out to be dependent on other factors. If individuals strongly shape and connect their sense of self-identify with perceptions of the group's identity, the result is a high-consensus group. The theory offers insights into corporate loyalty and commitment.

In lower-consensus groups, there is less group identification. The formation of high-consensus groups clearly has relevance for leadership, team building and organisation development programmes. In leader–member exchange treatments, the leadership process is considered to operate in differing ways for a core group of selected colleagues, and for the others in the group. This is interpreted by some researchers as a process privileging members of an in-group, who in turn act to retain the special treatment through their actions. This approach is criticised as reducing the complex sets of interrelationships to simple dyadic (one-to-one leader–follower) exchanges. A social identity perspective rejects this on several counts: it fails to consider the possibility that a leader–member relationship is benchmarked in relative ways against other known leader–member relationships, both in the subgroup and across subgroups.

> Leadership, and the nature of leader–subordinate relationships, needs to be understood in the context of a deeper textured analysis of group processes, intergroup behavior, and the nature of group membership . . . In addition, the notion of 'member' needs to address the member's self-concept.[9]

One conclusion from a social identity perspective is that leaders have to be aware of the consequences of offering 'individualised consideration' to members of the group. A privilege granted for one member will be interpreted differently in high-consensus and low-consensus groups. Just to make the issue more complex, the leader accepted in a high-consensus group is less immediately vulnerable to charges of favouritism, as actions will be interpreted more generously by other group members as being in the interests of the group.

Social identity theory and charisma

The concept of charisma now shifts. We see the greater potential for recognising charisma within high-consensus groups. These groups are particularly prone to construct or interpret leader behaviours on social identity grounds, which intimately connects the leader with values and aspirations of the group. These processes will thus be linked to the charismatic processes we have encountered earlier. There is one big difference, however: the attribution of charisma now derives primarily from group processes and aspirations, rather than personality traits. (We may still hold to the possibility that traits associated with charismatic leaders may favour selection within such a model of leadership.)

This explanation suggests that a leader helps members retain their cherished identity as an in-group member and helps differentiate them from members of out-groups. The work derives from classic studies of prejudice, and in-group/out-group identification processes.

More speculatively, we may see promise in social identity theories in exploring the contentiously termed *thought leadership* processes. The term can be found within knowledge-based maps of leadership suggesting the possessor had potent organisational knowledge perhaps of strategic goals or motivating corporate visions. A more popular consulting use appears to associate thought leader with someone whose ideas are setting an agenda for change. In either case, a social identity approach offers promise for future mapping.

The dilemma of the prejudiced leader

Social judgement theories offer means of studying and understanding power relationships in ways which challenge more established leadership beliefs. Powerful people are not necessarily powerful by virtue of superior powers of understanding and insight of their subordinates.[10] Leaders in a wide range of studies consistently show bias in their judgements of subordinates so as to stereotype them and derogate them as a matter of course. In short, many leaders are in practice consistently prejudiced and biased in their judgements of their subordinates.

It is perhaps a further indicator that the heroic model of leadership is at very least incomplete. According to social identity theorists, dominance may be maintained if followers are perceived as no competitive threat, through stereotyping and derogating (retained negative beliefs about subordinates). Similar processes sustain socially constructed status differences, and may well explain workplace bullying and teasing rituals. Several power-retaining benefits may well be accruing from such stereotyping, which may be consciously or unconsciously conducted.

As a general principle, such power-driven and cognitively biased strategies will always suffer from restricted authentic information, and risk longer-term failure as a consequence. We may have to dig more deeply into the processes and implications of social identities, status, and the maintenance of power in understanding the dilemmas of leadership.

Emotional intelligence and leadership

As the twentieth century drew to a close, there was a surge of popular interest in a concept known as emotional intelligence (EI) as a predictor of leadership effectiveness.

For (almost) the last time we invite the reader to apply the approaches suggested in this book for evaluating the concept of EI for its leadership implications. We set the challenge in the following terms. You have heard about a book describing the concept of EI, and have learned that its main claim is that EI is a far better predictor of leadership effectiveness than is general intelligence (IQ). That's all you need to know for you to develop your own map, perhaps to help you study the book in a more critical and attentive fashion. Our challenge is what broadly is suggested by your readings of earlier leadership maps about the link between leadership capabilities and performance? What is different about the proposed EI maps? Are there dilemmas that you would wish the author would address, in the book you are about to read? We suggest that you spend a few minutes on considering this, before examining the approach we took to the challenge (which will be found in the following paragraphs).

Putting EI in context

Intelligence has been one of the most thoroughly examined human characteristics. The most established tests of intelligence have been recognised as only a subset of mental activities. For most of the twentieth century (1900–1970), intelligence and emotions were largely separate fields of study. In the 1970s and 1980s, precursors to EI began to emerge. Work on social intelligence, a concept suggested by Edward Thorndike as early as the 1920s, has been deepened by contemporary workers to indicate the possibility of multiple intelligences, within a structure of intellect.[11] In the 1990s, EI research developed, and formal studies were popularised.[12]

A major review clarified the concept, suggesting that it involves the processing of emotional information, including the adaptive regulation of emotion (a means of personal development).

Goleman's EI map

Popular interest in the EI concept is easily traced to a best-selling book entitled *Emotional Intelligence*.[13] This is the book that we would have to examine to understand the most widely held beliefs about EI. Its author, David Goleman, was a brilliant communicator of ideas that had been emerging in the social sciences. In particular, he had assembled evidence that conventional intelligence as measured by IQ tests was not a particularly strong indicator of leadership performance. In contrast, differences in leadership characteristics suggested that emotional ('affective') skills explained a significantly greater proportion of the differences in leader performance.

For Goleman (and for many readers of his book) this led to the conclusion that the special leadership skills were due to emotional intelligence, and that emotional intelligence was the 'something special' that differentiated leaders. In empirical studies, the differences that could be explained by IQ were estimated as less than 50 per cent of the differences unexplained, and attributed to emotional intelligence. After the book was published, several assertions gained common currency. It was assumed that EI was far more important than IQ for leadership effectiveness. It was also assumed that a leader could become far more effective by developing his or her EI skills.

Evaluating the claims for EI

We suggested that readers might like to take Goleman's book as an important one to examine for the dilemmas of leadership it presents. By now, readers will be familiar with the approach. First, we take a look at our well-trusted maps of leadership. Second, we see what the new map is telling us, and how it differs from the more established maps.

For us, the maps of leadership have become more complex. The early (trait) maps promised us that leadership was directly connected to leadership performance. Our more recent maps point out that the relationship is highly *mediated*. Yukl's integrative model in this chapter shows us even more complexities. Goleman seems to be offering maps from the old and simpler tradition. Leadership has two main differentiating features, formal and emotional intelligence.

Without any further knowledge of Goleman's work, we would be able to approach the book to see how it deals with the other situational variables. Will it suggest that EI always determines effective leadership? The dilemma for us would be that if Goleman's claims are true, he has cast into doubt the validity of the development in leadership studies of more complex models.

This dilemma has been studied more deeply by other researchers who have pointed out that the formal definition of EI has changed in more popular treatments (including Goleman's) to embrace a wide range of leader characteristics such as well-being, motivation and various social skills, which fall outside the definition of cognitive capability (IQ). As the definition changes, so must the means of measuring the phenomenon. The scales considered most reliable, and in accord with the formal construction of emotional intelligence, are ones most remote from direct behaviours; the most accessible scales, including self-report, are the most suspect. Such considerations demonstrate that the popular claims that EI is twice as important as IQ for leader success have limited scientific justification at present.

Rescuing EI

It would be a mistake to dismiss the EI concept only on the grounds that its popular treatment has been found methodologically suspect. Interest in EI has drawn attention to non-cognitive leadership competences that have been under-regarded. Critical evaluations of the concept currently consider that it may well offer such insights, which go beyond related constructs such as practical intelligence and social intelligence.

The work reminds us that emotions convey valued information, and that awareness and reaction to emotions of others and self may well provide indicators for leadership and leadership development. At the very least, we are able to approach areas of existing interest in leadership armed with new maps, of leadership competences, some of considerable reliability. Future work may help us appreciate the skills associated with transformational leadership, and possibilities for their development. Practical trials have begun applying EI in personal development programmes.

Positive turbulence

Countless books have been written describing the increasingly uncertain business environment facing leaders. A popular term is that of turbulence. Turbulence is an unstable and largely unpredictable condition of complex systems. The term is borrowed from studies of physical systems (air and water turbulence) and used to imply unpredictable and unstable organisational environments. Extreme turbulence has become a popular application for the new mathematical ideas of chaos theory

One non-mathematical analysis offering practical advice for dealing with turbulence was written by Stan Gryskiewicz.[14] He identified Eric Trist, a pioneer of the action research methods of the Tavistock Institute, as having popularised the term's metaphoric use for a dynamically uncertain business environment.

Drawing on extensive experiences as a vice-president for global initiatives at the Center for Creative Leadership, Gryskiewicz argues that turbulence is now widely accepted as the inevitable context of work life and is often presented as a threat and undesirable. This results in a tendency for leaders to seek to manage and control the impact of uncertainties in the traditional manner for organisational problem-solving and risk management. He argues for an approach that faces turbulence head on and that actively seeks out ways of using turbulence constructively. To direct efforts towards control of turbulence is misplaced. Strategies of 'riding the waves' and working with the conditions are more appropriate. Positive turbulence seeks to seize opportunities through appropriate strategies.

The approach acts to overcome a natural tendency under turbulent conditions for an organisation to seek the protection of preserving the status quo in its actions and strategies. This may be contrary to what will ensure corporate survival and renewal.

Innovation occurs on the margins

Gryskiewicz believes that innovation occurs at the periphery of knowledge boundaries. A general principle is to accept the potential benefits of encouraging contact with information that comes from outside the organisation's dominant experiences and mapping (including people who are information carriers). By bringing together people who use different maps of their world, it becomes easier to challenge assumptions. Central to his approach is the belief that the chaotic conditions at the interfaces of two organisations can be constructively harnessed.

He instances ways in which companies have successfully institutionalised procedures which support positive turbulence. Intel since the 1980s actively encouraged its employees to challenge ideas regardless of their source. Open communications were also encouraged which cross the typical status barriers of experience and corporate rank. Honda had a similar corporate story of enthusiasm for accepting change. This is hardly surprising from a corporation whose CEO Konosuke Matshita publicly stated the importance of intense efforts of all employees to face up to environmental turbulence.

Diversity

Turbulence calls for team-based activities. The teams are likely to be highly diverse in terms of experiences and knowledge bases. The management of diversity requires a highly facilitative and supportive style from the team leader encouraging improvisation and offering scope for testing innovative ideas. This captures the broad principles of a creative leadership style developed by the so-called founding fathers of creativity research, including one of Gryskiewicz's early mentors, Don MacKinnon.[15] It also draws on ideas of improvisation.

Multiple perspectives

Various strategies are proposed for harnessing diversity. Team members are encouraged to have good networks of experts in their specialised fields. In addition, specialists should be regularly introduced to the ideas of experts from outside the set of competences of the existing team in search of the unexpected and fortuitous connections between the fields of knowledge. Creativity authority Edward De Bono has argued similarly for the benefits of actively seeking rich new knowledge fields in search of innovation. Readers will recognise the principles of critical map-testing (the comparative method) within the strategy for harnessing diversity.

Intensity of support systems

Under turbulent conditions teams benefit from high-intensity support systems – leaders. There is an absence of well-established guidelines in high-intensity environments. Support systems for change become as vital for organisational health as are control systems for production quality in traditional environments.

Receptivity

Implicit in the other three strategic perspectives is a leadership approach which is receptive of new ideas. This captures many of the procedures outlined as a form of creative or trust-based leadership in Chapter 6. (It may also be compared with the facets of transformational leadership described in Chapter 4.) The leader is creative at the level of the team and with a focus directed towards encouraging the creativity of each team member.

Getting personal

We have repeatedly affirmed that our intention is to offer leaders – existing and prospective ones – a chance to take a fresh look at personal leadership goals and ways of addressing them so as to benefit from other people's ideas ('maps'). We did not set out to write yet another book on leadership, but one on how an individual leader may be able to reorient his or her ideas and actions.

In previous chapters we have directed this section at the personal views of the readers. Here, it seems important to introduce a few personal remarks from the perspective of the two authors. The convention in books like this is to give a voice to the authorial 'we'. Whenever someone such as a leader speaks of 'our' vision, and how well 'we' are doing, the same verbal convention occurs, with its implication of the merging of individual views into a social identity. We have used that convention throughout, and will continue to do so, without further emphasis of its textual significance. That is not to say that we, the two authors of this text, hold identical value systems or decision preferences. As we constructed the maps, sometimes individually, sometimes working together, there was enough diversity and management of diversity to enrich the process and (we hope) the outcome. The process seems consistent with an overall treatment of leadership as a personal journey, and one within which the traveller was always bumping into ambiguities and dilemmas in thought and actions.

We learned and refined our views through interacting within our networks of students, colleagues and leaders. At the simple level, we found considerable variation among our contacts (and sometimes between ourselves) regarding the relative merits of the maps we were suggesting. This confirmed us in the view that each reader would be advised to put something personal into the process of map-making.

We could have concluded this chapter by carrying out the same kind of critique on the emerging themes as we did in previous chapters. It seems less appropriate, and too directive. Our conclusions and extrapolations from earlier maps are signalled in our choice of materials in this chapter.

You may well have tired of our insistent metaphor of map-making and map-reading. You can probably anticipate our suggestion, if that is the case. There are plenty of metaphors to help your thinking about leadership. Ours seems to work for us. It is consistent with the more recent ideas of leadership as sense-making, and about managing meaning. But it would also be consistent with your autonomy in thought and action as a leader to stick with the metaphor – or to find some other way to make sense of it all, drawing on your own experience, beliefs and assumptions (Box 10.1).

How power differs from influence

Power and influence can be terms which are as difficult to disentangle as leadership and management. Power is considered as a *relationship resulting in compliance* according to the balance or gradient of power. Influence is considered to be *a process resulting in acceptance* of views, with the intention of achieving willingness to act according to the balance or gradient of influence. The possibilities for confusing the

Box 10.1 Why there is no perfect definition of leadership

Joseph Rost argues that our understanding of leadership is seriously damaged by its well-known multiplicity of definitions. After investigating the definitions to be found in the work of the twentieth century, he concluded that the multiplicity concealed an underlying unity of beliefs within what he termed the paradigm of the industrial era. In a less formal way, we have referred to the different definitions and descriptions as maps of leadership. Rost is saying that the maps are all dealing with the same territory, but from different perspectives. He then attempts to capture the 'master maps' of leadership for the twentieth and twenty-first centuries. The twentieth-century definitions, he says, tell us how leadership was believed to operate in the industrial era. Management was the essential feature of industrial activity; leadership was a special kind of management. The definitions helped define not just leadership, but also beliefs about the industrial era and its working practices.

Rost then developed a definition that could be argued is more appropriate for the postindustrial era:

> Leadership is an influence relationship among leaders and followers who intend real changes that reflect their mutual purposes.

The definition attempts to remove the 'old' connotations of the industrial era (which accept the rights of a leader to give orders, control workers, set objectives) and replace them with a new set of values of collaboration, diversity, moral intentions (even if moral intentions may turn out to have morally disturbing consequences). An organisation has a legally constituted obligation to its shareholders, but they are part of the community of leaders who engage in establishing the moral agenda of the organisation.

Rost has arrived at a conclusion shared by many critics of the ways of thinking and acting about what he called the industrial era. The old ways have also been described as modernist, and have been particularly associated with rationality, and a belief in an objective and scientifically controllable reality. (Terms such as 'real leadership' and 'real change' force us to wonder about that deeper reality.)

Various radical proposals for a change in our 'master map' have been proposed, with terms such as postmodernism and interpretationalism.[16] These proposals challenge the fundamental beliefs of the modernists in progress achieved through rationality and control. Belief in the existence of absolute facts and definitions is replaced by beliefs in the representation of beliefs, that is to say, in the processes through which groups accept or challenge their knowledge bases. Rost offers glimpses of a postmodern view in his critique definitions of leadership of the industrial era. His attempt to provide a universal definition is less thoroughly postmodern, as it implies a belief in an absolute definition.

continued

> Whereas Rost suggests there is a universalistic replacement to leadership thinking and acting appropriate to the industrial era, a postmodern approach would consider that very belief (in absolute definitions) as one of the features of modern (industrial era) thinking. He wrestles with the difficulties of the modernist approach – seeking to locate leadership as something quite different, while retaining the same terminology as far as possible. The past experience of connotations of words cannot be fully exorcised. This provides difficulties for present-day Germans, whose term for leader is *Führer*. Rost's replacement of follower with collaborator would also imply connotations of compliance with an occupying power.

two are obvious. Another distinction sometimes made is that influence is directed towards *beliefs*, and power is directed towards *actions*.

Power is sometimes split into *position power* and *personal power*. Studies of power and influence often raise issues of legitimacy of the form of power relationship or the influence methods.

Two traditions of power relationships

We have mostly accepted a view throughout this book which assumes that the position power of leaders of organisations is legitimate, unless abused. Furthermore, we assume a further trickle-down effect so that others legitimately exercise power on behalf of the organisation, as indicated by its leaders. From this perspective, resistance to these legitimate activities comes from dissident forces, the most obvious example of which would be organised labour. We might add resistance from other views of those seeking redress for unfair treatment experienced by disadvantaged individuals or groups.

From another perspective, deriving from Marx and Weber, power arises in structural factors in organisations as in society forces, producing dominance of one group over others. From this perspective, organisational design and restructuring may be justified on grounds of economic rationality, but serves to strengthen the grip of those in power. It is, in essence, the process of institutionalisation of power. The creation of task forces, special projects, formal investigations or reorganisations would all be seen as institutionalising power to the benefit of the existing power elite.

Power within organisational departments

Different organisational departments appear to have different levels of power. This is hard to explain in the classical scientific management idea of the organisation as a machine, controllable in a rule-based way from the top down. Labour theorists have argued that the modern organisation cannot be totally subdivided into functional groups, each having fully defined operational routines. The level of control over activities seems strongly dependent on a subgroup or department's responsibilities for dealing with uncertainties. Specific strategic factors will determine the power distribution. This *strategic contingency* approach has shown how groups with highly prescribed structures and roles tend to have less power.[17] For example, if the market environment is uncertain and fast-moving, marketing subgroups will have more power than manufacturing subgroups whose work environment is more predictable.

The battles for power

Subgroups such as departments and influential individuals compete for the scarce resources needed for them to achieve their goals. These internal processes are often regarded as power struggles, as departments withhold information from one another, and compete as vigorously against one another as they compete against external competitive forces.

Power-based maps and trust-based maps

The comparative method of map-testing will reveal the dilemmas of power often concealed in maps of leadership. In new leadership maps *empowerment* is generally presented as desirable while the consequences of voluntary release of control is glossed over.

In the previous section, Gryskiewicz demonstrated why under turbulent conditions traditional attempts to lead through control are ill advised. His strategies amount to a manifesto for creative leadership. The leader creates the environmental freedom for a group to discover mutually acceptable and innovative future opportunities.

As was suggested in Chapter 6, the processes of creative problem-solving and trust-based leadership are well aligned, as alternatives to traditional power-based mappings of leadership. The leader acts as a facilitator in the management of group meaning. The maps require more widespread understanding of creativity as a socially mediated process than as the earlier mapping of an individualistic enterprise. Such maps are now receiving more attention, particularly through the efforts of Teresa Amabile, who has refocused attention on the social construction of creativity.[18]

We are living in a more complex business environment. The new fast-growing companies are more virtual and global and their products more intangible. To lead in such an environment requires more complex leadership maps (Box 10.2).

The dilemmas of charismatic and even transformational modes of leadership have left the way open to the maps of distributed leadership within teams and networks. Knowledge and information leadership appear to be directing attention towards learning and developmental models of leadership. See Box 10.3.

Box 10.2 GLOBE: a leadership project for the twenty-first century

The GLOBE (Global Leadership and Organizational Behavior Effectiveness) project is one of the most comprehensive collaborative studies of leadership ever undertaken. Inspired by Robert House, the project has developed since the early 1990s, and in a decade of work one hundred and fifty research collaborators have collected information from many thousands of middle managers in over sixty countries, across three major industry sectors. The project seeks to add to our understanding of those aspects of leadership which are more universal, and those which are more culture bound. Their definition of leaders focuses on the ability of an individual to influence, motivate and enable others to contribute to effectiveness and success of the organisations of which they are members.[19]

The GLOBE model proposes a set of interactions between cultural, organisational and leadership dimensions, with additional influences through strategic contingencies. The model addresses leadership at multiple levels (the individual, the organisation, the culture), drawing on the two traditions of cultural research, the psychological and the anthropological (qualitative and case-based methodologies).[20]

Leadership dimensions and styles

Nine relevant dimensions have been identified and studied:

- uncertainty avoidance
- future orientation
- power distance
- institutional collectivism
- humane orientation
- performance orientation
- family collectivism
- gender egalitarianism
- assertiveness.

Five leadership styles have been identified:

- charismatic
- team oriented
- humane
- autonomous
- self-protective.

Cultural clusters   The researchers have begun the process of data simplification by identifying what they see as primary clusters of shared cultural characteristics. They arrived at ten such clusters: South Asia, Anglo, Arab, Germanic Europe, Latin Europe, Eastern Europe, Confucian Asia, Latin America, sub-Sahara Africa and Nordic Europe.[21]

At the start of the twenty-first century, GLOBE was moving to stage two of its planned four stages. The project offers thorough, evidence-based benchmarks for cultural aspects of leadership practices. The richness of the data collected means that future research will be able to benchmark new ideas against extensive empirical evidence.

Box 10.3 It's up to you

At some stage on any journey a leader has to accept that no one else can provide them with further guidance or assistance. We hope you agree with us that the time has come and our value as guides has come to an end. We assume that if you stayed with us this long, you have found value in the maps we have provided during your leadership journeys. We now assume you can carry on without help from any more maps provided by us. That's not to say we believe you will not need to study any more maps in the future. Rather, that you know how to carry out the map-reading, -testing and -making.

So, it's over to you. Up to you to retrace your journey by referring back to the maps you have already made and perhaps seeing where your map-making has changed. Up to you to make further map-making efforts to support your leadership plans. Up to you to reject as much as you like. That's our final piece of unsolicited advice. We offer it not because we do not care what you do, but from precisely the opposite motives.

Summary

Around the year 2000 many books were written speculating on the leadership context of the twenty-first century. Futurology is notoriously difficult, so we may treat these maps with particular caution. There are some widely shared assumptions and from them we can compile a set of elements of the future context in which organisational leaders will operate. We would expect newer leadership maps to pay more attention to these elements although we also 'expect the unexpected' from innovative map-makers in the decades to come.

The survival of the old in the new maps

Our future understanding of leadership will be reflected in our future maps. As Yukl pointed out in his map on the future of leadership, new maps will not replace and wipe out all knowledge gained from earlier maps. More typically the new maps hold on to old ideas, sometimes reworking them in a new context. We have seen how this process occurred within the ancient ideas of charismatic leadership, which were subsequently reworked within maps of transformational leadership.

As we review the maps we have encountered throughout this book, we have seen how older maps could be tested and remade into newer ones by critical examination revealing their dilemmas. To take a significant example, the long-lived dominance of trait-based maps never succeeded in resolving the dilemmas of definition. Additionally there was the dilemma of *trait variability* among leaders – the failure of research to identify a universal set of traits identifying 'the right stuff' of the great leader.

These dilemmas helped map-makers to replace trait theories by behavioural ones. The context shifted towards leadership operating levels throughout organisations, and from what leaders were to what they did. As proposed by Yukl, such new mappings did not completely eliminate the influence of older maps. The new maps retained the assumptions of leader as the prime factor in achieving excellent performance. They also retained the importance placed on rationality (rational leaders, rational expectations of followers). Also, evaluation of leader success in terms of measureable performance remained largely unchanged.

Increasing complexity in leadership maps

The shift from trait to behavioural maps increased the complexity of maps in some ways (more variables) while retaining the fundamental simplicity of leadership as a prime causal factor which influenced follower behaviours to achieve organisational objectives. Yukl had been pointing out for some years that the maps failed to account for reciprocal or mutual influence processes. An example of such reciprocal processes would be leadership behaviours influencing followers whose behaviours also influence leaders. The turbulence of the environment is likely to grow in importance within future mappings. The shift will support mappings that examine knowledge and learning models of leadership.

Increasing complexity in leader maps

We deliberately distinguish complexity of leadership maps and leader maps. The rationale of developing your skills at personal map-making is the idea developed by Peter Senge that each leader has a mental map which requires a complexity appropriate for the environmental challenges.[22]

The management of meaning

The shift to new leadership maps helped place more emphasis on perceptual processes – including the importance of the management of meaning. The new leadership maps retained much from the older maps, while leaving unanswered some of the earlier dilemmas. The matter of a satisfactory definition of leadership persisted. Once again, however, older ideas were modified by context rather than completely exorcised. Studies of the symbolic and mythic aspects of leadership may provide additional life to the mapping of meaning.

Charisma and the fate of the heroic leader

Charisma became 'tamed' as the measurable aspects of transformational leadership. The new leadership maps still revealed dilemmas. The heroic leader remained an important figure within transformational leadership mapping. Difficulties remained concerning the malevolent and tyrannical leader who achieved transformational changes (the Hitler effect).

The heroic leader is a concept that appears vulnerable to further challenges as the frequently observed 'dark side of leadership' is more widely recognised through pioneering work of Kets de Vries and Barbara Kellerman. The symbolism of the mandrill leadership style serves as a warning of such behaviours. Here is some evidence that a more self-effacing and less self-serving style has considerable social and organisational benefits (the fifth level leader of Jim Collins is a promising example).

Rost's unification attempts

Rost's critique for the twenty-first century attempted to deal with the dilemmas of the contemporary leadership maps. His proposal was for a definition he believed to be implied in the multiple other definitions of leadership. He would define leadership as *an influence relationship among leaders and followers who intend real changes that reflect their mutual purposes*. He thus excludes leaders who do not operate according to principles of mutuality of purpose. He argues that such a mapping helps escape from an industrial age definition and suggests new mappings of distributed leadership (as indicated in the work of Manz and Sims, for example). Such attempts to claim priority for one definition over all others risks the very dilemma it seeks to address, namely the right of one perspective to dominate over all others.

Social identity processes

Emerging perspectives include a *social identity* mapping for leadership. This is suggested almost in passing by earlier map-makers (leader–member exchange would be an example). The mapping seems to address several of the dilemmas we have touched upon. It also gets us closer to a broad theory of influence processes. The mapping does not appear to be a revolutionary shift from the maps of new leadership. The currently favoured methodological approach of prototypicality seems to be within older traditions of essentialist mappings of leadership processes. However, it offers promise of more grounded examination of influence processes with rich empirical possibilities. The approach may also help map concepts of knowledge management and thought-leadership.

Emotional intelligence

Emotional intelligence has become another emerging theme of late-twentieth-century leadership maps. We have indicated how a comparative analysis of prevailing maps reveals challenging dilemmas of diagnostic accuracy and distance of the empirical measures from real-world leadership competences. More careful work is needed to explore such dilemmas.

Power and trust as alternative mappings

Leadership maps of the twentieth century conceal dilemmas of power and control which are revealed only through careful and comparative reading. Rost's appeal for leadership only as directed towards mutually accepted purposes is one attempt to smooth out the potential conflict. Enthusiasm in new leadership maps for shared visions and missions is another. The concept of empowerment tends to conceal dilemmas of multiple constituencies in organisations with different values and goals. The power-based maps have not adequately dealt with the dilemmas of power, coercion and conflict resolution.

A less investigated mapping is the one we have identified in these pages as trust-based leadership. Power is redistributed within a values framework which places a high priority on mutuality of goal setting as a creative and social process.

Notes

1 Yukl, G. A. (1999) 'An evaluative essay on current conceptions of effective leadership', *European Journal of Work and Organizational Psychology* 8(1): 33–48.
2 Rost, J. C. (1993a) *Leadership for the 21st Century*, Westport, CT: Praeger; Gini, A. (1995) 'Too much to say about something', *Business Ethics Quarterly* 5(1): 143–155.
3 Ciulla, J. B. (1995) 'Leadership ethics: mapping the territory', *Business Ethics Quarterly* 5(1): 6–28.
4 Rost, J. C., *Leadership for the 21st Century*, pp. 180 and 145 [see note 2].
5 Ibid., p. 102.
6 Manz, C. C. and Sims, H. P., Jr (1991) 'Superleadership: beyond the myth of heroic leadership', *Organizational Dynamics* 19: 18–35.
7 Rost, J. C. (1993b) 'Leadership development in the new millennium', *Journal of Leadership Studies* 1(1): 91–110; Rost, J. C. (1995) 'Leadership: a discussion about ethics', *Business Ethics Quarterly* 5(1): 129–141.
8 Hodgkinson, G. P. and Sparrow, P. R. (2002) *The Competent Organization: A Psychological Analysis of the Strategic Management Process*, Buckingham: Open University Press.
9 Hogg, M. A., Martin, R. and Weeden, K. (2003) 'Leader-member relations and social identity', in D. Van Knippenberg and M. A. Hogg (eds) *Leadership and Power: Identity Processes in Groups and Organizations*, London: Sage, p. 18.

10 Goodwin, S. (2003) 'A social-cognitive perspective on power and leadership', in Van Knippenberg and Hogg, *Leadership and Power*.

11 Gardner, H. (1983) *Frames of Mind*, New York: Basic Books.

12 Mayer, J. D. (2001) 'A field guide to emotional intelligence', in J. Ciarrochi, J. P. Forgas and J. D. Mayer (eds) *Emotional Intelligence in Everyday Life*, New York: Psychology Press.

13 Goleman, D. (1995) *Emotional Intelligence*, New York: Bantam.

14 Gryskiewicz, S. S. (1999) *Positive Turbulence: Developing Climates for Creativity, Innovation and Renewal*, San Francisco, CA: Jossey-Bass.

15 MacKinnon, D. W. (1978) *In Search of Human Effectiveness: Identifying and Developing Creativity*, Buffalo, NY: Creative Education Foundation.

16 Boje, D. M., Gephart, R. P., Jr and Thatchenkery, T. J. (eds) (1996) *Postmodern Management and Organization Theory*, Thousand Oaks, CA: Sage.

17 Hickson, D. J., Hinings, C. R., Lee, C. A., Schneck, R. E. and Pennings, J. M. (1971) 'A strategic contingencies theory of intraorganizational power', *Administrative Science Quarterly* 16(2): 216–229.

18 For example, Amabile, T. M. (1988) 'A model of creativity and innovation in organizations', *Research in Organizational Behavior* 10: 123–169; Amabile, T. M., Schatzel, E. A., Moneta, G. B. and Kramer, S. J. (2004) 'Leader behaviors and work environment for creativity: perceived leader support', *Leadership Quarterly* 15(1): 5–33.

19 House, R., Javidan, M., Hanges, P. and Dorfman, P. (2002) 'Understanding cultures and implicit leadership theories across the globe: an introduction to Project GLOBE', *Journal of World Business* 37: 3–10.

20 Geertz, C. (1973) *The Interpretation of Cultures*, New York: Basic Books; Kluckhohn, F. and Strodtbeck, F. L. (1961) *Variations in Value Orientations*, Evanston, IL: Row Peterson.

21 See the reports in the 2002 special issue of *Journal of World Business* 37(1).

22 Senge, P. M. (1990) *The Fifth Discipline: The Art and Practice of the Learning Organization*, New York: Doubleday.

Index